Journal of the

INDIAN WARS

Volume One, No. 2

Savas Publishing Company

202 First Street SE, Suite 103A, Mason City, IA 50401

Subscription and Publishing Information

Journal of the Indian Wars (*JIW*) is published quarterly by Savas Publishing Company, 202 First Street SE, Suite 103A, Mason City, IA 50401. Publisher: Theodore P. Savas. (515) 421-7135 (voice); (515)-421-8370 (fax); E-mail: cwbooks@mach3ww.com. Our online military history catalog of original books is found at www.savaspublishing.com.

SUBSCRIPTIONS to *JIW* are available at $29.95/yr. (four books); Canada and overseas is $39.95/yr. Write to: Savas Publishing Company, *JIW* Subscriptions, 202 First Street SE, Suite 103A, Mason City, IA 50401. Check, MO, MC or V accepted. Phone, fax or E-mail orders welcome. All subscriptions begin with the current issue unless otherwise specified.

DISTRIBUTION in North America is handled by Peter Rossi at Stackpole Books, 5067 Ritter Road, Mechanicsburg, PA 17055-6921. 800-732-3669 (voice); 717-976-0412 (fax); E-mail: prossi@stackpolebooks.com. European distribution is through Greenhill Books, Park House, 1 Russell Gardens, London NW11 9NN, England; E-mail: LionelLeventhal@compuserve.com; Back issues of *JIW* are available through Stackpole Books or your local bookseller. Retail price is $11.95 plus shipping ($4.00 for the first book and $1.00 for each additional book). Check, money order, MC/V, AE, or D are accepted. Contact Stackpole Books for quantity discounts.

MANUSCRIPTS, REVIEWS, AND NEWS SUBMISSIONS are welcome. For guidelines, consult our web site (www.savaspublishing.com) or send a self-addressed stamped envelope to Michael A. Hughes, Editor, *Journal of the Indian Wars*, 834 East Sixth Street, Box E, Ada, OK 74820. Proposals for articles (recommended) should include a brief description of your topic, a list of primary sources, and estimate of completion date. Manuscripts should be accompanied by a 3.5" disk with copies in both WordPerfect 6.1 (or lower) and Rich Text (RTF) formats. Persons interested in reviewing books should send a description of their qualifications, areas of expertise, and desired titles and topics. News submissions should include a brief abstracted version of any information. Submitted news may be posted on our web site at our discretion. Enclose a SASE if requesting a reply and include your E-mail and fax number. Publications (which may include page proofs) and videos for potential review should be sent to the managing editor.

JIW is published with the cooperation of Jerry Russell and the Order of the Indian Wars. Without Jerry's non-too-gentle proddings and earnest supplications, it would not have come to fruition. For more information, please write to OIW, P.O. Box 7401, Little Rock AR 72217.

Savas Publishing Company

Publisher
Theodore P. Savas

Editorial	Graphics	Cartography
Kim Burton	Jim Zach	Mark A. Moore
William Haley		

Marketing	Indexing
Nancy Lund	Lee W. Merideth

Journal of the Indian Wars

Editor
Michael A. Hughes

Editorial Consultants	Advertising/Circulation
Brian Pohanka, Jerry Keenan,	Nancy E. Lund
Neil Mangum, Jerry Russell,	Carol A. Savas
and Ted Alexander	

Associate Editors: Patrick Bowmaster and Eril B. Hughes

Civil War Regiments Journal

Managing Editor
Mark A. Snell

Assistant Editor	Circulation	Advertising
Mark Bell	Carol A. Savas	Nancy Lund

Book Review Editor		Desktop Publishing
Archie McDonald		Albert Pejack, Jr.

Contributors

John Alden Reid is a longtime National Park Service employee who previously worked at the military historical parks of Fort McHenry and Morristown. He is now chief of interpretation at Horseshoe Bend National Military Park in Alabama.

Patrick J. Jung is an adjunct professor of history and a full time administrator at Marquette University in Milwaukee, Wisconsin.

Michael D. Carter is a former captain in the U. S. Army field artillery and an adjunct history professor at Trinity College in Washington, D.C.

S. Matthew Despain recently completed the requirements for a doctorate in history at the University of Oklahoma. Most of his articles to date have been on the fur trade and the Indian wars.

G. Michael Pratt is a professor of Anthropology and director of the Archaeology Laboratory of Heidelberg College in Tiffin, Ohio. He is also associated with the college's Center for Historical and Military Archaeology.

Patrick Bowmaster is an associate editor and contributor to *Journal of the Indian Wars*. A freelance writer, Patrick resides in upstate New York.

Cindy Bedell is the site manager of the Tippecanoe Battlefield Museum of the Tippecanoe County [Indiana] Historical Association.

Rodney G. Thomas, a previous contributor to the journal, retired this year from the U.S. Army. He has a book coming out soon from Upton & Sons on the Indian art of the Battle of the Little Bighorn.

Journal of the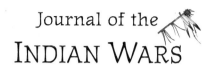
INDIAN WARS

Table of Contents

continued

Table of Contents (continued)

Editor's Preface

Michael A. Hughes

In the premiere issue of *Journal of the Indian Wars*, we noted that "*JIW* will be unique in its breadth and depth. . . . While the majority of our articles will focus on warfare in the West from 1848 to 1890, *JIW* will not ignore the fascinating Indian wars history east of the Mississippi River." This issue, which is dedicated to battles and leaders of the early United States east of the Mississippi River, confirms our dedication to diversity.

Eastern battles remain the most obscure in the history of Indian conflicts, and those fought in the "Old Southeast" are the most obscure of all. While the names of Andrew Jackson's victories at Emuckfaw and Enotochopco will never be household words—even though they catapulted Jackson to national prominence—John Alden Reid's essay on these battles, "Prelude to Horseshoe Bend: The Battles of Emuckfaw and Enotochopco," will undoubtedly resurrect interest in them. Reid, a park interpreter at Horseshoe Bend National Military Park, has penned a richly detailed account of these battles, two of bloodiest engagements of the Creek (Muskogee) War of 1812. As Reid aptly points out, Emuckfaw and Enotochopco paved the way for Jackson's later victory at Horseshoe Bend, which happens to be the subject of Reid's second contribution to this issue, "The Carnage was Dreadful": The Battle of Horseshoe Bend."

Indian leaders are too often described only in light of their relationship to whites. The famed patriot chief Black Hawk, for example, has often been portrayed as a passive victim of western expansion. Patrick J. Jung provides an alternative to this outlook in his innovative article on Black Hawk's desperate diplomacy among the tribes of what is now the midwestern United States. Like John Alden Reid's Creek War contribution, Jung's "The Black Hawk War Reconsidered: A New Interpretation of its Causes and Course" will reinvigorate study and interest in this aspect of Indian Wars history.

William Clark is best known for his participation in the continent-spanning Lewis and Clark Expedition. His activities in the Indian wars of the "Old Northwest" are far less well known. *JIW* is thus pleased to make Clark's journal of Anthony Wayne's 1794 campaign available once again. Clark's insights and observations are priceless and form the basis for much of our understanding of the campaign and the battle at Fallen Timbers. To the best of our knowledge, it has not seen the light of publication for seventy-five years. The fine introduction appended to Clark's entries was written by Associate Editor Patrick Bowmaster, who studied history under esteemed Civil War historian James I "Bud" Roberson. Pat's introduction represents his first written contribution to *JIW*.

Conflicts between whites and Indians are often treated as a sideline of United States history. As this issue of *JIW* makes clear, however, the Indian wars east of the Mississippi River had a dramatic effect on development of the United States. Michael A. Carter articulates this well in "'Fighting the Flames of a Merciless War': Secretary of War Henry Knox and the Indian War in the Old Northwest," 1790-1795." According to Carter, the Indian issue embodied most of the larger questions that had to be addressed by the new American government: the power of the Federal government, the federal debt, foreign policy, the role of a peacetime military, and and race relations.

Archaeologist G. Michael Pratt has consented to publication of his excellent perspective on the Battle of Fallen Timbers, the climax of the 1794 campaign. His article, adapted from his keynote lecture at the bicentennial commemoration of the battle in August 1994, is followed with an exclusive interview with Dr. Pratt on his rediscovery of the "lost" site of the Fallen Timbers engagement.

Several other items of interest round out this issue of *JIW*. When the inaugural issue of this publication hit the stands, we hoped it would encourage contributors to come forth with new documents and information on the Indian wars. As our "Custer at the Washita and Little Bighorn" issue went to press, we were approached by Matthew Despain, a graduate student who had access to the famed Walter Mason Camp Collection at Brigham Young University. Despain offered to provide an article based on previously unpublished material by Capt. Albert Barnitz on the Battle of the Washita. The result, "Captain Albert Barnitz and the Battle of the Washita: A New Document," demonstrates how much information is still "out there," waiting for the right researcher.

Two other contributions round out this issue. Cindy Bedell, the site manager of the Tippecanoe Battlefield Museum of the Tippecanoe County [Indiana] Historical Association, offers this edition's travel and museum article. Tippecanoe is often regarded as the action that completed the process of Indian defeat begun at Fallen Timbers. Rod Thomas, a contributor to our first issue and now a *JIW* associate editor, kicks off his new column, "Thomas Online," which will feature a wide variety of topics for our readers. His first offering is "A Beginner's Guide to Researching the Indian Wars Online." Regular web surfers, too, will find the information in Rod's article useful.

Major General Andrew Jackson

Horseshoe Bend National Military Park

Prelude to Horseshoe Bend:

THE BATTLES OF EMUCKFAW AND ENOTOCHOPCO,

January 1814

John Alden Reid

For four desperate years, 1811-1814, a series of vicious and genocidal campaigns were fought to determine once and for all the future of the continent west of the Appalachian Mountains. A handful of patriot chiefs, inspired by visions of a unified Indian America, faced an equally determined set of commanders intent on crushing resistance to United States expansion. The Indian wars associated with the War of 1812 may have had far greater consequence than that larger conflict. Yet, the decisive campaigns fought against the Indians of the "Old Northwest" and "Old Southwest" are even more obscure than the now largely overlooked war with Britain.

Emuckfaw and Enotochopco are two little-known battles waged during the almost forgotten Creek War. A bitter and cruel clash of cultures, the Creek War erupted in 1813 as a civil war between factions of the Creek (or Muskogee) Nation. The conflict sucked in American armies of Georgians, Mississippians, and Tennesseans against the Red Sticks, the Creek war party. The January 1814 battles on the creeks at Emuckfaw and Enotochopco, tributaries of the Tallapoosa River, were bloody frontier combats between Red Stick warriors and Tennessee Militia under Andrew Jackson. The combats at Emuckfaw and

Enotochopco occurred during Jackson's second militia campaign to chastise the Red Sticks.

The Red Sticks, Alabama Creeks from towns along the Coosa and Tallapoosa Rivers, sought a revival of their traditional life, relying upon game meat and the primitive cultivation of maize for their diet. The trade in deer skins, along with the staple of venison, was intrinsic to their way of life. Red was the color of war to the Creek or Muskogee, and the Red Sticks painted or dyed their skin with red ochre for battle, while the red-painted war club was a symbol of war. Tecumseh, during his mission to the Creeks in 1811, purportedly offered bundles of red-painted sticks as a primitive calendar. The Shawnee Tecumseh (born of a Muskogee mother) had eloquently predicted a war against the whites during his sojourn among the Creeks. Tecumseh's vehement appeal converted the Red Stick Muskogee to lift the war club, or atasa, against the white Creeks and the white Americans. The Creeks hostile to white Americans were thus known either as "Red Sticks" or "Red Clubs."[2]

The Lower or White Creeks hailed from along the Chattahoochee and Flint Rivers of Georgia. They had embraced white civilization, largely because of their proximity to white settlement and the influence of Indian Agents like Benjamin Hawkins. Emulating white farmers, the White Creeks tilled the soil with the plow and bred cattle. Initially embroiled in the civil strife with the Red Sticks that had sundered the Creek Nation, the White Creeks were enlisted as native auxiliaries, along with Cherokee native allies, in the American armies of the Creek War. The skirmish of Mississippi militia with Red Sticks at Burnt Corn Creek in July 1813, followed by the retaliation of the Red Sticks at the Fort Mims Massacre on August 30, 1813, galvanized the frontier. Militias were mustered in the surrounding states to punish the Red Sticks. Since white was the color of peace to the Muskogee, white feathers, plumes, or deer tails in the hair were worn to distinguish themselves and their Cherokee allies from their enemy.[3]

Three American columns were organized to march and converge in west central Alabama against the Red Sticks. The first, 1,000 men under Gen. John Floyd, moved west from Georgia while Gen. F. L. Claiborne led a second column of similar strength east from Mississippi. The third and largest wing of the movement was under the command of Andrew Jackson, a Tennessee lawyer and major general of militia. Jackson's army marched south from Fayetteville, Tennessee. The Tennessean's men fought battles at Tallusahatchee on November 3, 1813 (where frontier scout David Crockett declared that the Red

Stick Muskogee were "shot. . .like dogs"), and Talladega on November 9, 1813 (where Crockett claimed Creek warriors "came rushing forth like a cloud of Egyptian locusts . . . then broke like a gang of steers"). Some 500 Red Sticks were killed in these combats, while Jackson's army suffered casualties of 20 killed and 126 wounded.[4]

The victorious Tennessee militia went into camp on the Coosa River at Fort Strother. Inadequate supplies, the rigors of active campaigning, and expiring enlistments caused severe discontent amongst the militia. The militia victories had garnered nothing but famine and mutiny, the former a result of rations delayed by unscrupulous contractors. David Crockett remembered well the gnawing hunger and spreading desperation:

> No provisions had yet reached us, and we had now been for several days on half rations. However we went back to [Tallusahatchee] on the next day, when many of the carcasses of the Indians were still to be seen. They looked very awful, for the burning had not entirely consumed them. . . . It was, somehow or other, found that the house had a potatoe [sic] cellar under it . . . We found a fine chance of potatoes in it, and hunger compelled us to eat them, though I had a little rather not . . . for the oil of the Indians we had burned up on the day before had run down on them, and they looked like they had been stewed with fat meat. We then again returned to the army, and remained there for several days almost starving, as all our beef was gone. We

Jackson quelling the mutiny. *Horseshoe Bend National Military Park*

commenced eating the beef-hides, and continued to eat every scrap we could lay our hands on.[5]

The hardships described by Crockett and suffered by everyone caused many of Jackson's men to abandon their officers and quit the encampment at Fort Strother to travel to their homes in Tennessee. The American effort to crush the Red Sticks was temporarily abandoned.

The state of affairs at Fort Strother disgusted Jackson. His men had scored two victories, and retreat was simply not in his nature. Substantial contingents of both regular army and newly-raised militia reinforcements, however, soon allowed him to resume his campaign against the Creeks. The foray of Jackson's second militia army was merely a prelude to his subsequent and better known victory over the Red Stick Creeks at Horseshoe Bend on March 27, 1814, in the bloodiest battle of the savage Creek War.

The recently raised Tennessee volunteer militia, some 800 troops and officers, was ordered to hasten its march south to join Jackson by the 10th of January, but did not arrive in the camp at Fort Strother until the 15th. Troops waiting there from the former army included the artillery company with its 6-pounder, two companies of "spies" or scouts of Capts. John Gordon and William Russell, of approximately thirty troops each, a company of volunteer

officers commanded by Brig. Gen. John Coffee, and an infantry company of forty-eight soldiers. Jackson's revitalized army now numbered about 930 soldiers and would soon be reinforced by 200 native warriors (65 Cherokees and the remainder White Creeks) gathered at Talladega. Captain Reid described the inauspicious departure of the militia:

General John Coffee

Horseshoe Bend National Military Park

Seldom, perhaps, has there been an expedition undertaken fraught with greater peril than this. A thousand men, entirely unacquainted with the duties of the field, were to be marched into the heart of an enemy's country, without a single hope of escape, but from victory, and that victory not to be expected, but from the wisest precaution, and most determined bravery.[6]

The term of service for this new round of militia recruits was already approaching expiration and, as the militia was "expensive to the government [to maintain], and full of ardor to meet the enemy," Jackson determined to employ them on a brief but effective campaign. "The ill effects of keeping soldiers of this description long stationary and idle, I had been made to feel too sensibly already," Jackson explained, referring to the mutiny of militia in November.[7]

Despite the hazards everyone anticipated, Jackson ordered the army to move out on January 17. The militia marched on January 17, 1814, encamping the following night at Talladega, where the native troops joined the expedition. The army continued it march south to the Hillabee creeks, and on January 20 encamped at Enotochopco. Jackson, observing his raw army on the march into the wilderness, perceived "how little knowledge my spies [scouts] had of the country . . . . The insubordination of the new troops and the want of skill in most of their officers, also became more and more apparant." However, he added, "their ardor to meet the enemy was not diminished" despite their lack of discipline and experience. Much of the general's confidence in final victory was centered upon his "sure reliance upon the Guards, the company of old volunteer officers and upon the spies." This body of 125 veterans comprised the backbone of Jackson's otherwise neophyte army. According to Captain Reid, "Troops unacquainted with service are often times more sanguine than veterans. The imagination too frequently portraying battles in the light of a frolic, keeps danger concealed, until suddenly springing into view, it seems a monster too hideous to be withstood." Jackson's militia, anxious to experience combat, would soon have their fill of fighting.[8]

On the morning of January 21, the army marched from Enotochopco for the bend of the Tallapoosa River. During the march scouts encountered two Red Sticks. Although Jackson's men strove to capture the warriors, the Muskogees managed to evade that fate and escaped. With the approach of dusk, the army discovered trails converging on a "road, much beaten and lately traveled." The fresh signs of Red Sticks and gathering dusk prompted Jackson to order his army to encamp "in a hollow square . . . upon the eminences of Emuckfaw," so as to reconnoiter the Muskogee encampment, the obvious destination of the

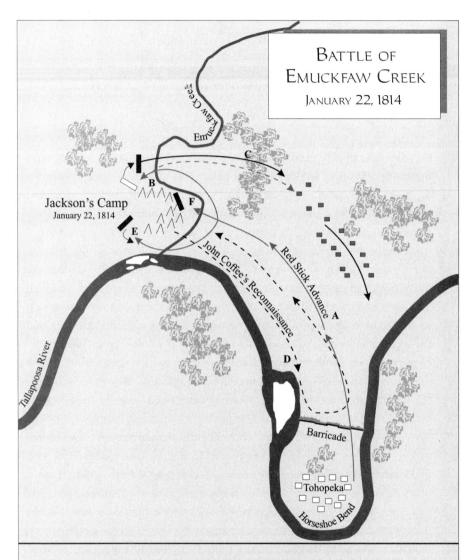

BATTLE OF EMUCKFAW CREEK

JANUARY 22, 1814

A. The Red Sticks advance against Jackson's men early on the morning of January 22, 1814;

B. The sharp attack strikes the left side of Jackson's camp and threatens the rear of his army;

C. Reinforcements are sent to the left, and under Gen. John Coffee, a bayonet charge is launched, throwing back the Red Sticks;

D. Jackson orders Coffee to take 400 men and reconnoiter the Red Stick encampment, which Coffee deems too strong to attack;

E. The Red Sticks launch another attack, this time against Jackson's right, which is successfully driven back by General Coffee;

F. While feinting against Jackson's right, the Red Sticks launch another attack against the American left flank, which is also successfully met, effectively ending the battle.

Theodore P. Savas

beaten road. Scouts were dispatched to investigate the road and discover the Red Sticks' refuge, pickets were posted, and sentinels doubled to guard against an attack during the shroud of night. One of the pickets glimpsed three Red Sticks and fired his flintlock in their direction, killing one. The corpse, hidden by the rapid onset of darkness, was discovered the following morning.[9]

Jackson's scouts soon returned to report their discovery of the Tohopeka encampment some three miles from the militia camp at Emuckfaw. There they had witnessed shrieking and dancing Red Sticks, who were seemingly aware of the approach of Jackson's army. The Muskogees were in ritual purification for combat, but were also removing women and children from the encampment, as reported by a native scout. The reconnaissance report convinced Jackson that the Red Sticks were either contemplating an attack against him or planning an escape before dawn. Either way, his army was prepared to either meet an attack or launch an attack with the onset of daylight. Jackson remarked to his wife about the irony of the expected assault, which would likely occur on January 22, the first anniversary of the 1813 River Raisin (or Frenchtown) Massacre. That slaughter had taken place when a contingent of Red Sticks who had journeyed north to Canada to support Tecumseh participated in the killing of Gen. James Winchester's Kentuckians. Jackson confided to Rachel that the Red Sticks' expectation was "to make my fate the fate" of the slaughtered militia at Frenchtown a year ago.[10]

At "dawn of day," about 6:00 a.m. on January 22, a spattering of musketry announced the opening of an assault by the Red Sticks against the left flank of Jackson's army, which was held by men commanded by Colonel William Higgins. Muskets flashed and thundered along the line as sentinels sounded the alarm, accompanied by the "shrieks and savage yells" of the Creek warriors. "Tho raw" the militia displayed "firmness and undaunted resolution" in repulsing the assault, Jackson later wrote. The "vigorous attack on . . . [the] left flank . . . was as vigorously met." The battle moved around the left flank and threatened the left rear of Jackson's line, raged for about half an hour. The commanding general later mentioned the conspicuous courage of General Coffee and Colonels William Carroll, James Sitler, and William Higgins, who had mounted their horses to gallop to the threatened parts of the line. The officers encouraged the militia, which stood firm in the face of repeated attacks despite their thinning line of battle.[11]

As the sun rose higher in the eastern sky and the combat continued, a charge was contemplated to repulse the Red Sticks. Jackson ordered reinforcements of raw infantry from Captain Larkin Ferrell's company, and the men were briskly fed into the line by Colonel Carroll. When all was ready, General Coffee ordered the charge at the point of the bayonet, and the men routed the Red Sticks and drove them back in retreat. The infantry pursued the fleeing warriors for two miles, inflicting "considerable slaughter" in the process (twenty-four corpses were later counted).[12]

Despite the intensity of the attack, Colonel Higgins' line of militia suffered only five killed and twenty wounded. According to Captain Reid, the militia's campfires played a significant role in minimizing losses. The fires were kindled beyond the boundary of the camp outside of the hollow square, he explained, providing the soldiers with illuminated targets, silhouetting the attacking Red Sticks warriors while the militia remained concealed in the shadows.[13]

The native troops fighting with Jackson (Cherokees and White Creeks) joined the militia in the pursuit of the Red Sticks. When the troops returned and the men had reorganized, Jackson ordered General Coffee with 400 militia and the native troops to march upon the Red Sticks' encampment at Tohopeka. Coffee was cautioned by Jackson to reconnoiter the place carefully and be particularly wary of enemy fortifications. As Coffee's detachment approached the Horseshoe of the Tallapoosa, a log and dirt barricade was indeed discovered. Coffee determined that an infantry attack was hazardous considering the imperviousness of the Red Stick barricade to musketry. According to General Jackson: "On viewing the encampment and its strength, the Genl. [Coffee] thought it most prudent to return to my encampment and guard the artillery thither."[14]

While Jackson had been working to effect an attack against the Red Sticks, however, the Creeks had been moving to attack the Americans a second time. Soon after Coffee returned to camp, a fresh assault threatened the right portion of Jackson's line. "A considerable body of the enemy made its appearance on my right flank and commenced a brisk fire on the party of men who had been on the picquet guard," Jackson later reported. Soldiers from Captain John Gordon's company, who had been searching for the Red Stick corpse shot by their picket on the eve of the battle, were the initial targets of the heavy and sudden enemy fire.[15]

Coffee, who beheld the assault on the right, replete with its "prodigious yelling," requested 200 troops to counterattack and blunt the Red Sticks' charge. Coffee's intent was to thrust his mounted men against the flank of the Red Sticks and turn their left. Soldiers in the rear of the detachment, however, refused to join in the attack, so only fifty-four men rode with Coffee into action. Among them were the volunteer officers of Coffee's brigade, soldiers of Captain Eli Hammond's company, scouts from Captain Russell's company, and troops under the command of Captains George Elliott and Thomas Mann.[16]

Coffee's men struck the Red Sticks, who were concealed in brush on a ridge of pine trees. The rough terrain prompted the brigadier to dismount his men and charge them on foot into the thicket to dislodge the "savages" from their refuge. The spirited attack drove the Red Sticks from the ridge to the banks of a reed-choked creek, but not without cost. Coffee suffered a painful wound through the body, while his aide-de-camp, Maj. Alexander Donelson, "who bravely fought and bravely fell," was killed, shot through the skull. Three other soldiers of the "little Sparten band" were also slain in the attack.[17]

Jackson, meanwhile, ordered up some 150 to 200 native troops as reinforcements for Coffee's counterattack. Before the Cherokees and White Creeks could be dispatched to succor Coffee, yet another Creek attack was launched against the Americans. Jackson quickly realized that the Red Stick attack on the right was a diversion to weaken the left of his line, and he ordered his men there to stand firm. Thus the Red Stick feint, which General Coffee had met so successfully, failed to draw sufficient numbers of men from the left side of the line to make it vulnerable to assault. Jackson personally encouraged his troops to stand firm and ordered reinforcements to counter the new threat. "The whole line met the enemy with astonishing entrepidity," Jackson recalled with pride, "and having given a few fires, they forthwith charged with great vigor." Captain Reid also witnessed the attack, which was "opposed with great gallantry." The Red Sticks fired at the militia from behind fallen logs, "prostrating themselves after firing, and re-loading, they would rise and again discharge their guns."[18]

The stalemate on the left was finally broken with a charge ordered by Colonel Carroll. Unable to stand against infantry armed with bayonets, the Red Sticks were thrown into confusion by the charge, routed from behind their logs, and pursued for one and one-half miles in a precipitous retreat and slaughter. Carroll's men slew some twenty-three Red Sticks in the charge and pursuit, made possible only because of the distinguished initial stand made Colonel Higgins and his regiment.

As Higgins and Carroll were beating back the attack in their sector, John Coffee's men continued to attack the Red Sticks on his front in an attempt to drive them from their shelter along the creek. The new position frustrated his forays to dislodge the Red Sticks, who, concealed in the reeds, were all but immune to American musketry. In an attempt to lure the Indians from their position and entice them to attack, Coffee ordered his men to retire to their horses. The ruse worked. The aggressive Red Sticks left the protection offered by the reeds and attacked the troopers. Although the men were "exhausted with fatigue," they stood firmly in the face of the new onslaught.[19]

Meanwhile, Carroll's pursuit of the Red Sticks from the left of Jackson's front was abandoned and the American soldiers and native troops returned to camp to reform their lines. With Coffee's battle still raging in front of his right flank, Jackson again ordered reinforcement for the beleaguered troops. The friendly Indians of James Fife, chief of the White Creeks, hastened to relieve Coffee. With these fresh supports to bolster his thinning line of battle, Coffee ordered his men forward in a final attempt to rout the Red Sticks from the field. The attack was well timed, and the Indians "fled in consternation and were pursued with dreadful slaughter." Forty-five Red Stick corpses were discovered during the three-mile pursuit.[20]

Jackson's dead were carried into the camp for burial while the wounded were collected on litters fashioned from the skins of slain horses. As the long day waned, the camp was fortified. Axes felled timber for a breastwork. Although the day had been won, the seesaw battle had drained the energy and enthusiasm from the volunteers, most of whom had never before fired a shot in anger. As Jackson related to his wife, "my wounded was so increased, my horses starving [and] my men in some degree began to be panic struck." Captain Reid also commented on the morale, remarking that, "the spirits of our troops, most of whom had never before seen an enemy, were observed visibly to flag, towards the evening" within the breastwork of logs fortifying the camp. Another Red Sticks attack on the militia was anticipated during the night, and "it was with the utmost difficulty the sentinels could be kept at their posts, who, expecting, every minute, the appearance of the enemy, would, at the least noise, fire and run in."[21]

Although his militia had successfully reconnoitered the encampment of Tohopeka and had encountered the Red Sticks and inflicted severe casualties at Emuckfaw, General Jackson determined it was time to return to Fort Strother. His own army had suffered enough casualties to dishearten his volunteers, and as Jackson explained it, the militia expedition "had not set out prepared or with a view to make a permanent establishment." The general "considered it worse than useless to advance and destroy an empty encampment." It was not

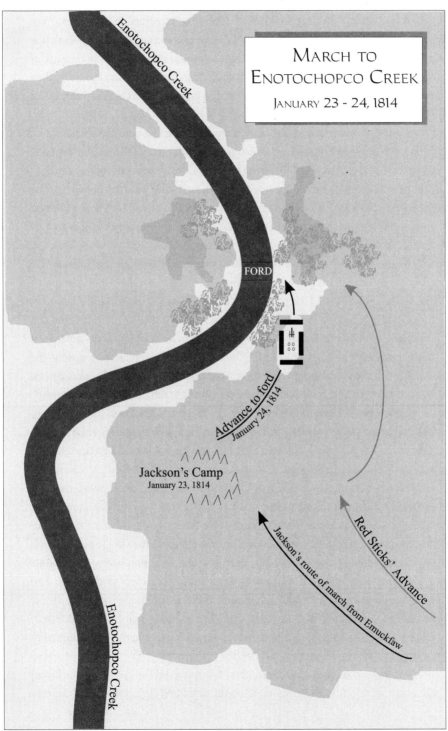

Enotochopco Creek

MARCH TO
ENOTOCHOPCO CREEK
JANUARY 23 - 24, 1814

FORD

Advance to ford
January 24, 1814

Jackson's Camp
January 23, 1814

Jackson's route of march from Emuckfaw

Red Sticks' Advance

Enotochopco Creek

Theodore P. Savas

necessary "or prudent to proceed any farther," he explained in his report. "Not necessary because . . . by commencing a return, which having to them the appearance of a retreat would inspirit them to pursue me: not prudent because of the number of my wounded . . . of the starving condition of my horses, they having had neither corn nor cain [sic] . . . [and because] of the scarcity of supplies."[22]

Supplies were indeed short. The native Creek and Cherokee soldiers with Jackson's army were described as being "destitute," while the militia's rations were scarce. The horses, upon which the entire army depended, were grazing on cane after having consumed the last of their corn fodder. Jackson hoped to draw the Red Sticks away from their encampment in a diversion for General Floyd, who at this time was marching his own men toward Calabee Creek, where he would meet the Red Sticks in battle on January 27.[23]

Abandoning his breastwork at Emuckfaw at 10:30 a.m. on January 23, Jackson began marching his fatigued army toward Enotochopco, "a deep creek and between two hills." During the march the men passed a "harycane," or what Jackson described as a "dangerous defile occasioned by a hurricane," a collection of timber felled by a tornado. When the Enotochopco was reached at dusk, the men promptly began cutting trees to built a log breastwork around the camp to protect them against an attack. The miserable and backbreaking work was conducted under a cold rain, which continued to fall throughout the night.[24]

Jackson was expecting the Red Sticks to attack him in the morning. In order to avoid an ambuscade at the ravine of Enotochopco Creek, he had his "guide and fatigue" troops to cut a road through the thickets to a crossing on the waterway. Although reeds grew along the banks of Enotochopco, they were thin at this ford. Jackson's intention was "to draw the enemy after me over a peace of ground, that I could slaughter the whole of them." On the morning January 24, the militia army prepared for its march. The flanks and rear were arranged to meet an attack, while the wounded were transported in litters in the center of the column with the army's artillery. Before long the slow-moving columns approached Enotochopco and began descending the ridge to the ford. The advance guard and some of the flanking columns made it safely over the creek, as did the litters carrying the wounded. The artillery was in the process of crossing, the frigid water reaching up to the hubs of the wheels, when musketry erupted in the army's rear.[25]

When Jackson heard the alarm, he "felt rejoiced, the ground was of [his] choosing, and [he] knew if the men would stand and fight [he] would destroy every nine of ten of the enemy." Since the attack (or ambush) was anticipated, Jackson later claimed he heard the musketry "without surprise, and even with pleasure, calculating with the utmost confidence on the firmness of [his] troops. The general planned to meet the attack by wheeling his right and left columns into line, recrossing the creek and falling upon the flanks and rear of the Red Sticks. Once contact was made, Jackson would order his militia to envelop the attackers and cut off their retreat with a ring of bayonets. The plan was to trap the Red Sticks in a move reminiscent of Jackson's earlier pair of victories at Tallusahatchee and Talladega. The rear guard, which was turning back to meet the advancing Red Sticks, was composed of the regiments commanded by Colonel Nicholas Perkins and Lieutenant Colonel John Stump. Captain Ferrell's company was posted to guard the wounded, whose litters were being carried up the bank as the alarm sounded.[26]

"Old Hickory" awaited the deployment of his trap, confident of victory. "But to my astonishment and mortification," he later wrote, "I beheld the right and left columns of the rear guard precipitately give way. This shameful retreat was disastrous in the extreme." To his wife, Jackson confessed that the columns in the rear "broke like Bullocks." As confusion erupted up and down the line, Jackson spurred his horse to the creek bank to arrest the retreat, harshly admonishing the fugitives to stand and face the enemy. "I attempted to draw my sword, it had become hard to draw, and in the attempt I had like to have broke my left arm," Jackson explained to his wife, claiming that if he had been able to unsheath his sword, he would have halted the stampede. The colonels of the fleeing regiments, Perkins and Stump, proved no help at all and in fact contributed to the confusion by leading the stampede rearward. Only Colonel Carroll and a meager collection of twenty-five soldiers led by Captain John Quarles, whom Carroll had managed to halt and form for action, together with Captain William Russell's company of scouts, stood firm in the face of the onslaught, volleying their muskets into the Red Sticks.[27]

When the attack struck the rear of the army, Captain David Deaderick's artillery company was in the process of crossing the creek, the artillerists and horses straining to pull the harnessed cannon and limber wagon through the deep water. The guns were under the immediate command of Lieutenant Robert Armstrong, since Deaderick was absent, "confined by sickness." As Jackson later noted, "With his wonted bravery, [Lieutenant Armstrong] ordered the guards to form, [and] unharnish the artillery." Some of the musket-carrying artillerists, in obedience to orders and in the face of a galling fire from the

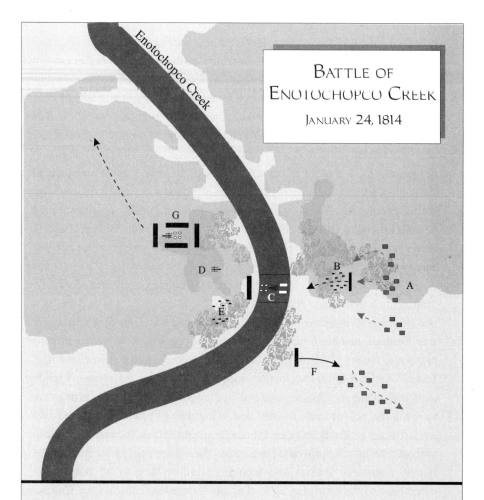

A. The initial Red Stick assault;

B. Jackson's rear guard stampedes in the face of the sudden attack, and drops back in the direction of the ford on Enotochopco Creek;

C. The ford, showing the first position of the artillery piece and litters;

D. The second position of Jackson's artillery. His artillerists made a gallant stand on a small hill above the creek, and probably saved the army from a devastating defeat;

E. Jackson rallies his fleeing soldiers, and guides them back over the creek to attack the Red Sticks' left flank;

F. The Red Sticks are finally repulsed and pursued back to Tohopeka, in the bend of the Horseshoe on the Tallapoosa River. This site will witness the climax of Jackson's campaign against the Red Sticks on March 27, 1814, at the Battle of Horseshoe Bend;

G. Jackson reassembles his column and resumes his march to Fort Strother.

opposite bank, formed atop a small hill, leveled their firearms and fired "tremendous" volleys into the enemy. Under the cover of this fire, five cannoneers in company with Lieutenant Armstrong managed to drag the 6-pounder from the mud of the creek and haul its carriage to the summit of the hill. General Jackson's "heart bled for [these] brave" cannoneers. Although he ordered reinforcements to assist them, his orders went unheeded in the reigning chaos. The artillerists, he later explained, were "obliged to conquer or die."[28]

With nothing but sweat and muscle, the men deployed their piece for action. In the confusion of unlimbering the gun, however, the rammer and priming wire (or pricker) were misplaced. Despite the loss of the tools of their trade, two artillerists, Constantine Perkins and Cravan Jackson, refused to retreat and somehow managed to load the cannon with grapeshot. In lieu of the pricker or priming wire ("picker"), Jackson stuck his ramrod through the vent of the cannon at its breech to puncture the grapeshot cartridge in its flannel bag. As he did so, he tore a musket cartridge with his teeth to prime the vent, rather than inserting a priming quill or pouring loose powder from a priming horn. Perkins, meanwhile removed his bayonet and used the muzzle of his musket to ram the cartridge of grape down the cannon tube. A smoldering match held by a linstock was prepared to discharge the cannon.

As Perkins and Jackson continued their work unscathed, others around them were not so fortunate. Captain William Hamilton, who had been abandoned by his troops at Fort Strother when their terms of enlistment expired, was serving as an artillerist and suffered a fatal wound. The gallant Lieutenant Armstrong was also struck down with a mortal and painful wound in the groin. The stricken officer, fearing the loss of the gun to the enemy, continued to shout encouragement to his artillerists. "Some of you must perish!" he yelled, urging them to save the cannon. According to Captain Reid, "every man who there fought, [the artillerists, and Quarles's and Russell's companies under Colonel Carroll] seemed to prefer death to flight."[29]

Despite Armstrong's fears, Perkins, Jackson and the rest of the cannoneers had no intention of losing their artillery piece. One of them leaned over with the linstock and discharged the cannon, sending a hail of grapeshot into the mass of Red Sticks. "The cannon fired, the muskets roared . . . [and] the cannon roared again [then] this Spartan band charged" with fixed bayonets, reported General Jackson. Armstrong's men, he wrote with no little pride, acted with "deliberate bravery"[30]:

[I]n the hurry of the moment, in separating the gun from her limbers—the rammer and picker of the cannon was left tied to the limber. As soon as they were about to fire, this was discovered. Jackson amidst the galling fire of the enemy pulled out the Iron ramrod of his musket, used it as a picker, primed with a cartridge and fired the cannon, Perkins pulled off his bayonet, used his musket as a rammer, drove home the load with the muzzle of his musket, Jackson again used the ramrod as a picker, the cartridge as a powder horn, and fired her again.[31]

While the artillerists held their ground, Jackson and his staff, including the wounded General Coffee, endeavored to restore order within the ranks of the army. Coffee had been carried on a litter on the march from Emuckfaw but, anticipating the battle, had mounted his horse that morning. The wounded officer displayed "calm and deliberate firmness"[32] in the demoralized stampede of the militia. Of General Jackson, Captain Reid remarked:

In that moment of confusion, he was the rallying point, even for the spirits of the brave . . . . Cowards forgot their panic, and fronted danger, when they heard his voice, and beheld his manner; and the brave would have formed round his body a rampart of their own. In the midst of showers of balls, of which he seemed unmindful, he was seen performing the duties of subordinate officers, rallying the alarmed, halting them in their flight, forming his columns, and inspiriting them by his example. An army, suddenly dismayed, was thus rescued from the destruction that lately appeared inevitable.[33]

Captain Gordon's company of scouts from the advance guard had hastened across the creek to strike the Red Sticks on their left flank. Broken by the musketry and thrown into confusion by the shower of grapeshot, the Indians began retreating, pursued by the troops of Carroll and the reinforcements mustered by Jackson and his staff. "The enemy . . . were stricken with alarm, and fled away, leaving behind their blankets, and whatever [other equipment] was likely to retard their flight," Captain Reid remembered. Captain Quarles, "preferring death to the abandonment of his post," was mortally wounded in the head during the firm stand of his troops. Twenty-six Red Stick corpses were tallied, but Jackson estimated some 200 were killed in the carnage at Enotochopco and in the pursuit of the broken Muskogees. Most of the corpses of the Red Sticks were carried from the field by surviving warriors.[34]

It had been a near thing, but Jackson once again emerged victorious. The future American president's militia had suffered twenty killed and seventy-five wounded, four mortally, in the battles at Emuckfaw (January 22) and Enotochopco (January 24), while inflicting heavy casualties on the Red Stick Creeks, who lost at least 189 slain, their dead counted by the victors. The latter victory was gained in spite of Colonel Perkins and Lieutenant Colonel Stump, who had fled rearward with their men at the beginning of the fight. To Jackson, such an act was unforgivable. "Had it not been for the cowardly conduct of those two officers (for the men were brave if the officers had shew the example) I should have killed the most of these barbarians without half the loss I , sustained," he complained to his wife. "[The officers] are now under an inquiry before a court martial. They ought to be shot." Stump was not executed but he was cashiered, while the Court of Inquiry exonerated Perkins of cowardice.[35]

Jackson claimed "a signal victory over [the Red Sticks], they lost their packs and was never saw or heard of more, during [his] return march" to Fort Strother. The militia marched for the fort "no more disturbed by their yells." Jackson complimented his staff for performing their duty, firmly maintaining their assigned posts, and restoring order from chaos at Enotochopco.[36] For their exertions in distributing the general's orders, Jackson reported them as deserving of his gratitude.

To Richard K. Call, a volunteer officer who would later serve as Jackson's aide-de-camp, the general wrote a laudatory letter describing his appreciation of the peril menacing his army at the Alabama creek and his gratitude to the courageous cannoneers who preserved his militia from rout and massacre. "[H]aving been abandoned by your company contrary to my express orders," he began,

> Having yourself remained at your post, followed me and bravely faught at Emuckfau and more bravely with the guards to whom you had attached yourself at the battle of Enotachapco. There the guards and those attached to them covered themselves with glory, and by their bravery Saved my rear from havack and distruction . . . .
>
> On your retirement you carry with you my grateful acknowledgment for your Services and the bravery you displayed with the artillery Company on the banks of Enotachapco on the morning of the 24th Instant.[37]

The campaign's accomplishments were amazing. With a raw militia army Jackson had penetrated into enemy territory, defeated the Red Stick Muskogee in two pitched battles, performed a reconnaissance which helped divert attention away from General Floyd's column of Georgians operating along the

Tallapoosa, and prevented a planned enemy attack upon Fort Armstrong on the Coosa River. Jackson remarked in his report to General Pinckney that the battles at Emuckfaw and Enotochopco "hastened the termination of the creek war." Captain Reid agreed: "perhaps the greatest good that resulted . . . was the effect produced on the minds of the people at home, from whom was to be collected a force sufficient to terminate the war. Experience has often proved the facility with which numbers are brought to a victorious standard. . . ."[38]

With their terms of enlistment expiring, the victorious militia were discharged and sent home to encourage others to join the "victorious standard." The final campaign of the war two months later, with its culminating victory at Horseshoe Bend, wiped away any lingering blemish from the colors of the militia. After that victory, Jackson would write his wife about the conduct of his soldiers, claiming, "There never was more heroism or roman courage displayed." He continued the praise in his report of the campaign, lauding both Regulars and militiamen: "Never were men more eager to be led to a charge . . . . The spirit which animated them was a sure augury of the success which was to follow. . . . [T]he militia . . . charged with a vivacity and firmness, which would have done honour to regulars."[39]

Jackson's palpable anxiety regarding militia, engendered by their near-rout at Enotochopco ("after the retreat of the rear guard, they seemed to have lost all their collectedness, and were more difficult to restore to order than any troops I have ever seen"[40]) would be erased by his March 27, 1814, victory at Horseshoe, Bend, as he would report to Tennessee Governor Willie Blount:

> The conduct of the militia on this occasion has gone far towards redeeming the character of that description of troops. They have been as orderly in their encampments and on the line of march, as they have been signally brave in the day of battle.[41]

The prosecution of the cruel war with the Creeks was approaching its climax. Jackson, who received widespread recognition for his victories after his battle report made its appearance in the newspapers, cobbled together yet another militia army for the final effort to crush the Red Sticks. This third legion was stocked with infantry from the Thirty-Ninth U. S. Regiment to inculcate discipline into the militia ranks. The bitter tarnish of Enotochopco Creek was about to be polished into the luster of final victory.

NOTES

1. John Reid and John Henry Eaton, *The Life of Andrew Jackson* (Philadelphia: M. Carey, 1817), 124, 137.

2. "The war clubs were immediately seen . . . particularly among the . . . hordes residing near the Alabama." (Ibid., 29). "[War] clubs when painted red, [are] consider[ed] a declaration of war. They are formed of a stick . . . with a strong piece of sharp iron affixed at the end; and in appearance resemble a hatchet." (Ibid., 29 n). "These sticks Tecumseh caused to be painted red. It was from this . . . that these Indians were called Red Sticks." (Benjamin Drake, *Life of Tecumseh* [New York: Kraus Reprint Co., 1969], 144).

3. Andrew Jackson to John Coffee, Camp Blount, October 7, 1813, John Spencer Bassett, ed., *The Correspondence of Andrew Jackson* (New York: Kraus Reprint Company, 1969), vol. 1, 328.

4. David Crockett, *A Narrative of the Life of David Crockett of the State of Tennessee* (Lincoln: University of Nebraska Press, 1987), 88, 92.

5. Ibid., 89-90.

6. Reid and Eaton, *Life of Andrew Jackson*, 124.

7. Jackson to Thomas Pinckney, January 29, 1814, Bassett, *The Correspondence of Andrew Jackson*, 448

8. Ibid., 449; Reid and Eaton, *Life of Andrew Jackson*, 126.

9. Jackson to Thomas Pinckney, January 29, 1814, Bassett, *The Correspondence of Andrew Jackson*, 449; Reid and Eaton, *Life of Andrew Jackson*, 126.

10. Jackson to Rachel Jackson, January 28, 1814, Bassett, *The Correspondence of Andrew Jackson*, 444.

11. Reid and Eaton, *Life of Andrew Jackson*, 126; Jackson to Rachel Jackson, January 28, 1814, and Jackson to Thomas Pinckney, Bassett, *The Correspondence of Andrew Jackson*, 444, 449.

12. Reid and Eaton, *Life of Andrew Jackson*, 126; Jackson to Rachel Jackson, January 28, 1814, and Jackson to Thomas Pinckney, Bassett, *The Correspondence of Andrew Jackson*, 444, 449.

13. Reid and Eaton, *Life of Andrew Jackson*, 126.

14. Jackson to Thomas Pinckney, January 29, 1814, Bassett, *The Correspondence of Andrew Jackson*, 450."

15. Ibid.

16. Reid and Eaton, *Life of Andrew Jackson*, 126.

17. Ibid.; Jackson to Rachel Jackson, January 28, 1814, Bassett, *The Correspondence of Andrew Jackson*, 445."

18. Jackson to Thomas Pinckney, January 29, 1814," Bassett, *The Correspondence of Andrew Jackson*, 450; Reid and Eaton, *Life of Andrew Jackson*, 128.

19. Reid and Eaton, *Life of Andrew Jackson*, 128.

20. Ibid.

21. Jackson to Rachel Jackson, January 29, 1814, Bassett, *The Correspondence of Andrew Jackson*, 445; Reid and Eaton, *Life of Andrew Jackson*, 130.

22. Jackson to Thomas Pinckney, January 29, 1814, Bassett, *The Correspondence of Andrew Jackson*, 150, 151.

23. Ibid.

24. Jackson to Rachel Jackson, January 28, 1814," and "Jackson to Thomas Pinckney, January 29, 1814," Bassett, *The Correspondence of Andrew Jackson*, 445, 451.

25. Jackson to Rachel Jackson, January 28, 1814," ibid., 445.

26. Jackson to Thomas Pinckney, January 29, 1814," ibid., 451.

27. Jackson to Rachel Jackson, January 28, 1814," ibid., 445.

28. Jackson to Rachel Jackson, January 28, 1814, and Jackson to Thomas Pinckney, January 29, 1814," ibid., 446, 452.

29. Reid and Eaton, *Life of Andrew Jackson*, 134.

30. Jackson to Thomas Pinckney, January 29, 1814, ibid., 452.

31. Ibid.

32. Reid and Eaton, *Life of Andrew Jackson*, 135.

33. Ibid., 135, 136-137.

34. Ibid., 135; Jackson to Thomas Pinckney, January 29, 1814, Bassett, *The Correspondence of Andrew Jackson*, 452.

35. Jackson to Rachel Jackson, January 28, 1814, ibid., 447.

36. Jackson to Rachel Jackson, January 28, 1814, and Jackson to Thomas Pinckney, January 29, 1814," ibid., 447, 452.

37. Jackson to Richard K. Call, January 30, 1814, Bassett, *The Correspondence of Andrew Jackson*, 454.

38. Ibid.; Reid and Eaton, *Life of Andrew Jackson*, 138.

39. Jackson to Rachel Jackson, April 1, 1814, and Jackson to Thomas Pinckney, March 28, 1814, Bassett, *The Correspondence of Andrew Jackson*, 493, 489.

40. Jackson to Thomas Pinckney, January 29, 1814," ibid., 453, 489.

41. Ibid., and Jackson to Willie Blount, "Battle of Tehopiska [sic], or the Horse Shoe," March 31, 1814, Bassett, *The Correspondence of Andrew Jackson*, 492.

"The Carnage was Dreadful"

The Battle of
HORSESHOE BEND
March 27, 1814

John Alden Reid

> "The bend of the Tallapoosa...resembles in its curvature that of a horse shoe. . . .Nature furnishes few situations so eligible for defence; and barbarians have never rendered one more secure by art. Across the neck of land which leads into it. . .they had erected a breast-work, of greatest compactness and strength—from five to eight feet high, and prepared with double rows of port-holes very artfully arranged. The skill which they manifested in their breast-work, was really astonishing."[1]

With these words General Andrew Jackson of the Tennessee Militia described the log and dirt barricade of the Red Stick Creeks of Chief Menawa and the Prophet Monahee. Jackson's army of regulars from the Thirty-Ninth U.S. Infantry and Tennessee militia brigades took the barricade by storm at the point of the bayonet in the bloodiest battle of the Creek War in the then-wilderness of Alabama. On March 27, 1814, Jackson's army managed to crush the Red Sticks despite their strong fortified position and conspicuous bravery. The slaughter claimed some 800-900 of the 1,000 Creeks arrayed for battle behind the barricade. In a battle noted for its savagery, Jackson's army suffered 49 killed and 154 wounded, many mortally.

The Battle of the Horseshoe was one of the bloodiest of the War of 1812, and is perhaps the worst slaughter suffered by natives at the hands of an American army. The power of the Creeks (also known as Muskogee) was forever broken by the carnage on the banks of the Tallapoosa River; the hopes of the Red Sticks, the traditionalist Creeks who sought to halt white expansion by force, were immolated in the fires of the war's desolation.

Andrew Jackson's stunning victory earned him his first laurels of martial fame, catapulting him into the national limelight. Nine months later on January 8, 1815, he would vanquish the British Redcoats at Chalmette in the Battle of New Orleans, the last battle of the War of 1812 and the worst defeat suffered by the British on American soil. From the spoils of Jackson's victory at Horseshoe Bend came Alabama, the twenty-second state admitted to the Union, a state born out of the embers of war. Jackson's triumphs over Red Sticks and Redcoats carried him to the White House in 1829, when he was inaugurated the seventh president of the United States.

*   *   *

The Red Stick Creeks of the northern Tallapoosa River towns began concentrating at the refugee encampment of Tohopeka in the horseshoe-shaped bend of the Tallapoosa—or, in their Muskogee tongue, *Cholocco Litabixee*, or "horse's hoof"—at the narrowest neck of the peninsula. There, a strong log and dirt barricade had been constructed to protect the crude log huts erected in the "toe" of the horseshoe. The encampment of Tohopeka, which in Muskogee meant "fence" or "fortification," attracted Red Sticks from the surrounding towns of Oakfuskee, New Yauca, Eufaula, Oakchaya, the Fish Ponds, and the Hillabee towns, all of which were abandoned as the threat of war with Americans approached yet again.

Andrew Jackson's militia had crushed Red Stick resistance to the north during his first campaign nearer to the Coosa River, at the battles of Tullusahatchee on November 3, 1813, and Talladega six days later. The defeats convinced the survivors and fugitive Red Sticks to flee south to the Tallapoosa River towns. Hillabee warriors had also suffered at the hands of the militia, although their defeat was the result of a tragic mistake. The Hillabees had delivered a peace overture to General Jackson, who in turn made arrangements to deliver it to Tennessee militia general John Cocke. Unfortunately, Cocke had already ordered General James White's Tennessee militia and Cherokee allies to attack the hostile Indians living along Hillabee Creek. On November 18, 1813, White's combined force swept into the area and proceeded to slaughter the unprepared Indians. Jackson's message about the peace negotiation and surrender of the Hillabees reached Cocke after the "Hillabee Massacre." The survivors believed the attack was the result of Jackson's perfidy and resolved to never again surrender or contemplate peace.

Other events also worked to effect the gathering of the Indians within the Horseshoe. The town of New Yauca, situated on the opposite bank of the Tallapoosa River near the Horseshoe, was razed in December 1813 by a Georgia militia raid commanded by Gen. David Adams. The surviving Red Sticks concentrated with the refugees of the Hillabee towns and other Red Sticks within the peninsula behind the barricade. Unfortunately for the surviving Indians, the Horseshoe's ostensible strength was but a chimera.

Jackson's second militia campaign in January 1814 had penetrated all the way to the Tallapoosa River. This expedition witnessed another pair of American victories at the battles of Emuckfaw (January 22) and Enotochopco (January 24), two bitter clashes that severely weakened the Red Sticks' ability to wage war. It was during the former battle that the Americans got their first look of the powerful barricade at Tohopeka, when General John Coffee and his mounted troops reconnoitered the position but deemed it too strong to directly attack. After his battlefield successes, Jackson returned to Fort Strother on the Coosa River and began planning the decisive campaign to exterminate the Red Sticks, who after their devastating defeats at Emuckfaw and Enotochopco withdrew to Tohopeka to reorganize and await Jackson's inevitable advance.

Reinforced with new levies of militia and the Regulars of the Thirty-Ninth U.S. Infantry, Jackson moved down the Coosa and established Fort Williams. Using axes to cut a rough road through the wilderness and dragging two cannon with them, Jackson's Tennessee Army marched from Fort Williams on the Coosa River and encamped at Emuckfaw Creek on March 26, 1814. Emuckfaw, the scene of Jackson's earlier victory, stirred emotions, bringing about the hope that this time the Americans would inflict an even more decisive defeat. The Red Sticks were now within striking distance.

Early the following morning, Jackson detached Gen. John Coffee's brigade of 700 mounted militia, Col. Gideon Morgan's regiment of 500 Cherokees, and Maj. William McIntosh's 100 "White" Creeks, to ford the Tallapoosa and surround the large bend in the waterway, a deft move which simultaneously prevented reinforcements from reaching the Red Sticks and cut off their line of retreat. The Indians' wall, proclaimed Jackson, "became a snare" where they were "penned for the slaughter."[2]

While his blocking column moved into position, Jackson and the troops of the Thirty-Ninth U.S. Infantry and the Tennessee Militia Infantry, about 2,000 soldiers, marched into the peninsula of the Horseshoe to confront the 1,000 Red Sticks behind their log and dirt barricade. The cannoneers of the pair of small

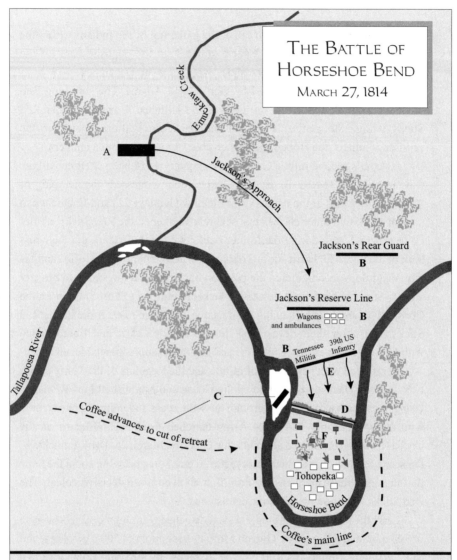

THE BATTLE OF
HORSESHOE BEND
MARCH 27, 1814

Emuckfaw Creek

Jackson's Approach

A

Tallapoosa River

Jackson's Rear Guard
B

Jackson's Reserve Line
Wagons and ambulances   B

B   Tennessee Militia   39th US Infantry
E

C

D

Coffee advances to cut of retreat

F

Tohopeka

Horseshoe Bend

Coffee's main line

A. Jackson's column approaches Horseshoe Bend

B. Jackson's army prepares for battle. He forms his Tennessee militia and U.S. Regulars in the main line of battle, with a second line and his ambulances and wagons in reserve. A small rear guard is also posted.

C. General Coffee's cavalry is dispatched to either attack from the rear or cut off the retreat of the Red Sticks. Meanwhile, Bean's militia takes up a position on an island in the Tallapoosa River opposite the left flank of the main Red Stick line of battle.

D. The Red Sticks form their main line of battle behind the dirt and log barricade.

E. Jackson's main attack overruns the Red Stick position.

F. Overwhelmed, the Red Sticks stream rearward deeper in the Horseshoe, which in reality is little more than a death trap.

artillery pieces accompanying Jackson, (a three-pounder and six-pounder belonging to Capt. Joel Parrish's Militia Artillery Company), were ordered to bombard the log wall from a knoll 80 yards distant from the barricade. Jackson hoped the bombardment would breach the barricade and rout the "savages" taking shelter behind it. Jackson "endeavoured to levell the works with. . .cannon, but in vain." For two hours his guns and riflemen let loose "a brisk. . . galling fire," a hail of iron shot and lead balls which splintered the bark of the logs, but the "balls passed thro the works without shaking the wall. . . ." Although nearly "every shot penetrated. . . and carried with it death," explained Jackson, "still such was the strength of the wall that it never shook."[3]

Some 70 three- and six-pound solid shot were fired in the cannonade, but the round shot embedded itself in the logs and dirt of the rampart or passed through, leaving the wall standing. When Jackson realized his first bombardment would not create a breach through which his infantry could charge, he contemplated a bayonet assault upon the barricade using the core of his army, the regulars of the Thirty-Ninth, as the vanguard.

Meanwhile, Cherokees and White Creeks from Jackson's blocking column swam the Tallapoosa despite its frigid depth and swift current, stole canoes stashed along the bank by the Red Sticks, and ferried militia soldiers back across the stream. The troops attacked the Red Sticks from the rear, burning the crude log huts of Tohopeka and capturing the 300 women and children who cowered there. "Notwithstanding the determined bravery" of these soldiers, they were too few to overwhelm the Red Sticks, or as Jackson later reported, "wholly insufficient to dislodge the enemy." The move, however, distracted the Indians and forced them to fight the battle on two fronts. Already outnumbered, the move against the rear of their position sealed their doom.[4]

Determined to rely on his Regulars, Jackson ordered an infantry charge with fixed bayonets to rout the determined Red Sticks from behind the logs. The men moved out and quickly reached the flaming barricade, which was shrouded in a sulphurous, choking haze. The combat raged "muzzle to muzzle, through the port-holes," where the lead "balls were welded to the bayonets of . . . musquets." Major Lemuel Montgomery of the Thirty-Ninth U.S. Infantry was killed in the assault, shot through the skull. Another participant with better luck was Ensign Samuel Houston, who would later become famous for his association with the state of Texas. Houston was the victim of a grievous wound inflicted by a barbed arrow in his thigh.[5]

A fanciful depiction of the wounding of Sam Houston at the barricade.

Horseshoe Bend National Military Park

Red Stick Chief Menawa

Horseshoe Bend National Military Park

Jackson's bloody gamble, however, was a smashing success and the Red Sticks were driven from the barricade at the point of the bayonet. The routed Indians fled into the thickets around the banks of the Tallapoosa. Jackson's cannons had been dragged to the barricade after it fell under the weight of his infantry. The pieces were fired into the retreating Indians, many of whose leaders were killed or wounded in the flight. The Prophet Monahee was "shot in the mouth by a grape shot" and killed.[6]

Somehow the chief of the Red Sticks, Menawa, managed to escape with his life despite suffering seven wounds. Tulwa Tustunuggee, a Hillabee Red Stick warrior, was wounded nine times and carried from the butchery by his brother, Emathlahutky. The battle itself lasted about five hours, explained Jackson, "but the firing and slaughter continued until it was suspended by the darkness of the night." The slaughter moved even Jackson. "The carnage was dreadfull," he explained to his wife Rachel in describing the nature of the action following the fall of the barricade:

> The event could no longer be doubtful. The enemy altho many of them fought to the last with that kind of bravery which desperation inspires, were at length entirely routed and cut to pieces. The whole margin of the river which surrounded the peninsular was strewed with the slain. Five hundred and fifty seven were found by officers of great respectability whom I had ordered to count them; besides a very great number who were thrown into the river by their surviving friends, and killed. . . .

"Both officers and men who had the best opportunities of judging,"concluded Jackson, "believe the loss of the enemy in killed not to fall short of eight hundred."[7]

The battle wiped out the cream of the Red Stick warriors. Fugitive Red Sticks fled south to the Seminoles in Spanish Florida, while others, suffering from starvation, surrendered to Jackson's army as it marched south to build Fort Jackson at the confluence of the Coosa and Tallapoosa rivers in April 1814. Jackson dismissed his militiamen in May and returned with them to Tennessee after eight months of campaigning in the Alabama wilderness. Promoted to major general in the Regular Army (he had been a general of militia), Jackson returned to dictate the Treaty of Fort Jackson to the Creeks in August 1814. The accord ceded some 20 million acres of land to the United States.

The Horseshoe of the Tallapoosa after the battle, Jackson poetically announced to his men after their return march to Fort Williams on April 2, 1814, appeared as a "wilderness which wither[ed] in sterility and seem[ed] to mourn the desolation which overspread it."[8] Although Jackson's army left the corpses of 557 Red Sticks to rot, some were gathered for burial after the Americans vacated the area. The Tallapoosa, too, was a cemetery for the slain of the battle. Jackson's killed (except for Maj. Lemuel Montgomery, who was buried on the field) were sunk in the river to prevent the mutilation of their corpses, a rather ironic burial alongside some 300-400 Red Sticks who were shot or drowned in the same waterway.

According to Andrew Jackson, the men who died at the Horseshoe Bend of the Tallapoosa "fell gloriously."[9] Although his words were intended to honor only the men in his army, the same can be said for the Red Sticks, who sacrificed their lives in the defense of their culture and way of life. The ground at Horseshoe Bend was hallowed by the bravery of those who struggled in the combat, and the national military park is itself a monument to all who fell there.

NOTES

1. Andrew Jackson to Governor Blount, "Battle of Tehopiska [sic], or the Horse Shoe," John Spence Bassett, ed., *The Correspondence of Andrew Jackson* (New York: Kraus Reprint Company, 1969), vol. 2, p. 490. Very few firsthand accounts of the fighting at Horseshoe bend exist. The bulk of our knowledge of what transpired there is based upon Jackson's correspondence, and this article is based on that source as well as this author's familiarity with the terrain.

2. Proclamation by Jackson, April 2, 1814, ibid., p. 494.

3. Jackson to Blount, "Tehopiska," and, Jackson to Rachel Jackson, April 1, 1814, ibid., p. 490, 493.

4. Ibid.

5. Jackson to Blount, "Tehopiska," ibid., p. 490.

6. Ibid.

7. Ibid.

8. Proclamation by Jackson, April 2, 1814," ibid., p. 494.

9. Jackson to Blount, "Tehopiska," ibid., p. 492.

BLACK HAWK
This engraving, which shows Black Hawk wearing a blue
military frock coat, is based upon paintings made after his capture.

The Sauk and the Black Hawk War, with Biographical Sketches, etc.

THE BLACK HAWK WAR RECONSIDERED

A New Interpretation of its Causes and Consequences

Patrick J. Jung

"Black Hawk has done nothing for which an Indian ought to be ashamed. He has fought for his countrymen . . . against white men who came, year after year, to cheat them and take away their lands. You know the cause of our making war. It is known to all white men. They ought to be ashamed of it."

— attributed to Black Hawk at his surrender,
as quoted from Wayne Moquin, ed., *Great Documents of American Indian History*

The Black Hawk War has generated a tremendous amount of interest among the general public and scholars since it was fought in 1832. Much of the interest in this small war derives from the fact that it was one of the few Indian uprisings in the Old Northwest that was not fought as part of a larger imperial conflict. While the events of the war are well known, historians continue to disagree about its causes. Participants and observers, including the Sauk warrior Black Hawk (Makataimeshekiakiak), penned the earliest books on the war. These works tended to castigate either the Sauks and Mesquakies (the latter also known as the Foxes) or the scheming, land-hungry white settlers and their political allies for starting the conflict. Other works appeared in the late nineteenth century and throughout the twentieth century that added little to the debate and simply restated the two earlier arguments.[1]

After the Second World War, the intersection of cultural anthropology and history brought about a series of important works that examined the war from the standpoint of tribal politics and internal division. The focus of these works was the conflict between Black Hawk and his nemesis, Keokuck. Black Hawk's leadership of the anti-American faction of the Sauk and Mesquakie tribes set him against the treaty-abiding faction under Keokuck, who advocated removal westward in order to avoid a war. These studies have shed much light upon the internal dynamics of the two tribes and the rise to prominence of Black Hawk and Keokuck, neither of whom was born into a leadership clan, within the confederated tribes of the Sauk and Mesquakie.[2]

What all of these studies have failed to consider is the larger picture of Indian culture throughout the Old Northwest, for the Sauks and Mesquakies did not live in a vacuum. Certain events, particularly the 1827 Winnebago Uprising, illustrate that the Black Hawk War was not an isolated incident but was instead the product of powerful ideological forces that existed among all the tribes of the region. Moreover, the suppression of the Winnebago Uprising had definite consequences for the outcome of the Black Hawk War. The other phenomenon that must be considered is the escalation of intertribal warfare during the 1820s and early 1830s. The wars fought between the tribes not only prevented Black Hawk from consolidating Indian support but led to more Indians fighting against him than for him.

The forces that led to the Black Hawk War had existed among the tribes of the Old Northwest for almost one hundred years. During the eighteenth century, the Indians of the trans-Appalachian West experienced what Gregory Dowd calls an "awakening" of nativistic spirit. Despite their cultural and linguistic differences, the tribes began to see themselves as sharing a common racial bond. Moreover, they all suffered the effects of white expansion. Among many of the tribes, religious prophets arose who freely mixed Indian and Christian beliefs and preached against white expansion in general and American expansion in particular. This movement reached its height under Tecumseh, who was influenced by the teachings of his brother Tenskwatawa, the Shawnee Prophet. Tenskwatawa and Tecumseh preached that all Indians could find redemption by abstaining from alcohol, foregoing the trappings of white culture, and fighting American expansion.[3]

Winnebagos, Kickapoos, Shawnees, Ottawas, Ojibwas, Sauks, Mesquakies, and members of other tribes flocked to Prophetstown in present-day Indiana to hear the message preached by Tenskwatawa and join Tecumseh's pan-Indian confederacy. The movement under Tecumseh and Tenskwatawa occurred at a time when relations between the United States and Great Britain were at a crisis point. While many Americans believed that British Indian agents in Canada were behind this pan-Indian resistance movement, the reality was that both the British and the Indians opposed United States expansion into the trans-Appalachian West, and this common goal brought them into a military alliance.[4] The first blood came at the Battle of Tippecanoe in November 1811, when American troops under the command of Indiana Territorial Governor William Henry Harrison skirmished with Indian warriors at Prophetstown. Within seven months, the United States declared war upon Great Britain, thus signalling the beginning of the War of 1812.[5]

The Indians at Prophetstown dispersed to their home villages after the Battle of Tippecanoe. Even before this, the teachings of Tenskwatawa and Tecumseh had reached virtually every Indian village in the trans-Appalachian West. The tribes of the region overwhelmingly supported the British against the United States during the war, and this added to the strong anti-American sentiments that were already evident in native communities.[6] The conclusion of the war brought an end to the Anglo-American struggle for the Old Northwest, but it did not end the anti-Americanism that had become manifest in the region. Indeed, most tribes, to include the Sauk and Mesquakie, continued to harbor large factions that seethed with a hatred for the United States and its white settlers. What emerged in the years after 1815 is best defined as an ideology, a set of conscious beliefs that advocate a particular course of action.[7] As with any ideology, the beliefs that made up this anti-Americanism were flexible and differed from tribe to tribe and even individual to individual. For example, the Sauks and Mesquakies received many of Tenskwatawa's teachings from a Potawatomi named Main Poc, but his admonitions to the two tribes often diverged significantly from those of Tenskwatawa, particularly in regard to abstinence from alcohol and the idea that all Indians were brothers. Nevertheless, both Main Poc and Tenskwatawa shared a common opposition to American expansion.[8]

Many Sauks and Mesquakies received further indoctrination during visits to Prophetstown, and while the numbers are difficult to discern, it is known that a party composed of about eleven hundred Sauks, Mesquakies, and Winnebagos visited in 1810. Black Hawk rejected these teachings because he believed that joining Tecumseh's pan-Indian confederacy threatened his own political ambitions. However, this did not stop him from fighting with the British during the War of 1812.[9] Moreover, Black Hawk and other Sauks and Mesquakies, even those not directly influenced by Tecumseh and Tenskwatawa, harbored anti-American sentiments due to events that were particular to the two tribes. The most significant incident was the treaty that the two tribes signed in 1804. The second article of the treaty ceded almost the entire western half of present-day Illinois and southwestern Wisconsin to the United States. The details of the treaty conference are sketchy since the

American officials kept no journal of the proceedings. The tribes had not authorized members of the delegation to sell any land, but the delegates returned home and stated that they had been plied with alcohol and had not been told of the treaty's provisions.[10] The Sauk and Mesquakie leadership was stunned when informed of the transaction, and Black Hawk later noted that the treaty "has been the cause of all of our difficulties."[11]

Later treaties reaffirmed and reinforced this mistrust. The Treaty of Ghent ended the War of 1812 and required the United States to restore to Great Britain's Indian allies all rights and possessions that they held before the war. Federal commissioners invited the tribes to Portage des Sioux in present-day Illinois to conclude treaties of peace, but many of the Sauks and Mesquakies refused to end the hostilities and even continued to commit depredations against Americans.[12] The two tribes initially sent only low-ranking warriors who had no authority to make peace. The young delegates treated the commissioners contemptuously and reiterated that neither tribe would recognize the 1804 treaty. Moreover, even as they attended the council, their villages had war parties out raiding white settlements in the Lower Mississippi Valley.[13]

The Sauks and Mesquakies finally decided to make peace with the United States and sent appropriate delegations to Portage des Sioux, the Mesquakies in the autumn of 1815 and the Sauks in the spring of 1816. Black Hawk attended this conference and signed the treaty. According to his autobiography, the American treaty commissioners told neither him nor any of the other Sauk signatories that by signing, they accepted the land cession outlined in the 1804 treaty. The treaty signed by the Mesquakies eight months earlier contained a similar provision. Black Hawk later stated that "Here for the first time, I touched the goose quill to the treaty—not knowing, however, that, by this act, I consented to give away my village. Had that been explained to me, I should have opposed it, and never would have signed the treaty."[14]

This second act of deception further intensified anti-American sentiments among members of two tribes. They so distrusted the United States and its agents that they refused to sign even the most innocuous documents. In exchange for selling their land in 1804, the United States promised to pay the Sauks and Mesquakies one thousand dollars in goods per year. The government required their Indian agent, Thomas Forsyth, to have the chiefs sign receipts for the goods, but, according to Forsyth, they refused to sign them fearing that the documents "might come back in another shape, alluding . . . that their lands would be claimed."[15] At a later annuity payment, Forsyth again explained to the

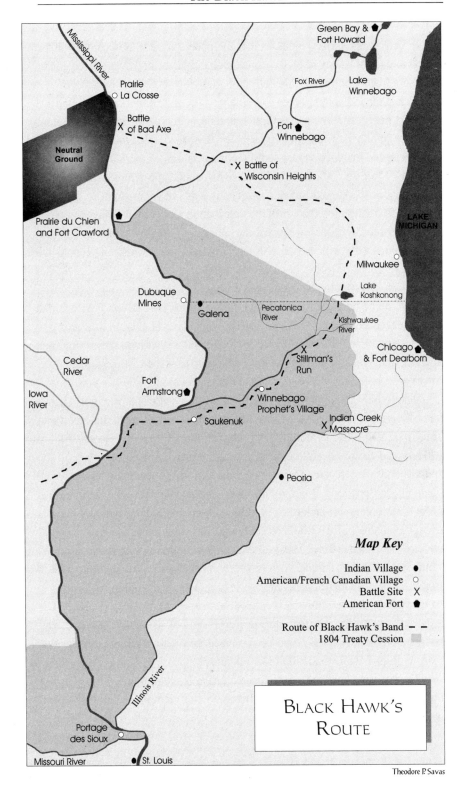

Map Key

Indian Village	●
American/French Canadian Village	○
Battle Site	X
American Fort	⬟

Route of Black Hawk's Band − −
1804 Treaty Cession ▨

BLACK HAWK'S
ROUTE

Theodore P. Savas

assembled Sauks and Mesquakies that the papers were only receipts, but the chiefs refused to let any of their people touch the papers and even posted guards to ensure that no one signed them.[16]

While the Indian resistance movement of Tecumseh and Tenskwatawa and the 1804 treaty were the most significant factors in creating an anti-American ideology among the Sauks and Mesquakies, there were other forces at work that reinforced and magnified these sentiments, particularly British Indian agents in Canada. While the War of 1812 decisively ended the struggle for the Old Northwest in the United States's favor, this was not so apparent in the years immediately following the conflict. Both Britain and United States retained a large measure of suspicion toward the other. American attempts to conquer Canada during the war led British authorities to maintain strong ties to the Indians in Old Northwest in case they would be needed as allies to defend Canada against American designs in the future.[17]

The main bases for British operations after 1815 were Fort Malden opposite Detroit and a series of posts in the Upper Great Lakes. For the next two decades, thousands of Indians from the United States flocked to these posts each spring to receive presents from Indian agents and hear speeches that urged them to continue in the service of their Great Father in Britain.[18]

The Indians remained wary of British promises after the war, particularly since their allies had given the Old Northwest over to the United States without consulting them. In the months after the war, British Indian agents and army officers had the unenviable task of explaining the terms of the peace to the Indians and often received stinging rebukes by tribal leaders who displayed "haughty indignation" at being "deceived and abandoned . . . by the British Govt."[19] Despite their lack of faith in the British, the Indians had few choices except to maintain their allegiance because they knew that the United States coveted their lands. Black Hawk attended these gatherings and expressed the sentiments of many Indians when he subtly reminded the British of the broken promises they had made during the war in order to gain the fidelity of the tribes. Nevertheless, Black Hawk concluded one speech by stating that "The Americans according to their stories are Masters of us and our Lands" who possessed "sweet tongues," and he promised to remain a British ally for this reason, despite "some bad blood that remains."[20]

The British agents in Canada faced a difficult situation when dealing with the tribes, for they had to keep the Indians within Britain's diplomatic orbit without provoking them into precipitating another war with the United States.

British agents patiently listened as the Indians detailed the injustices they suffered under American sovereignty. The British held out the promise of future military aid in the event of another conflict, but they also counseled restraint. The British did not desire another war with the United States, but their speeches revealed that they believed that another conflict was on the horizon. This resulted in an ambiguous message that was open to a number of interpretations. Warriors and chiefs who harbored intense anti-American sentiments often read more into these speeches than British Indian agents intended, and this gave them hope that future hostilities would be accompanied by British aid.[21]

Another reason the Indians hoped for a successful conflict with white Americans was the Americans' greed for mineral resources on Indian lands. Most of the pressure upon the tribes in the upper Mississippi River Valley came from hordes of whites flocking to the region to extract lead ore from ground. This region had been known for its rich mineral deposits since the time of the French, and American miners entered the area as early as 1811. By the 1820s, the federal government began granting leases to white miners who wanted to take part in the burgeoning lead trade centered around Galena, Illinois. Soon, miners swept up the tributaries of the Fever (now the Galena) River and set up small mining operations. The population of the Fever River district exploded from 150 in 1825 to 1500 by the end of 1826. Many of the tribes, particularly the Winnebagos and the Mesquakies, had mined lead in this area for many years and often exchanged the ore for trade goods.[22] The federal government set aside certain areas for white miners, but these parcels were based upon a faulty understanding of which tribes had claims to these lands and thus were of dubious legality. However, by the late 1820s, white miners flaunted even these ill-conceived boundaries and openly began to extract ore on land that unequivocally belonged to the Winnebagos.[23]

The Mesquakies suffered similar trespasses at Dubuque's Mines, a site on the west bank of the Mississippi that they jealously guarded from the covetous eyes of whites on the other shore. The first incursion came in May 1830 when the Mesquakies abandoned the area due to attacks by the Santee Dakotas (also called the Sioux) and the Menominees. Whites heard of the tribe's absence and quickly rushed in and began to mine and smelt ore. By early June, about one hundred miners occupied Dubuque's Mines, and William Clark, the superintendent of Indian affairs at St. Louis, had to send federal troops to remove them.[24] When the Mesquakies abandoned the site the next year for fear of Santee Dakota attacks, the army sent a permanent military detachment under the command of a young lieutenant named Jefferson Davis to prevent whites from overrunning the site once again.[25]

The pan-Indian resistance movement, the treaties with the federal government, the hope of future British military aid, and the incursions of white miners all combined to reinforce and intensify the anti-American ideology among the Indians of the Old Northwest, particularly those in the Upper Mississippi Valley. The Sauks and Mesquakies were not the only tribes affected by these events, as the case of the Winnebagos readily demonstrates. The strong anti-Americanism of the Winnebagos was visibly evident in the years preceding the War of 1812. Most members of the tribe eagerly accepted the message of Tecumseh and Tenskwatawa and joined them at Prophetstown. William Henry Harrison stated that the Winnebagos constituted the Shawnee brothers' principal strength in 1810, and according to one old Winnebago chief, his young men "breathed nothing but war against the United States."[26] Indeed, it was the Winnebagos at Prophetstown who initiated the skirmish that resulted in the Battle of Tippecanoe. During the War of 1812, the Winnebagos proved to be staunch British allies.[27]

In the period after the war, many Winnebagos were reluctant to make peace with the United States. Only one band signed the 1816 treaty of peace with the United States at Portage des Sioux. The Winnebagos also demonstrated their anti-American sentiments in other ways, namely as criminal acts that were motivated by ideology rather than material gain.[28] In 1819, after returning from British posts in Canada where they heard a series of inflammatory, anti-American speeches from British Indian agents, the Winnebagos partook in a series of criminal acts such as shooting at federal soldiers on Lake Winnebago and harassing an American military party near the portage of the Fox and Wisconsin Rivers. The next year, three Winnebagos killed two United States soldiers at Fort Armstrong near Rock Island. Interrogations of the perpetrators of the Fort Armstrong murders and meetings between army officers and tribal leaders revealed a deep-seated hatred for the United States and the soldiers that the federal government had stationed in their midst.[29] The Winnebagos were hardly unique in their sentiments, for throughout the 1820s other tribes such as the Ojibwas and Menominees also engaged in criminal acts that ranged from petty theft to assault and even murder. In every case, anti-American sentiments were the root cause, and they were all directed against American soldiers and fur traders.[30]

The line between criminal acts and overt resistance was thin in such circumstances as later events illustrated. In the spring of 1826, a party of Winnebagos killed a French-Canadian family at a sugar-making camp near Prairie du Chien. While the act itself had little or nothing to do with anti-Americanism, the efforts by federal officials to apprehend the suspects revealed the enmity that the Winnebagos posited toward the United States. Tribal leaders consistently refused to fully cooperate with the federal authorities assigned the task of apprehending the responsible parties.[31] The army ultimately arrested two of the perpetrators and later transferred them to Fort Snelling at the confluence of the Minnesota and Mississippi Rivers. During the summer of 1826, many of the more intensely anti-American Winnebagos, particularly those of the Wisconsin River bands, explored the possibility of leading a general uprising against the United States. The anti-American members of the Santee Dakota evinced strong interest in such a plan, and both parties redoubled their efforts toward consolidating an alliance in 1827.[32]

The culmination of these efforts brought about a short-lived uprising by the Winnebagos and the Santee Dakotas in June 1827. The Winnebagos were spurred to action by unfounded rumors that the two Winnebagos arrested the year before had been murdered at Fort Snelling. Moreover, the army had abandoned Fort Crawford at Prairie du Chien the year before, and many Winnebagos interpreted this as a sign of United States weakness and fear.[33] Members of the Prairie La Crosse band under the leadership of Wanuk-chouti, or Red Bird, decided to initiate the revolt by going to Prairie du Chien in order to murder an American trader who lived there. When they found out that he was not at home, they settled instead upon murdering members of a French Canadian family. They killed a trader named Registre Gagnier and his hired man and severely wounded Gagnier's baby daughter. Afterward, the Prairie La Crosse Winnebagos sent war belts to other tribes urging them to rise up against the United States, but only the Santee Dakotas remained interested.[34] Two days after the Gagnier murders, the warriors of the Prairie La Crosse band and their Santee Dakota allies attacked two American keelboats descending the Mississippi River. The warriors killed two men and wounded four others. The number of Winnebagos and Santee Dakotas involved in the attack is difficult to determine but probably numbered between one hundred and two hundred persons.[35]

The army and Indian Department moved quickly and put down the uprising and prevent the disaffection from spreading to other tribes. By September 1827, the perpetrators had been apprehended and the troubles quelled.[36] Despite the limited nature of the revolt, the actions of the Indians throughout the Mississippi Valley and Upper Great Lakes revealed the persistence of anti-Americanism among the tribes. The Rock River and Fox River Winnebago bands did not participate directly in the uprising, but upon hearing that their kinsmen were engaged in fighting the United States, members of these seemingly quiescent bands harassed American miners and virtually shut down wagon and river traffic between Peoria, Illinois, and the lead mining region. The Fox River Winnebagos were engaged in a treaty council with the United States during the uprising, which prevented a more active response. However, they used the occasion to complain about white miners on their lands and even burned down buildings that American negotiators had erected at the treaty grounds.[37]

The Winnebagos were not alone in using the uprising to express anti-American sentiments. Anti-American Potawatomis also expressed support for the uprising, and although they did not join the Winnebagos, they threatened to do so, creating a sense of panic among the French Canadian and American settlers at Chicago. Near Peoria, other Potawatomis committed robberies against Americans. As for the Santee Dakotas, even more would have joined the Winnebagos had not the influential Santee Dakota Chief Wabasha prevented his warriors from do so.[38] None of this was lost to American officials in the army and Indian Department. Thomas L. McKenney, the commissioner of Indian Affairs, noted that while there were no more "Pontiacs or Tecumthes [sic] to form and lead on confederated bands," the danger was real enough, and had the uprising not been put down quickly, the Winnebagos, Santee Dakotas, and Potawatomis "would have broken out . . . into acts of a general violence."[39]

The forces that led to the 1827 Winnebago Uprising are important to understand, for they were the same ones that led Black Hawk to resist the United States five years later. It was the product of an anti-American ideology that had come into being over the course of the previous century, and it was endemic to all the tribes. The 1827 Winnebago Uprising was also significant because it revealed the limits of forging an intertribal confederacy among the Indians of the Old Northwest. The anti-American factions of the Sauks and Mesquakies had little interest in supporting the uprising since the Winnebagos tended to side with the Santee Dakotas in intertribal wars, while the Sauks and Mesquakies tended to side with Ojibwas, the sworn enemies of the Santee Dakotas. Indeed, the Ojibwas sent the wampum belts and messages to their Sauk and Mesquakie allies urging them not to support the Winnebagos.[40]

Intertribal warfare was not a new phenomenon, but it intensified a great deal in the 1820s and early 1830s. The longest running rivalry was between the Ojibwas and the Santee Dakotas for control of the lands to the south of Lake Superior and at the headwaters of the Mississippi. These two groups began fighting in the 1730s, and after about 1805, the Sauks and Mesquakies began to expand north and west into the lands of the Santee Dakotas and other Siouan-speaking tribes in the trans-Mississippi West.[41] These dual expansions created two alliance systems that while loosely constructed became more entrenched during the 1820s and 1830s. The Ojibwas, Sauks, and Mesquakies became allies because they shared a common enemy, the Santee Dakotas. The Kickapoos in Illinois and the Iowas of the western prairies often joined the Sauks and Foxes in their forays, as did the confederated bands of the Ojibwas, Ottawas, and Potawatomis along the western shore of Lake Michigan.[42] Other tribes, particularly the Menominees and the Winnebagos, sided with the Santee Dakotas. The Menominees had long enjoyed peaceful relations with both the Santee Dakotas and the Ojibwas and even hunted in the contested area that stood as a "no man's land" between the two tribes. However, the murders of Menominees by Ojibwas in the contested area forced them to join the Santee Dakotas, and murders of Menominees by the Sauks and Mesquakies reinforced this alliance. The Winnebagos had traditionally been the allies of the Santee Dakotas, and murders committed by the Sauks and Mesquakies against Winnebagos increased the enmity between them.[43]

The United States went to great lengths to quell intertribal conflicts because war parties often attacked white traders, miners, and settlers in addition to Indian enemies. Federal treaty commissioners concluded a series of three treaties at Prairie du Chien in 1825, Fond du Lac on Lake Superior in 1826, and Little Lake Butte Morts in 1827 to establish boundaries between the tribes.[44] However, by 1828, efforts at bringing about peace had failed when the Santee Dakotas and Ojibwas began fighting again. By the next year the fighting spread to the south when Sauk and Mesquakie war parties raided Santee Dakota villages. By 1830, the Menominees and Winnebagos became involved on the side of the Santee Dakotas.[45] The United States hoped to avert further escalations by inviting the Sauks, Mesquakies, Santee Dakotas, and members of other tribes to a treaty council at Prairie du Chien in 1830. However, the council was stymied even before it began when a party of Santee Dakotas and Menominees slaughtered fifteen Mesquakie chiefs in retaliation for the killing of a Winnebago woman the previous year. The federal commissioners ultimately produced a treaty in spite of this obstacle, and they went one step further than the earlier treaties by separating the Santee Dakotas from the Sauks and Mesquakies with a strip of land forty miles wide and two hundred miles long called the Neutral Ground that neither side could enter.[46]

However, this buffer zone failed to stem the tide of intertribal war. In July 1831, a war party of about forty Sauks and Mesquakies invaded the lands of the Santee Dakotas and killed two tribal members. Other depredations soon followed. All hopes for peace were deflated that same month when a Sauk and Mesquakie war party killed twenty-five Menominees at Prairie du Chien in retaliation for the killing of the Mesquakie chiefs the previous year. The Menominees were shocked by the killings, and while they promised federal Indian agents that they would remain at peace, they demanded swift justice from the United States against the Sauks and Mesquakies.[47]

These two events—the 1827 Winnebago Uprising and the escalation of intertribal warfare—explain why the Black Hawk War happened and why it took the course that it did. Anti-Americanism continued to exist after the War of 1812 in variety of forms, mainly as criminality and open revolt, and the Winnebago Uprising and the Black Hawk War were simply manifestations of this ideology. However, not all Indians who championed this ideology were willing to go war. Indeed, only the Prairie La Crosse band participated in the 1827 uprising despite the fact that about two thirds of the Winnebagos were estimated to be steadfastly anti-American. Indeed, the Rock River bands and those of the Fox River Valley sat out the war or were content to commit criminal acts instead. In the period after the War of 1812, many Indian tribes in the Old Northwest saw war against the United States as futile and dangerous, and often times even the most staunchly anti-American Indians shied away from open revolt.[48]

The federal government also reinforced the region militarily after the Winnebago Uprising, which made open revolt more risky. In 1826, the United States had only 680 soldiers stationed at the three posts west of Lake Michigan: Fort Howard at Green Bay, Fort Armstrong, and Fort Snelling. After the uprising, the army reoccupied Fort Crawford and Fort Dearborn at Chicago. The federal government also established a new post, Fort Winnebago, at the portage of the Fox and Wisconsin Rivers in the heart of the Winnebagos' country. By the end of 1828, these six posts possessed a total of 801 troops.[49]

The increase in federal military power was accompanied by the further erosion of Indian unity due to Intertribal fighting. However, the situation for

Black Hawk was far more tenuous than it had been for the Prairie La Crosse Winnebagos five years before because he had the support of only a fraction of the Sauk and Mesquakie tribes. His rival, Keokuck, was every bit as anti-American as Black Hawk, but he believed that the two tribes had little to gain by defying the United States despite the odious nature of earlier treaties.[50] Black Hawk's band totalled about one thousand members, about eight hundred of whom were Sauks and Mesquakies. The other two hundred were members of the anti-American faction of the Kickapoos and Sauk-Winnebago mixed bloods from the village of the Winnebago Prophet. The total population of the Sauk and Mesquakie tribes was about 6,600 members; therefore, Black Hawk had the support of only one eighth of the two tribes. William Clark estimated that one sixth of the Sauks and Mesquakies supported Black Hawk, which corresponds closely with other sources. Moreover, the traditional allies of the two tribes—the Ojibwas and the confederated villages of Potawatomis, Ottawas, and Ojibwas along the western shore of Lake Michigan—were reluctant to support what they saw as a renegade band that did not have backing within the Sauk and Mesquakie tribes.[51] Black Hawk did gain some aid and encouragement from Indians outside his two tribes during the war, but this had less to do with the vision that he had for his people than with the persistence of anti-Americanism in the region.

The events that directly precipitated the Black Hawk War began in 1828, when the federal government opened up the land of the 1804 cession for settlement. While both the treaty-abiding faction under Keokuck and the anti-American faction under Black Hawk (now called the British Band) wanted to remain on the west side of the Mississippi, the members under Keokuck left for the Iowa River valley in order to avoid conflict. The British Band remained at its main village, Saukenuk, on the Rock River and soon was engaged in almost daily quarrels with newly-arrived white settlers.[52] In 1830, the British Band returned to Saukenuk despite the exhortations of federal Indian agents and the faction under Keokuck. Black Hawk fulfilled his promise to return to Saukenuk again in 1831, and during the course of this year the British Band became reinforced by the arrival Mesquakies who had participated in the massacre of the Menominees at Prairie du Chien and by Kickapoos from southern Illinois who also protested earlier land cessions made by their tribe.[53]

The return to Saukenuk in 1831 turned out to be a fiasco for the British Band and a personal humiliation for Black Hawk. The governor of Illinois, John Reynolds, called up seven hundred militia for the express purpose of forcing the

British Band across the Mississippi. A federal force of ten companies under the command of General Edmund P. Gaines joined the militia, and Gaines used Keokuck and other influential members of the treaty-abiding faction to persuade members of the British Band to depart. Gaines decided to move the regular troops and militia against Saukenuk in order to break the stalemate that ensued. When the force arrived at Saukenuk at the end of June, they discovered that the British Band had slipped across the river the night before. A few days later on June 30th, Gaines met with Black Hawk and forced him to sign articles of capitulation. In addition to recognizing the Sauks' and Mesquakies' previous treaties, Black Hawk promised to remain on the west side of the Mississippi.[54]

The entire matter would have ended in 1831 had Black Hawk not accepted the counsels of two other Indians. The first was Wabokieshiek, better known as the Winnebago Prophet. He was actually of Winnebago and Sauk parentage, and although little is known about his religious teachings, he was said to have contact with the spirit world. Like other Indian prophets who had risen up in the trans-Appalachian West, he gained a personal following, and while his teachings failed to spark the same level of interest in militant nativism as those of Tenskwatawa, he attracted about two hundred followers, many of whom were also Sauk-Winnebago mixed bloods, to his village along the Rock River.[55]

During the winter of 1828-1829, Black Hawk made his first visit to Wabokieshiek, who advised him not to leave Saukenuk. Wabokieshiek repeatedly told Black Hawk that the Americans would do nothing to dislodge his people from Saukenuk because they had promised the British after the War of 1812 that they would not disturb the Indians. The two men soon developed a relationship that closely resembled that which Tecumseh and Tenskwatawa enjoyed twenty years earlier. In 1830, Black Hawk and Wabokieshiek even sent emissaries as far away as Texas to gain Indian allies to support the British Band's cause.[56]

The most influential adviser that Black Hawk consulted between 1831 and 1832 was another Sauk named Neapope. Like other Indians in the region, Black Hawk and Neapope frequently visited Malden to receive presents and renew their pledge of fealty to the British. While the British Band was involved in the standoff with Gaines in the summer of 1831, Neapope was at Malden. When he returned, he brought news that the British supported Black Hawk in his efforts to remain at Saukenuk and would provide his followers with guns, ammunition, and provisions that would be sent to Milwaukee. Moreover, the confederated

KEOKUCK

This engraving is based upon portraits made of
Keokuck late in his life.

The Sauk and the Black Hawk War, with Biographical Sketches

Illinois Governor
John Reynolds

My Own Times

bands of the Ojibwas, Ottawas, and Potawatomis would assist them, as would the Winnebagos. If they were defeated, the British promised Black Hawk and his band refuge in Canada.[57] Other tribal leaders, most notably Keokuck, quickly dismissed Neapope's promises as mere lies, but Black Hawk, who had been dejected after evacuating Saukenuk in 1831, was buoyed by the news. Certainly, his anti-American sentiments made him overly receptive to such grandiose promises. He stated that he was "pleased to think that, by a little exertion on my part, I could accomplish the object of all my wishes."[58]

The counsels of Wabokieshiek and Neapope convinced Black Hawk that he could successfully reoccupy Saukenuk in the spring of 1832, and in April of that year he and his band crossed the Mississippi. Most federal officials did not think that this act meant that hostilities had been initiated, and Black Hawk for his part did not plan to start a war. He simply intended to move up the Rock River, plant corn for his band at Wabokieshiek's village, and take possession of the British supplies at Milwaukee. The British Band would not resort to violence unless the army attacked them first, but they would stand firm in their right to live peaceably on the east side of the Mississippi.[59] Moreover, Indian agents and military officers were far more concerned about stemming intertribal warfare. Indeed, as Black Hawk crossed the Mississippi, he saw General Henry Atkinson headed north to Prairie du Chien with a steamboat full of troops to arrest the Mesquakie warriors who perpetrated the massacre against the Menominees the previous year so that further bloodshed could be prevented.[60]

Black Hawk's situation seemed at first to confirm that he might succeed, but he did not receive as much good news as he expected. The chiefs and headmen of the Rock River Winnebagos paid him a visit with their subagent, Henry Gratiot, who ordered Black Hawk to return to the west side of the river immediately. Without Gratiot's knowledge, the Rock River Winnebagos, particularly those under White Crow, encouraged Black Hawk to continue his march up the Rock River, where he would find other tribes ready to support him. However, the Rock River Winnebagos maintained a cautious stand. They, too, were threatened with removal from their lands, and while their counsels to Black Hawk displayed a persistent anti-American ideology, they made repeated demonstrations of loyalty to Gratiot. The United States's response during the 1827 Winnebago Uprising had made a deep impression upon them, and although they wanted Black Hawk to succeed, they wanted him to do so without their support.[61] Black Hawk later met with the Potawatomis at the Kishwaukee River, but they were even less facilitating than the Winnebagos. When they told him that no British warship could be expected to land at Milwaukee, Black Hawk quickly saw the promises of Neapope unravel.[62]

After meeting with the Potawatomis at Kishwaukee, Black Hawk determined that further resistance was useless and decided to return. His decision came too late, for the army and the Illinois militia had been marshalling forces to fight the British Band in the event of hostilities. The governor of Illinois called up the militia in April and ordered mounted volunteers to patrol the northern section of the state. On May 14, 1832, about thirty miles north of Dixon's Ferry (present-day Dixon, Illinois), a party of volunteers spotted members of the British Band who had been sent to announce Black Hawk's decision. A few of the militiamen, fearing a ruse, fired upon the Indians and killed two. About 270 mounted troops rushed to join the fray, but Black Hawk, hearing of the engagement, readied his followers and counterattacked. The militia panicked and broke ranks.[63] In this small engagement known as Stillman's Run, only eleven militiamen and five of Black Hawk's followers died. The news shocked settlers in Illinois, and it was made worse by the fact that Black Hawk's men, adhering to Indian custom, scalped the dead. Prior to this battle, the war had been avoidable, but once blood had been spilled, both the British Band and the citizens of Illinois cried out for revenge, and war became inevitable.[64]

As with the 1827 Winnebago Uprising, the commencement of hostilities gave the anti-American factions of the Potawatomis and Winnebagos an excuse to commit depredations against Americans. About fifty Potawatomi warriors joined in the uprising, but they had little interest in the British Band's cause. Their participation resulted instead from earlier confrontations they had had with white settlers in Illinois. The anti-American party of fifty Potawatomis, accompanied by three Sauks, committed the next act of the war after Stillman's Run when they murdered sixteen whites at Indian Creek, Illinois, and took two young women captive. However, this was the only act of violence committed by any Potawatomis, and they did not travel with the British Band thereafter.[65]

After the Indian Creek Massacre, Black Hawk and his followers went further up the Rock River and camped near Lake Koshkonong in the country of the Rock River Winnebagos, who displayed the same cautious attitude they had from the beginning. It was no secret to Black Hawk that they were aiding both his band and the Americans. The Rock River Winnebagos provided the British Band with food and horses, and at the same time a group of them returned the two captive women to their family. At this point, Black Hawk's warriors went out in small war parties and terrorized white settlers, particularly those in the lead mining region to the west. The anti-American faction under White Crow supplied about fifty warriors for Black Hawk's war parties.[66]

However, Black Hawk's position at Lake Koshkonong was precarious, and he decided that he had to retreat west toward the Mississippi. Five Rock River Winnebagos guided his band to the Wisconsin River, but at this point, according to Neapope, the Winnebagos "discovered that the Sacs [i.e., Sauks] would be whipped, they turned their faces and went back, and turned against the Sacs."[67]

The Wisconsin River Winnebagos also exhibited their persistent anti-Americanism, but it was much more latent and passive than that of the Rock River Winnebagos under White Crow. When a Menominee force fighting on the side of the United States descended the Fox and Wisconsin Rivers, the Wisconsin River Winnebagos urged them not to fight the British Band because "the [A]mericans were enemies of all red-skins."[68] Even Joseph Street, the Indian agent at Prairie du Chien who talked in glowing terms about the fidelity of the Wisconsin River Winnebagos, admitted that Winneshiek of Prairie La Crosse befriended Black Hawk. However, the only act committed by the Wisconsin River Winnebagos in support of Black Hawk consisted of at least two of Winneshiek's sons acting as guides for Black Hawk's band as they made their way to the Mississippi.[69]

General Henry Atkinson

Wakefield's History of
the Black Hawk War

While these actions demonstrated the persistence of anti-Americanism, the participation of Indians on the side of the United States illustrates the limited nature of this phenomenon and the intense rivalries that existed between the tribes. The United States took advantage of these two facts and recruited large numbers of Indians to fight the British. General Henry Atkinson commanded the forces against Black Hawk, and in the early weeks of the war called for Indians to act as scouts. By early June 1832, he had 225 Indian scouts at Prairie du Chien, forty of whom were Menominees, at least eighty of whom were Santee Dakotas, and the balance were Winnebagos. At Chicago, many Potawatomis joined scouting parties led by local fur traders.[70]

The Santee Dakotas, Menominees, and Winnebagos who assembled at Prairie du Chien were initially utilized to help defend the mining region, and small parties went out to find and harass Black Hawk's people. Henry Dodge, the commander of a mounted force of white militia, had a contingent of these warriors with him as scouts for much of the war. During one small action near the Pecatonica River, Dodge's men killed eleven Sauks. When he allowed his Indian scouts to take the scalps, he noted that the "[f]riendly Indians appeared delighted with the scalps [and] they went to the ground where the Indians were killed and cut them literally to pieces."[71]

The first major battle of the war after Stillman's Run came on July 21, 1832, at the Wisconsin River. Commonly called the Battle of Wisconsin Heights, the action involved a chance encounter between Dodge's battalion and the main body of Black Hawk's band. As they had done at the Pecatonica River, the Winnebago guides who accompanied Dodge scalped the dead, and some of the white volunteers took scalps as well.[72]

More dramatic was the participation by Menominee and Santee Dakota auxiliaries as soldiers. Atkinson needed men in late May 1832, and the Menominees and Santee Dakotas were more than willing to fight their old adversaries. This was particularly true of the Menominees, who were still incensed at the murders committed against their people at Prairie du Chien the previous year. Within a week of Stillman's Run, Atkinson called upon Indian agents in the region to gather Menominees and Santee Dakotas to join his army.[73] The bulk of the Menominees were at Green Bay when the war began. Even before they received word of Atkinson's request, the tribe had assembled at Green Bay to protect the Green Bay settlement. The Menominees were eager for the opportunity to join the war, particularly since many of the perpetrators of the Menominee massacre were with Black Hawk. The Green Bay Indian agent, Samuel Stambaugh, organized 232 Menominee volunteers as a battalion composed of two companies with himself as the battalion commander, local fur traders as junior officers, and tribal war chiefs as sergeants.[74]

While these preparations were underway, the commander at Fort Crawford sent a delegation to convince the Santee Dakotas under Chief Wabasha to fight the British Band. They agreed and supplied 150 warriors to intercept Black Hawk's retreating followers. Only a few them arrived in time to participate in the final battle of the war, the Battle of Bad Axe, on August 2, 1832, at the confluence of the Bad Axe and Mississippi Rivers. The carnage of the battle was heightened by the fact that Atkinson had a steamboat armed with a cannon firing at the panic-stricken members of the British Band as they attempted to escape the militia and regular troops on the east bank of the Mississippi and the Santee Dakotas on the west bank.[75]

When the bulk of the Santee Dakotas arrived the next day, the commander at Fort Crawford assigned them the duty of capturing stray members of Black Hawk's band. They were not content, however, to simply capture them alive. A Santee Dakota party found a camp of Black Hawk's followers along the Cedar River in present-day Iowa and attacked them at dawn. The members of the British band were too tired and confused to put up a fight, and the Santee Dakotas proceeded to Prairie du Chien after their attack with sixty-eight scalps and twenty-two prisoners.[76] The Menominees also arrived late and had to settle for rounding up escaped prisoners. Stambaugh gave his Menominee companies explicit orders to avoid fighting if at all possible, but they were also eager to bring vengeance down upon their enemies. According to one of the officers, the Menominees were "fierce for a fight" when they found a small party of Sauks. The Menominees immediately killed the two Sauk men in the party, and in the mad melee that followed, one of the lieutenants took an accidental gun shot to the arm from one of his own men.[77]

In the end, Black Hawk faced an overwhelming force of white militiamen and federal soldiers, but he faced a large number of Indian warriors as well. It is safe to estimate that at least 752 Indians fought on the side of the United States during the war. Black Hawk, on the other hand, only managed to attract about fifty Potawatomis and fifty Winnebagos to his standard, and they did not stay with him for the duration of the war but instead used the conflict as an excuse to settle old scores with white settlers and miners in their respective localities.[78] Moreover, the vast majority of Indians in the region simply remained neutral and flocked to local Indian agencies and army posts to avoid the conflict. Although their numbers are difficult to determine, it was literally in the thousands.[79] Even when Black Hawk and Wabokieshiek tried to escape to their Ojibwa allies after the Battle of Bad Axe, Black Hawk's humiliation did not end, for both men were captured near Prairie La Crosse by a Winnebago warrior named Chaasjan-ga, who delivered them to Prairie du Chien.[80]

Black Hawk died among his people six years after the war. He had no desire to fight Americans anymore and even went out of his way to make them feel welcome in his home.[81] He was an old Indian warrior who realized that he could no longer hold back the tide of white settlement as Tecumseh had sought to do in an earlier age. Anti-Americanism did not die after the Black Hawk War, but it no longer manifested itself in warfare as it had for more than half a century. Intertribal warfare did not die out either until the press of white settlement put indissoluble barriers between the tribes.

Thus, the Black Hawk War stands as the culmination of two phenomena that had existed in the Old Northwest for years before Black Hawk's birth. Any understanding of the war he led against the United States must take both into account if we are to understand the causes of the war and the course that it followed.

NOTES

1. For the early works by observers and participants, see Ma-ka-tai-me-she-kia-kiak (or Black Hawk), *Black Hawk, An Autobiography*, ed. Donald Jackson (1833, reprint edition, Urbana: University of Illinois Press, 1955); John Wakefield, *Wakefield's History of the Black Hawk War*, ed. Frank Stevens (1834; reprint edition, Madison, WI: Roger Hunt, 1976); Benjamin Drake, *The Life and Adventures of Black Hawk; With Sketches of Keokuck, The Sac and Fox Indians, and the Late Black Hawk War* (Cincinnati: G. Conclin, 1838); John Reynolds, *My Own Times; Embracing also a History of My Life* (Belleville, IL: B. H. Perryman and H. L. Davison, 1855). For works written during the late nineteenth century and the twentieth century, see Perry Armstrong, *The Sauks and the Black Hawk War, With Biographical Sketches, Etc.* (1887; reprint edition, New York: AMS Press, 1979); Reuben Thwaites, "The Story of the Black Hawk War," in Lyman Draper, et al., eds., *Collections of the State Historical Society of Wisconsin*, 31 vols. (Madison: State Historical Society of Wisconsin, 1855-1931), 12:217-65 (hereafter cited as *WHC*); Frank Stevens, *The Black Hawk War* (Chicago: Blakely Printing Company, 1903); Jacob Van der Zee, "The Black Hawk War and the Treaty of 1832," *Iowa Journal of History and Politics* 13 (July 1915): 416-28; Jacob Van der Zee, "The Black Hawk War," *Iowa and War* 9 (March 1918): 1-32; Cyrenus Cole, *I Am a Man: The Indian Black Hawk* (Iowa City: State Historical Society of Iowa, 1938); Joseph Lambert, "The Black Hawk War: A Military Analysis," *Journal of the Illinois State Historical Society* 32 (December 1939): 442-73; Cecil Eby *"That Disgraceful Affair:" The Black Hawk War* (New York: W. W. Norton, 1973). For a historiographical assessment of these works, see Roger Nichols, "The Black Hawk War in Retrospect," *Wisconsin Magazine of History* 65 (Summer 1982): 244-45.

2. William Hagan, *The Sac and Fox Indians* (Norman: University of Oklahoma Press, 1958); P. Richard Metcalf, "Who Should Rule at Home? Native American Politics and Indian-White Relations," *Journal of American History* 61 (December 1974): 658-60; Anthony F. C. Wallace, "Prelude to Disaster: The Course of Indian-White Relations Which Led to the Black Hawk War of 1832," *Wisconsin Magazine of History* 65 (Summer 1982): 247-88; Roger Nichols, *Black Hawk and the Warrior's Path* (Arlington Heights, IL: Harlan Davidson, 1992).

3. Gregory Dowd, *A Spirited Resistance: The North American Indian Struggle for Unity, 1745-1815* (Baltimore: Johns Hopkins University Press, 1992), 23-190; Gregory Dowd, "Thinking and Believing: Nativism and Unity in the Ages of Pontiac and Tecumseh," *American Indian Quarterly* 16 (Summer 1992): 309-35. For information on Tecumseh and Tenskwatawa, see R. David Edmunds, *Tecumseh and the Quest for Indian Leadership* (Boston: Little, Brown and Company, 1984), 43-45, 93, 97, 109, 121-34; R. David Edmunds, *The Shawnee Prophet* (Lincoln: University of Nebraska Press, 1983), 28-39, 78; R. David Edmunds, "Tecumseh, The Shawnee Prophet, and American History: A Reassessment," *Western Historical Quarterly* 14 (July 1983): 261-76; Timothy Willig, "Prophetstown on the Wabash: The Native Spiritual Defense of the Old Northwest," *Michigan Historical Review* 23 (Fall 1997): 130-35.

4. For sources that discuss the Indians who supported Tenskwatawa and Tecumseh, see William Henry Harrison to the Secretary of War, 28 August 1810, Logan Esarey, ed., *Messages and Letters of William Henry Harrison*, 2 vols., *Indiana Historical Collections*, vols. 7 and 9 (Indianapolis: Indiana Historical Commission, 1922), 1:471 (hereafter cited as *WHHL*); Harrison to the Secretary of War, 25 July 1810, *WHHL*, 1:449; Harrison to the Secretary of War, 25 April 1810, *WHHL*, 1:417; Harrison to the Secretary of War, 15 June 1810, *WHHL*, 1:427; William Clark to the Secretary of War, 20 July 1810, *WHHL*, 1:449; Harrison to the Secretary of War, 7 August 1810, *WHHL*, 1:456; Harrison to the Secretary of War, 6 June 1811, *WHHL*, 1:513. For American opinions regarding British machinations among the Indians, see Thomas Jefferson to Harrison, 16 January 1806, *WHHL*, 1:186; William Wells to Harrison, 20 August 1807, *WHHL*, 1:242; William Hull to the Secretary of War, 16 June 1809, *WHHL*, 1:348; Harrison to the Secretary of War, 5 July 1809, *WHHL*, 1:349; Harrison to the Secretary of War, 25 April 1810, *WHHL*, 1:418. For discussions of why the British and Indians created an alliance, see Richard White, *The Middle Ground: Indians, Empires, and Republics in the Great Lakes Region, 1650-1815* (New York: Cambridge University Press, 1991), 5-16; Reginald Horsman, "British Indian Policy in the Northwest, 1807-1812," *Mississippi Valley Historical Review* 45 (June 1958): 52-59; Robert Allen, *His Majesty's Indian Allies: British Indian Policy in the Defence of Canada, 1774-1815* (Toronto: Dundurn Press, 1992), 110-15; Robert Allen, "The British Crown and the War of 1812," *Michigan Historical Review* 14 (Fall 1982): 1-11.

5. Harrison to the Secretary of War, 8 November 1811, *WHHL*, 1:618-31; Donald Hickey, *The War of 1812: A Forgotten Conflict* (Urbana: University of Illinois Press, 1989), 46.

6. Patrick Jung, "Forge, Destroy, and Preserve the Bonds of Empire: Euro-Americans, Native Americans, and Métis on the Wisconsin Frontier, 1634-1856" (Ph.D. diss., Marquette University, 1997), 152-72.

7. Scholars have reached a variety of conclusions concerning Indian-white relations in the Old Northwest after 1815. Richard White has articulated the concept of the middle ground to define a relatively coequal political relationship between the colonial powers and the tribes. White asserts that the American victory in 1815 effectively ended this relationship. See White, *Middle Ground*, 518-23. Other scholars have stressed that the cultural movements and political relationships that characterized the Old Northwest throughout the seventeenth and eighteenth centuries continued to exist, but only for a short time after 1815, and in a diminutive, muted fashion. See Colin Calloway, *Crown and Calumet: British-Indian Relations, 1783-1815* (Norman: University of Oklahoma Press, 1987), 240-57; Dowd, *Spirited Resistance*, 191-201; Allen, *His Majesty's Indian Allies*, 168-94. For definitions of ideology, see Malcolm Hamilton, "The Elements of the Concept of Ideology," *Political Studies* 35 (March 1987): 18-38; Clifford Geertz, "Ideology as a Cultural System," in *Ideology and Discontent*, ed. David. Apter (New York: Free Press, 1964), 47-76.

8. Dowd, *Spirited Resistance*, 144; R. David Edmunds, "Main Poc: Potawatomi Wabeno," *American Indian Quarterly* 9 (Summer 1985): 259-72. It should be noted that

any ideology will be accepted by people in a variety ways and with varying levels of commitment. See Philip Converse, "The Nature of Belief Systems in Mass Publics," in *Ideology and Discontent*, 206-61. A similar concept is that of popular ideology, which occurs when structured ideologies are freely mixed with older, traditional elements of societal belief systems. See George Rudé, *Ideology and Popular Protest* (New York: Pantheon Books, 1980), 27-38.

9. On the Sauks, Mesquakies, and Winnebagos at Prophetstown in 1810, see Harrison to the Secretary of War, 15 June 1810, *WHHL*, 1:427. For Black Hawk's rejection of Tenskwatawa and Tecumseh, see Ma-ka-tai-me-she-kia-kiak,*Black Hawk*, 66; Metcalf, "Who Should Rule at Home?," 658-59; Nichols, *Black Hawk*, 42-43.

10. Hagan, *Sac and Fox*, 16-25; Treaty with the Sauks and Foxes, 3 November 1804, Charles Kappler, ed., *Indian Affairs: Laws and Treaties*, 2 vols. (Washington, D.C.: Government Printing Office, 1903-1904), 2:74 (hereafter cited as *IALT*); Charles Royce, "Indian Land Cessions in the United States," in *Eighteenth Annual Report of the Bureau of American Ethnology* (Washington, D.C.: Government Printing Office, 1899), 666; Thomas Forsyth, Original Causes of the troubles with a party of Sauk and Fox Indians . . . , 1 October 1832, Thomas Forsyth Papers, Series T, vol. 9, pp 54-59, Lyman C. Draper Manuscript Collection, State Historical Society of Wisconsin, Madison, Wisconsin (hereafter cited as follows, Draper MSS, 9T:54-59).

11. Ma-ka-tai-me-she-kia-kiak,*Black Hawk*, 60-63.

12. Treat of Peace and Amity (Treaty of Ghent), 24 December 1814, John Haswell, ed., *Treaties and Conventions of the United States of America and Other Powers since July 4, 1776* (Washington, D.C.: Government Printing Office, 1889), 404-5; Robert Fisher, "The Treaties of Portage des Sioux," *Mississippi Valley Historical Review* 19 (March 1933): 495-97; James Monroe to Clark, Ninian Edwards, and Auguste Chouteau, 11 March 1815, *American State Papers: Indian Affairs*, 2 vols. (Washington, D.C.: Gales and Seaton, 1832-1834), 2:6 (hereafter cited as *ASP:IA*); Forsyth to the Secretary of War, 30 April 1815, *WHC*, 11:338; Clark, Edwards, and Chouteau to Monroe, 22 May 1815, *ASP:IA*, 2:7; Forsyth to the Commissioners, 30 May 1815, *WHC*, 11:340-41.

13. Fisher, "Treaties of Portage des Sioux," 500-3; Nicolas Boilvin to the Secretary of War, 11 January 1816, Clarence Carter and John Bloom, eds., *The Territorial Papers of the United States*, 28 vols. (Washington, D.C.: Government Printing Office, 1934-1975), 17:282 (hereafter cited as *TPUS*); Clark, Edwards, and Chouteau to the Secretary of War, 11 July 1815, *ASP:IA*, 2:8-9; Clark, Edwards, and Chouteau to the Secretary of War, 16 July 1815, *ASP:IA*, 2:8; Clark, Edwards, and Chouteau to the Secretary of War, 18 September 1815,*ASP:IA*, 2:9; Clark, Edwards, and Chouteau to the Secretary of War, 18 October 1815, *ASP:IA*, 2:10; *Missouri Gazette and Illinois Advertiser* (St. Louis), 8 July 1815, 15 July 1815, 22 July 1815; *Missouri Gazette* (St. Louis), 16 September 1815, 15 June 1816.

14. Treaty with the Foxes, 14 September 1815, *IALT*, 2:212-22; Treaty with the Sauk, 13 May 1816, *IALT*, 2:126-28; quoted from Ma-ka-tai-me-she-kia-kiak, *Black Hawk*, 95, 98.

15. Treaty with the Sauk and Fox Indians, 3 November 1804, *IALT*, 2:75; Forsyth to Clark, 3 June 1817, *WHC*, 11:347-48; quoted from Forsyth to Clark, 3 April 1823, Draper MSS, 4T:159-60.

16. Forsyth to William Lee, 3 July 1823, Draper MSS, 6T:25-26; Forsyth to Clark, 7 July 1823, Draper MSS, 4T:170.

17. On British suspicions of the United States and the need to retain Indian allies, see Robert McDonall [sic] to Secretary Foster, 15 May 1815, J. C. Holmes, et al., eds., *Collections of the Michigan Pioneer and Historical Society*, 40 vols. (Lansing: Michigan Pioneer and Historical Society, 1877-1929), 16:103-5 (hereafter cited as *MPHC*); McDonall [sic] to unknown, 7 August 1816, *MPHC*, 16:512; Catherine Sims, "Algonkian-British Relations in the Upper Great Lakes Region: Gathering to Give and Receive Presents, 1815-1843" (Ph.D. diss., University of Western Ontario, 1992), 55-64, 85-91; Colin Calloway, "The End of an Era: British-Indian Relations in the Great Lakes Region after the War of 1812," *Michigan Historical Review* 12 (Fall 1986): 6, 17-19.

18. Gordon Drummond to Earl Bathurst, 25 April 1815, *MPHC*, 25:625; Drummond to Bathurst, 27 August 1815, *MPHC*, 25:631-32; McDonall [sic] to unknown, 19 June 1816, *MPHC*, 16:468-69; Return of the Indians of Upper and Lower Canada . . . , *MPHC*, 23:108; Speech of Lieutenant Colonel McKay . . . , 29 June 1816, *MPHC*, 26:479-85; William Puthuff to Lewis Cass, 20 August 1817, *WHC*, 19:472; Extract from the Commissioner's Report . . . , 9 September 1825, *MPHC*, 23:443; Thomas Anderson to McKay, 20 July 1828, *MPHC*, 23:148-50; Names of Indian Tribes usually visiting Drummond Island . . . , 22 August 1828, *MPHC*, 23:151; Sims, "Algonkian-British Relations," 1, 44-47, 136-37; Calloway, "End of an Era," 12-19.

19. Ibid., 9-14; McDouall to unknown, 25 April 1815, Grignon, Lawe, and Porlier Papers, Box 1, Folder 5, State Historical Society of Wisconsin, Madison, Wisconsin (hereafter cited as GLP MSS); McDouall to Andrew Bulger, 25 April 1815, *WHC*, 13:133-34; McDouall to Robert Dickinson, 28 April 1815, *WHC*, 13:135; McDouall to Bulger, 1 May 1815, *WHC*, 13:135-39; quoted from McDonall [sic] to the Military Secretary, 17 June 1816, *MPHC*, 16:464.

20. Calloway, "End of an Era," 17-18; Ma-ka-tai-me-she-kia-kiak, *Black Hawk*, 110, 119; Minutes of a speech by Mayocantay the Winnebago Chief, 30 June 1830, *MPHC*, 23:144-47; David Armour, "From Drummond Island: An Indian View of Michigan History," *Michigan History* 67 (May-June 1983): 17-22; quoted from the Speech of the Black Hawk . . . , 3 August 1815, *MPHC*, 16:196-97.

21. McDonall [sic] to George Murray, 24 June 1815, *MPHC*, 16:137; McDonalls [sic] speech . . . , 28 June 1815, *MPHC*, 16:192; Speech of McDonall [sic] . . . , 17 September 1815, *MPHC*, 16:273-75; McDonall [sic] to unknown, 7 August 1816, *MPHC*, 16:508-12; Forsyth to Clark, 25 August 1826, Draper MSS, 4T:260; Anderson, Remarks on the Winnebago Chief Four Leg's Speech, 13 July 1828, *MPHC*, 23:147-48; Anderson to McKay, 20 July 1828, *MPHC*, 23:148-50; Minutes of a speech by Mayocantay the Winnebago Chief, 30 June 1830, *MPHC*, 23:144-47; Sims, "Algonkian-British Relations," 81-89.

22. Reuben Thwaites, "Notes on Early Lead Mining in the Fever (Or Galena) River Region," *WHC*, 13:271-92; Joseph Schafer, *The Wisconsin Lead Region* (Madison: State Historical Society of Wisconsin, 1832), 21-43; Duane Everhart, "The Leasing of Mineral Lands in Illinois and Wisconsin," *Journal of the Illinois Historical Society* 60 (Summer 1967): 117-23; M. Thomas to George Bomford, 30 September 1826, Executive Office, *Message from the President of the United States . . . in Relation to the Lead Mines Belonging to the United States . . .* , 19th Cong., 2d sess., 1826, Ho. Exec. Doc. 7 (Serial 149), 8; John Marsh to Cass, 20 November 1826, Records of the Michigan Superintendency of Indian Affairs, 1814-1851, Microfilm Publication M-1, Reel 19, Frame 106, Record Group 75, Records of the Bureau of Indian Affairs, National Archives, Washington, D.C. (hereafter cited as NA, M-1); Herbert Kuhm, "The Mining and Use of Lead by the Wisconsin Indians," *Wisconsin Archeologist* 32 (June 1951): 25-31; Janet Spector, "Winnebago Indians and Lead Mining: A Case Study of the Ethnohistoric Approach in Archaeology," *Midcontinental Journal of Archaeology* 2:1 (1977): 131-37.

23. Forsyth to Clark, 24 June 1822, Draper MSS, 4T:128-34; John Calhoun to Forsyth, 14 February 1822, Draper MSS, 5T:11-13; Forsyth to Calhoun, 24 June 1822, Draper MSS, 6T:5-6; Joseph Street to the Secretary of War, 15 November 1827, Letters Received by the Office of Indian Affairs, 1824-1881, Microfilm Publication M-234, Reel 696, Frame 45, Record Group 75, Records of the Bureau of Indian Affairs, National Archives, Washington, D.C. (hereafter cited as NA, M-234); Cass and Thomas McKenney to James Barbour, August 1827, War Department, *Letter . . . Transmitting a Report of Gov. Cass and Col. McKenney on the Subject of the Complaints of the Winnebago Indians, &c*, 20th Cong., 1st sess., 1828, House Doc. 117 (Serial 171), 5-6; Thomas to Bomford, 30 September 1827, War Department, *In Relation to the Lead Mines of the United States*, 20th Cong., 1st sess., 1828, House Doc. 45 (Serial 170), 7-8.

24. Clark to McKenney, 2 August 1828, NA, M-234, Reel 748, Frame 465; A. E. Wing to the Committee on the Territories, 10 January 1829, *TPUS*, 12:7-8; Lucius H. Langworthy, "Dubuque: Its History, Mines, Indian Legends, Etc., By Lucius H. Langworthy," ed. John Parish, *Iowa Journal of History and Politics* 8 (July 1910): 371-72; Jacob Van der Zee, "Early History of Lead Mining in the Iowa Country," *Iowa Journal of History and Politics* 13 (January 1915): 39-40; Lucius H. Langworthy, "Autobiographical Sketch of Lucius H. Langworthy," ed. John Parish, *Iowa Journal of History and Politics* 8 (July 1910): 321; Wyncoop Warner to Forsyth, 3 June 1830, Commissary General of Subsistence, *Correspondence on the Subject of the Emigration of the Indians*, 23d Cong., 1st sess., 1834, Sen. Doc. 512 (Serial 245), 64 (hereafter cited as Sen. Doc. 512); Clark to McKenney, 16 June 1830, NA, M-234, Reel 696, Frames 247-48; Clark to McKenney, 19 June 1830, Sen. Doc. 512 (Serial 245), 68; Clark to Andrew Jackson, 21 July 1830, William Clark Papers, vol. 4, p. 141, Kansas Historical Society, Topeka, Kansas (hereafter cited as Clark MSS).

25. William Williamson to Clark, 10 September 1830, Clark MSS, vol. 6, pp 1-2; Clark to P. G. Randolph, 11 April 1831, NA, M-234, Reel 728, Frame 107; Willoughby Morgan to Randolph, 23 July 1831, NA, M-234, Reel 728, Frames 160-62; McKenney

to Clark, 9 June 1830, Sen. Doc. 512 (Serial 245), 14; McKenney to Clark, 4 August 1830, Sen. Doc. 512 (Serial 245), 23; Clark to McKenney, 23 July 1830, Sen. Doc. 512 (Serial 245), 80-81; Langworthy, "Dubuque," 379; Langworthy, "Autobiographical Sketch," 321-22; Van der Zee, "Lead Mining in Iowa," 44-46; Jefferson Davis, "A Letter by Jefferson Davis," ed. Charles Aldrich, *Annals of Iowa*, 4 (October 1899): 230-32; George Davenport to Joseph Duncan, 11 February 1832, Sen. Doc. 512 (Serial 246), 221-23.

26. Wells to Harrison, 8 April 1809, *WHHL*, 1:338; Harrison to the Secretary of War, 25 April 1810, *WHHL*, 1:417; Harrison to the Secretary of War, 14 June 1810, *WHHL*, 1:427; Harrison to the Secretary of War, 25 July 1810, *WHHL*, 1:449; Lyman Draper, Tecumseh's Vincennes Conference, 1810, Draper's Notes, Series S, vol. 25, p. 91, Lyman C. Draper Manuscript Collection, State Historical Society of Wisconsin, Madison, Wisconsin; quoted from Harrison to the Secretary of War, 28 August 1810, *WHHL*, 1:471.

27. Matthew Elliot to Isaac Brock, 12 January 1812, *WHHL*, 1:616-81; Harrison to the Secretary of War, 24 December 1812, *WHHL*, 1:684; Harrison to the Secretary of War, 7 January 1812, *WHHL*, 2:4-5; Harrison to the Secretary of War, 13 May 1812, *WHHL*, 2:49; Jonathan Askin, Jr., to Louis Grignon, 28 January 1814, *WHC*, 10:101; Louise Kellogg, *The British Régime in Wisconsin and the Northwest* (Madison: State Historical Society of Wisconsin, 1935), 272, 276-79, 289, 295, 304.

28. For the 1816 treaty, see Treaty with the Winnebago, 3 June 1816, *IALT*, 2:130-31; Martin Zanger, "Red Bird," in *American Indian Leaders: Studies in Diversity*, ed. R. David Edmunds (Lincoln: University of Nebraska Press, 1980), 65. While there have been no studies of criminal acts as ideological expressions among North American Indians, there have been studies of this phenomenon among other cultures in colonial situations. In particular, see Ranjit Guha, *Elementary Aspects of Peasant Insurgency in Colonial India* (Delhi, India: Oxford University Press, 1983), 5-12.

29. On the 1819 acts, see Alexander Wolcott to Cass, 14 November 1819, NA, M-1, Reel 6, Frames 212-13; Lewis Morgan to Joseph Smith, 3 January 1820, *WHC*, 20:139; Smith to Jacob Brown, 5 January 1820, *WHC*, 20:139-42; William Whistler to Smith, 3 January 1820, NA, M-1, Reel 7, Frame 63; Whistler to John Bowyer, 13 January 1820, *WHC*, 20:142-43; Bowyer to Cass, 15 January 1820, *WHC*, 20:143-44; William Maddison [sic], to unknown, 5 October 1819, *WHC*, 20:126. For the murders at Fort Armstrong, see Martin Zanger, "Conflicting Concepts of Justice: A Winnebago Murder Trial on the Illinois Frontier," *Journal of the Illinois State Historical Society* 73 (Winter 1980): 263-76; Jonathan Johnson to Cass, 19 April 1820, *WHC*, 20:167; F. Barnard to John Hunt, 14 May 1820, *WHC*, 20:168-70; Henry Leavenworth, Interrogation of the Winnebago Prisoners, Clark MSS, vol. 2, pp 182-94; Lawrence Taliaferro to Clark, 12 June 1820, Letters Received by the Secretary of War Relating to Indian Affairs, 1800-1823, Microfilm Publication M-271, Reel 3, Frame 316, Record Group 75, Records of the Bureau of Indian Affairs, National Archives, Washington, D.C. (hereafter cited as NA, M-271); Clark to Calhoun, 25 June 1820, NA, M-271, Reel 3, Frame 320; Leavenworth to the Winnebagoes [sic], n.d., NA, M-271, Reel 3, Frame 322.

30. George Grosvenor to Smith, 2 January 1820, NA, M-1, Reel 7, Frame 62; George Johnson to Smith, 3 January 1820, NA, M-1, Reel 7, Frame 64; Smith to Brown, 5 January 1820, *WHC*, 20:140; James Doty to Henry Schoolcraft, 17 November 1821, *IPUS*, 11.176-77, Indictment of Ka ta koh . . . a Chippewa Indian for murder, 20 September 1821, Records of the Territorial Court of Michigan, 1815-1836, Microfilm Publication M-1111, Reel 2, Record Group 21, Records of District Courts of the United States, National Archives, Washington, D.C.; Schoolcraft to Cass, 31 August 1824, NA, M-234, Reel 419, Frames 87-88; Deposition of William Morrison relating the account of the Little Frenchman, 10 July 1825, NA, M-234, Reel 419, Frames 363-64; Deposition of William Aiken, et al., regarding the statements of O-quay-gun and Mee-toh-korsee-kanse, 16 July 1825, NA, M-234, Reel 419, Frame 365; Doty to the Secretary of War, 22 July 1825, NA, M-234, Reel 419, Frames 355-57; Joseph Rollette to O. N. Bostwick, 4 September 1824, Edward E. Ayer Manuscript Collection, No. 777, Newberry Library, Chicago, Illinois; Jung, "Forge, Destroy, and Preserve the Bonds of Empire," 335-55.

31. Boilvin, Depositions in the Methode Murder, 6-7 July 1826, Circuit Court File on the Methode Murder, 1827, Iowa Microseries 4, Reel 1, Records of the Iowa County Clerk of Court, University of Wisconsin-Platteville Area Research Center, Platteville, Wisconsin (hereafter cited as UWP-ARC, IMS-4); Doty to W. Morgan, 11 May 1826, NA, M-234, Reel 315, Frames 25-27; E. Reid to Cass, 19 June 1826, NA, M-1, Reel 18, Frame 114; Forsyth to Clark, 20 June 1826, Draper MSS, 4T:250-51; Council of W. Morgan with the Winnebagos, Sioux, and Menominees, 5 July 1826, UWP-ARC, IMS-4, Reel 1; Council of W. Morgan with the Winnebagos, 7 July 1826, UWP-ARC, IMS-4, Reel 1; W. Morgan to the Acting Adjutant General, 9 July 1826, NA, M-234, Reel 931, Frame 1; W. Morgan, Depositions in the Methode Murder, 18 July - 4 August 1826, Crawford and Iowa County Criminal Cases for the Additional Court of Michigan Territory, 1824-1836, Iowa Series 20, Box 1, Folder 84, Records of the Iowa County Clerk of Court, University of Wisconsin-Platteville Area Research Center, Platteville, Wisconsin; W. Morgan to the Assistant Adjutant General, 7 August 1826, UWP-ARC, IMS-4, Reel 1; W. Morgan to the Assistant Adjutant General, 10 August 1826, UWP-ARC, IMS-4, Reel 1; [William J. Snelling], "Early Days at Prairie du Chien and the Winnebago Outbreak of 1827," *WHC*, 5:126-28

32. Marsh to Cass, 20 November 1826, NA, M-1, Reel 19, Frame 106; Forsyth to Clark, 9 July 1827, Draper MSS, 4T:274-75; Forsyth to Cass, 10 September 1827, NA, M-1, Reel 21, Frame 102; John Kinzie to Cass, 3 August 1827, NA, M-234, Reel 419, Frames 789-91; Street to the Secretary of War, 15 November 1827, War Department, *Letter from the Secretary of War . . . In Relation to the Hostile Disposition of the Indian Tribes on the Northwestern Frontier*, 20th Cong., 1st sess., 1828, House Doc. 277 (Serial 175), 14-15 (hereafter cited as Ho. Doc. 277); Street to Edwards, November 1827, *WHC*, 11:360-61; Journal of the 1828 council with the Winnebago Indians, Documents Relating to the Negotiation of Ratified and Unratified Treaties with Various Tribes of Indians, 1801-1869, Microfilm Publication T-494, Reel 2, Frame 136, Record Group 75, Records of the Bureau of Indian Affairs, National Archives, Washington, D.C. (hereafter

cited as NA, T-494); [Snelling], "Early Days," *WHC*, 5:143-44; Zanger, "Red Bird," 69-70;

33. Ibid., 69; James Lockwood, "Early Times and Events in Wisconsin," *WHC*, 2:156, 158; [Snelling], "Early Days," *WHC*, 5:143-44; Taliaferro, Journal, 13-17 June 1827, Lawrence Taliaferro Papers, vol. 8, pp 15-16, Minnesota Historical Society, St. Paul, Minnesota (hereafter cited as Taliaferro MSS); Cass to Barbour, 10 July 1827, *TPUS*, 11:1101-2; McKenney to Barbour, 19 July 1827, NA, M-234, Reel 419, Frame 935; McKenney to the Secretary of War, 4 August 1827, NA, M-234, Reel 419, Frame 948; McKenney to the Secretary of War, 17 September 1827, Ho. Doc. 277, 9-10; Street to the Secretary of War, 15 November 1827, Ho. Doc. 277, 14-15; Street to Edwards, November 1827, *WHC*, 11:360-61.

34. Marsh to Clark, 30 June 1827, NA, M-234, Reel 748, Frame 92; Forsyth to Clark, 3 July 1827, NA, M-234, Reel 748, Frame 95; Marsh to Cass, 4 July 1827, *TPUS*, 11:1096-97; Doty, "Trials and Decisions in the Several Courts held in the Counties of Michilimackinac, Brown, and Crawford," pp 143-44, James D. Doty Papers, Box 3, State Historical Society of Wisconsin, Madison, Wisconsin; Thomas McKenney, *Memoirs, Official and Personal; With Sketches of Travels . . .*, 2d ed. (New York: Paine and Burgess, 1846), 127-31; Lockwood, "Early Times," *WHC*, 2:161-62; McKenney to the Secretary of War, 17 September 1827, Ho. Doc. 277, 9-12; Henry Atkinson to Edmund Gaines, 28 September 1827, War Department, *Annual Report of the Secretary of War for 1827*, 20th Cong., 1st sess., 1827, Ho. Doc. 2 (Serial 169), 157 (hereafter cited as *SWAR 1827*, Ho. Doc. 2) 155; Cass to Barbour, 4 July 1827, *TPUS*, 11:1093-95; Taliaferro to Clark, 1 August 1827, Taliaferro MSS, vol. 4, pp 95-96; Forsyth to Clark, 15 October 1827, Draper MSS, 6T:76-78.

35. Marsh to Cass, 4 July 1827, *TPUS*, 11:1096-97; Taliaferro to Clark, 9 July 1827, Taliaferro MSS, vol. 4, pp 91-92; Marsh to McKenney, 10 July 1827, NA, M-234, Reel 419, Frames 937-38; Marsh to Clark, 20 July 1827, NA, M-234, Reel 748, Frames 138-39; McKenney to Barbour, 26 July 1827, NA, M-234, Reel 419, Frame 942; Taliaferro to Clark, 17 August 1827, Taliaferro MSS, vol. 4, pp 101-2; Taliaferro to Clark, 8 August 1827, NA, M-234, Reel 757, Frame 20-21; McKenney to the Secretary of War, 17 September 1827, House Doc. 277, 10; Lockwood, "Early Times," *WHC*, 2:162-63; [Snelling], "Early Days," *WHC*, 5:144-52; Forsyth to Clark, 28 July 1827, Draper MSS, 6T:66; Atkinson to Gaines, 28 September 1827, *SWAR 1827*, Ho. Doc. 2, 155; Zanger, "Red Bird," 70-71.

36. Zanger, "Red Bird," 73-79; Roger Nichols, *General Henry Atkinson: A Western Military Career* (Norman: University of Oklahoma Press, 1965), 124-36; Francis Prucha, *The Sword of the Republic: The United States Army on the Frontier, 1783-1846* (London: Macmillan Company 1969), 163-67.

37. Forsyth to the Peoria Indian Agent, 7 July 1827, NA, M-234, Reel 132, Frames 24-25; John Dixon to Clark, 24 July 1827, NA, M-234, Reel 748, Frame 144; Clark to Barbour, 30 July 1827, NA, M-234, Reel 748, Frame 137; Depositions of David Crossin, et al., 10 March 1828, NA, M-234, Reel 748, Frame 505; Atkinson to Gaines, 28 September 1827, *SWAR 1827*, Ho. Doc. 2, 155-56; Forsyth to William Downy and

Charles St. Vrain, 27 August 1827, Draper MSS, 6T:74; Forsyth to Clark, 5 July 1827, NA, M-234, Reel 748, Frame 96; Cass to Barbour, 10 July 1827, *TPUS*, 11:1101-4; Clark to Barbour, 23 July 1827, NA, M-234, Reel 748, Frame 132; Marsh to Cass, 31 July 1827, NA, M 1, Reel 21, Frame 27; "Journal of the 1827 Butte des Morts Treaty," NA, T-494, Reel 2, Frames 26-27, 32-33; Robert Irwin to Cass, 5 January 1828, NA, M-1, Reel 22, Frame 1.

38. On the Potawatomis, see Zanger, "Red Bird," 73-74; Cass to Barbour, 23 July 1827, NA, M-234, Reel 132, Frames 12-13; Wolcott to Barbour, 25 July 1827, NA, M-234, Reel 132, Frames 28-31; Kinzie to Cass, 3 August 1827, NA, M-234, Reel 419, Frame 790. For the Santee Dakotas, see Zanger, "Red Bird," 70; Rollette to Cass, 16 November 1827, NA, M-1. Reel 21, Frame 176.

39. McKenney to Barbour, 19 July 1827, NA, M-234, Reel 419, Frame 933; McKenney to the Secretary of War, 4 August 1827, NA, M-234, Reel 419, Frames 946-48; quoted from McKenney to the Secretary of War, Ho. Doc. 277, p. 9-11.

40. Cass to Barbour, 4 July 1827, *TPUS*, 11:1094; Cass to John Connelly [sic], 5 July 1827, *TPUS*, 11:1097-98; Cass to Barbour, 10 July 1827, *TPUS*, 11:1102-3; Forsyth to Clark, 9 July 1827, Draper MSS, 4T:274-77; Clark to Forsyth, 14 July 1827, Draper MSS, 2T:50; Clark to John Eaton, 17 January 1831, NA, M-234, Reel 749, Frame 1126; Forsyth to Cass, 10 September 1827, NA, M-1, Reel 21, Frame 102; Forsyth to Clark, 15 June 1827, Draper MSS, 4T:271; Forsyth to Clark, 15 October 1827, Draper MSS, 6T:76-78.

41. Harold Hickerson, *The Chippewa and Their Neighbors: A Study in Ethnohistory* (New York: Holt, Rhinehart and Winston, 1970), 66, 76-90; Royce Kurtz, "Economic History of the Sauk and Mesquakie: 1780s-1845" (Ph.D. diss., University of Iowa, 1986), 37-54; Clark, Council with the Yancton Sioux, 26 September 1817, Clark MSS, vol. 2, pp 50-56; Forsyth to Calhoun, 18 August 1822, Draper MSS, 4T:103-5; Robert Stuart to Eaton, 9 February 1830, *TPUS*, 12:125-26.

42. Schoolcraft to George Porter, 15 August 1832, Ellen Whitney, ed., *The Black Hawk War, 1831-1832*, 2 vols., *Collections of the Illinois State Historical Library*, vols. 35-38 (Springfield: Illinois State Historical Library, 1970-1978), 2:1007 (hereafter cited as *BHW*); Forsyth to Clark, 30 September 1818, Draper MSS, 4T:61-62; Forsyth to James Latham, 30 April 1825, Draper MSS, 4T:224-25; Forsyth to Clark, 11 May 1825, Draper MSS, 4T:227-28; Forsyth to Clark, 6 May 1830, Draper MSS, 6T:125-26; Clark to Eaton, 17 May 1830, NA, M-234, Reel 749, Frame 943; Talk of the Messengers of Ta-oman, the Fox Chief, to Clark, 17 May 1830, NA, M-234, Reel 749, Frames 945-46; Clark to Eaton, 26 May 1830, NA, M-234, Reel 749, Frames 950-52.

43. On the Menominees, see Hickerson, *Chippewa and Their Neighbors*, 83-88; Cass to Calhoun, 6 April 1821, *TPUS*, 11:116-17; Street to Clark, 21 September 1830, NA, M-234, Reel 696, Frame 215; Street to Clark, 29 October 1830, NA, M-234, Reel 696, Frame 263; Street to Eaton, 2 March 1831, NA, M-234, Reel 315, Frames 609-10. For the Winnebagos, see Forsyth to Calhoun, 3 June 1823, Draper MSS, 4T:165-66; Marsh to Clark, 30 May 1827, NA, M-234, Reel 748, Frame 94; Marsh to Cass, 4 July 1827, *TPUS*, 11:1096; McKenney to Barbour, 26 July 1827, NA, M-234, Reel 419,

Frame 942; Forsyth to Cass, 10 September 1827, NA, M-1, Reel 2, vol. 1, pp 78-79; Stuart to Eaton, 9 February 1830, *TPUS*, 12:125-26; Street to Warner, 12 April 1830, NA, M-234, Reel 749, Frames 975-77; Talk of the Messengers of Ta-oman, the Fox Chief, to Clark, 17 May 1830, NA, M-234, Reel 749, Frames 945-46; Kinzie to Cass, 1 June 1830, NA, M-1, Reel 26, Frame 85.

44. On the Federal officials' rationale behind quelling intertribal conflicts, see Clark to Forsyth, 4 June 1820, Draper MSS, 1T:79-80; Clark to Forsyth, 1 May 1824, Draper MSS, 4T:33; Forsyth to J. H. Vose, 8 September 1824, NA, M-234, Reel 419, Frames 83-84; Street to Clark, 20 March 1829, NA, M-234, Reel 749, Frame 641; Street to Clark, 8 April 1829, NA, M-234, Reel 749, Frame 638; Clark to Eaton, 17 May 1830, NA, M-234, Reel 749, Frame 943; Clark to the Secretary of War, 17 November 1830, Clark MSS, vol. 4, p. 190. For the various treaty councils, see Clark to Calhoun, 22 December 1824, NA, M-234, Reel 747, Frames 126-27; Journal of the proceedings . . . at Prairie du Chien, August 1825, NA, T-494, Reel 1, Frames 711, 718-26, 746; Treaty with the Sioux, etc., 19 August 1825, *IALT*, 2:250-55; Cass and Clark to Barbour, 1 September 1825, NA, T-494, Reel 1, Frame 750; Cass to McKenney, 2 February 1826, NA, M-234, Reel 419, Frame 429; Cass to McKenney, 2 September 1826, NA, M-234, Reel 419, Frame 530; Thomas McKenney, *Sketches of a Tour to Lakes, Of the Character and Customs of the Chippeway Indians, And of Incidents Connected with the Treaty of Fond du Lac* (1827; reprint, Minneapolis: Ross and Haines, Inc., 1959) 457-76; McKenney, *Memoirs*, 83; Treaty with the Chippewa, 5 August 1826, *IALT*, 2:268-73; Treaty with the Chippewa, etc., 11 August 1827, *IALT*, 2:281-83; Cass and Clark to Barbour, 1 September 1825, NA, T-494, Reel 1, Frame 751.

45. Kurtz, "Sauk and Mesquakie," 47; Taliaferro, Daily Journal for all Occurrences at the St. Peter's Agency, 4 January 1829, Taliaferro MSS, vol. 8, p. 211; Street to Clark, 25 August 1828, NA, M-234, Reel 696, Frame 97; Schoolcraft to Cass, 29 October 1829, NA, M-234, Reel 420, Frames 360-61; Cass to unknown, 11 March 1830, NA, M-234, Reel 420, Frames 355-58; Francis Audrain to Schoolcraft, 8 June 1830, NA, M-1, Reel 26, Frame 103; Schoolcraft to Cass, 22 June 1830, NA, M-1, Reel 26, Frame 101; Taliaferro to Clark, 30 July 1830, NA, M-234, Reel 757, Frames 64-65; W. Morgan to Eaton, 30 July 1830, NA, M-234, Reel 696, Frame 167; W. Morgan to Eaton, 8 August 1830, NA, M-234, Reel 696, Frames 165-66; Clark to Eaton, 17 May 1829, NA, M-234, Reel 749, Frames 627-28; Clark to Eaton, 18 May 1829, M-234, Reel 749, Frames 726-27; Rollette to unknown, 3 July 1829, NA, M-234, Reel 759; Stuart to McKenney, 15 August 1829, *TPUS*, 12:59-60; Stuart to Eaton, 9 February 1830, *TPUS*, 12:125-26; Taliaferro to Clark, 3 May 1830, NA, M-234, Reel 749, Frame 935.

46. On the killing of the Mesquakie chiefs, see Jacob Van der Zee, "The Neutral Ground," *Iowa Journal of History and Politics* 13 (July 1915): 311-12; Forsyth to Clark, 28 April 1830, Draper MSS, 6T:118-20; Taliaferro to Clark, 3 May 1830, NA, M-234, Reel 749, Frame 935; Forsyth to Clark, 6 May 1830, Draper MSS, 6T:125-27; Joseph Hardy to Warner, 7 May 1830, NA, M-234, Reel 749, Frames 954-55; Clark to Eaton, 10 May 1830, NA, M-234, Reel 749, Frames 919-21; Clark to Forsyth, 10 May 1830, NA, M-234, Reel 749, Frames 925-27; Clark to Eaton, 17 May 1830, NA, M-234, Reel 749,

Frame 942-44; Taliaferro to Clark, 17 May 1830, NA, M-234, Reel 749, Frames 952-53; Talk of the Sacs and Foxes with Clark, 24 May 1830, NA, M-234, Reel 749, Frames 964, 967; Kinzie to Cass, 1 June 1830, NA, M-1, Reel 26, Frame 85. For the 1830 treaty council, see Extract of Minutes of a Council held at Prairie du Chien, 1830, NA, T-494, Reel 2, Frames 253, 258-64; Treaty with the Sauks and Foxes, etc., 15 July 1830, *IALT*, 2:305-10; Royce, "Indian Land Cessions," 726-27; Clark to the Secretary of War, 11 July 1830, Clark MSS, vol. 4, p. 131; Clark and W. Morgan to Eaton, 16 July 1830, Sen. Doc. 512 (Serial 245), 78-79; Van der Zee, "Neutral Ground," 312-31. There were actually two treaties signed at the Prairie du Chien council in 1830. The Menominees, Santee Dakotas, Sauks, Mesquakies, and Winnebagos signed the first on July 10, 1830, and it established peace between them but involved no land cessions. This treaty was not ratified, but the second, signed on July 16th, was the principal treaty that established the buffer zone. The July 10th treaty, although not ratified, did reaffirm the boundaries and state of peace established in the 1825 Treaty of Prairie du Chien. For the July 10, 1830 treaty, see Treaty of Peace and Friendship . . . , 10 July 1830, NA, T-494, Reel 8, Frames 47-53.

47. On the July 1831 attacks, see Van der Zee, "Black Hawk War," 416; Taliaferro to Clark, 8 August 1831, NA, M-234, Reel 749, Frame 1260; Taliaferro to Clark, 12 August 1831, NA, M-234, Reel 748, Frames 1261-62; Street to the Secretary of War, 31 August 1831, *TPUS*, 12:343-44; Street to Clark, 31 August 1831, NA, M-234, Reel 749, Frames 1262-63; Clark to Cass, 12 September 1831, NA, M-234, Reel 749, Frames 1257-58; Felix St. Vrain to Clark, 10 September 1831, NA, M-234, Reel 728, Frames 138-39; Rollette to Cass, 24 November 1831, NA, M-234, Reel 696, Frames 347-48; Street to Clark, 15 November 1831, NA, M-234, Reel 749, Frames 1324-26; Street to Clark, 21 December 1831, NA, M-234, Reel 750, Frame 37. For the Menominee massacre, see List of Menominees killed at Prairie du Chien by the Sauks and Foxes, 31 July 1831, NA, M-234, Reel 728, Frame 133; Street to G. Loomis, 31 July 1831, Sen. Doc. 512 (Serial 245), 518; Street to the Secretary of War, 1 August 1831, *BHW*, 2:116-19; Loomis to Street, 1 August 1831, Sen. Doc. 512 (Serial 245), 518-19; Street to unknown, 1 August 1831, NA, M-234, Reel 728, Frames 126-27; Street to the Secretary of War, 1 August 1831, *BHW*, 2:116-19; "Journal of proceedings by Samuel Stambaugh . . . and the principal chiefs of the Menominees," 15 August 1831, NA, M-234, Reel 315, Frames 530-40; Stambaugh to Cass, 16 August 1831, NA, M-234, Reel 315, Frames 527-29; Davenport to Duncan, 11 February 1832, Sen. Doc. 512 (Serial 246), 222-23.

48. Clark to Barbour, 11 July 1827, NA, M-234, Reel 748, Frame 89; Forsyth to Clark, 20 July 1827, Draper MSS, 4T:277-78; Forsyth to Clark, 7 August 1827, Draper MSS, 6T:71-72; Forsyth to Cass, 10 September 1827, NA, M-1, Reel 21, Frame 102; Cass and McKenney to Forsyth, 9 August 1827, Draper MSS, 2T:53; Forsyth to Clark, 28 July 1827, Draper MSS, 6T:66-67; McKenney to Barbour, 19 July 1827, NA, M-234, Reel 419, Frame 932-34; Kinzie to Cass, 3 August 1827, NA, M-234, Reel 419, Frame 791; McKenney, *Memoirs*, 73-76, 78-79; Journal of the 1827 Butte des Morts Treaty, NA, T-494, Reel 2, Frames 26-27, 32-33; Bernard Sheehan, *Seeds of Extinction:*

Jeffersonian Philanthropy and the American Indian (Chapel Hill: University of North Carolina Press, 1973), 190-91.

49. For the troop strength in 1826, see Brown to Barbour, 11 January 1826, *American State Papers: Military Affairs*, 7 vols. (Washington, D.C.: Gales and Seaton, 1832-1861), 3:215-16 (hereafter cited as *ASP:MA*); Position and Distribution of Troops in the Eastern Department . . . , November 1826, in Annual Report of the Secretary of War for 1826, *ASP:MA*, 3:339-40 (hereafter cited as SWAR 1826); Position and Distribution of Troops in the Western Department . . . , November 1826, SWAR 1826, *ASP:MA*, 3:341-42; Francis Paul Prucha, *A Guide to the Military Posts of the United States, 1789-1895* (Madison: State Historical Society of Wisconsin, 1964), 8, 68, 71. For the troop strength after the Winnebago Uprising, see Roger Jones to Winfield Scott, 14 August 1827, NA, M-1, Reel 21, Frame 57; Barbour to Cass, 16 August 1827, *TPUS*, 11:1113-14; Jones to Cass, 6 September 1827, NA, M-1, Reel 21, Frame 100; Atkinson to Gaines, 28 September 1827, *SWAR 1827*, Ho. Doc. 2, 158; Alexander Macomb to Peter Porter, November 1828, War Department, *Annual Report of the Secretary of War for 1828*, 20th Cong., 2d sess., 1828, Sen. Doc. 1, (Serial 181), 157; Fort Armstrong Post Returns, December 1828, Returns from U.S. Military Posts, 1800-1916, Microfilm Publication M-617, Reel 41, Record Group 94, Records of the Office of the Adjutant General, National Archives, Washington, D.C. (hereafter cited as NA, M-617); Fort Winnebago Post Returns, December 1828, NA, M-617, Reel 1454; Fort Crawford Post Returns, December 1828, NA, M-617, Reel 264; Fort Dearborn Post Returns, December 1828, NA, M-617, Reel 300; Fort Howard Post Returns, December 1828, NA, M-617, Reel 488; Fort Snelling Post Returns, January 1829, NA, M-617, Reel 1193.

50. Proceedings of the Commissioners for holding a treaty . . . for the cession of the mineral country . . . , 1829, NA, T-494, Reel 2, Frame 193; Wallace, "Prelude to Disaster," 264-74; Hagan, *Sac and Fox*, 92-105.

51. The numbers used to provide the numerical estimates are taken from Wallace, "Prelude to Disaster," 277-78; and Jeanne Kay, "The Fur Trade and Native American Population Growth," *Ethnohistory* 31:4 (1984): 275, 277. For William Clark's estimate, see Clark to Eaton, 17 January 1831, NA, M-234, Reel 749, Frame 1126. On the reluctance of the confederated villages of the Potawatomis, Ottawas, and Ojibwas to join Black Hawk, see Atkinson to John Reynolds, 5 May 1832, *BHW*, 2:348; Clark to Cass, 8 May 1832, *BHW*, 2:357; Thomas J. V. Owen to G. Porter, *BHW*, 2:383-84; Atkinson to Henry Dodge, 17 May 1832, *BHW*, 2:378 Owen to Steven Mason, 3 June 1832, NA, M-1, Reel 30, Frame 123; A Council held at Porters [sic] Grove . . . , 3-4 June 1832, *BHW*, 2:510.

52. Forsyth to Clark, 24 May 1828, Draper MSS, 6T:81-82; Forsyth to Clark, 16 June 1828, Draper MSS, 6T:86-87; Forsyth to Clark, 22 June 1828, Draper MSS, 6T:87-88; Forsyth to Clark, 6 July 1828, Draper MSS, 6T:92-93; Forsyth to Clark, 22 August 1828, Draper MSS, 6T:95; Forsyth to Clark, 17 May 1829, Draper MSS, 6T:97-99; Forsyth to Clark, 22 May 1829, Draper MSS, 6T:100-1; Forsyth to Clark, 1 October 1829, NA, M-234, Reel 749, Frame 1215; Clark to Eaton, 20 May 1829, NA, M-234, Reel 749, Frames 631-33; Forsyth to Clark, 17 May 1829, Draper MSS,

6T:97-99; Clark to the Secretary of War, 1 June 1829, NA, M-234, Reel 749, Frame 646; Forsyth to Clark, 17 June 1829, Draper MSS, 6T: 102-3; Ma-ka-tai-me-she-kia-kiak, *Black Hawk*, 111-16; Wallace, "Prelude to Disaster," 267-71.

53. Forsyth to Clark, 28 April 1830, Draper MSS, 6T:118-20; Forsyth to Clark, 30 April 1830, Draper MSS, 6T:212-22; Forsyth to Clark, 25 May 1830, Draper MSS, 6T:132; F. St. Vrain to Clark, 8 October 1830, NA, M-234, Reel 749, Frame 1217; F. St. Vrain to Clark, 15 May 1831, *BHW*, 2:7; Thomas Burnett to Clark, 18 May 1831, *BHW*, 2:8-9; F. St. Vrain to Clark, 28 May 1831, *BHW*, 2:21-22; Deposition of Rinnah and Samuel Wells, 10 June 1831, *BHW*, 2:43-44; Deposition of Citizens of the Rock River Settlement, 10 June 1831, *BHW*, 2:44-45; Ma-ka-tai-me-she-kia-kiak, *Black Hawk*, 120-23, 130; A. M. Gibson, *The Kickapoos: Lords of the Middle Border* (Norman: University of Oklahoma Press, 1963), 80-87; Wallace, "Prelude to Disaster," 272-75; Hagan, *Sac and Fox*, 120-26.

54. Reynolds to Clark, 26 May 1831, *BHW*, 2:13; Clark to Gaines, 28 May 1831, *BHW*, 2:16-17; Gaines to Jones, 30 May 1831, *BHW*, 2:25-26; Gaines to Jones, 14 June 1831, *BHW*, 2:47-50; Burnett to Clark, 29 June 1831; *BHW*, 2:81; Memorandum of Talks between Gaines and the Sauk, 4-7 June 1831, *BHW*, 2:27-31; George McCall to Archibald McCall, 17 June 1831, *BHW*, 2:55-58; Nathaniel Buckmaster to John Y. Sawyer, 30 June 1831, *BHW*, 2:84; Articles of Agreement and Capitulation between the United States and Sauk and Fox, 30 June 1831, *BHW*, 2:85-88; Gaines to Hugh White, 6 July 1831, *BHW*, 2:102-3; Wallace, "Prelude to Disaster," 275-76.

55. Forsyth to Clark, 24 May 1828, Draper MSS, 6T:82; Forsyth to Clark, 25 June 1828, Draper MSS, 6T:90; Forsyth to Clark, 1 July 1828, Draper MSS, 6T:91; F. St. Vrain to Clark, 28 May 1831, *BHW*, 2:21; Street to Clark, 6 July 1831, *BHW*, 2:104; Clark to the Secretary of War, 12 August 1831, *BHW*, 2:136; Henry Gratiot to Clark, 15 October 1831, NA, M-1, Reel 30, Frame 9; E. Wacker to Atkinson, 17 January 1833, NA, M-234, Reel 728, Frame 316; Black Hawk and the Winnebago Prophet to the President, n.d., NA, M-234, Reel 728, Frames 319-20; Dowd, *Spirited Resistance*, 193.

56. Ma-ka-tai-me-she-kia-kiak, *Black Hawk*, 112-13, 120, 124, 126-27; Gaines to Jones, 14 June 1831, *BHW*, 2:48; F. St. Vrain to Gaines, 15 June 1831, *BHW*, 2:51-52; Clark to Eaton, 29 June 1831, *BHW*, 2:83; F. St. Vrain to the Secretary of War, 6 September 1831, NA, M-234, Reel 728, Frame 165.

57. Ma-ka-tai-me-she-kia-kiak, *Black Hawk*, 110, 119, 132-33; Hagan, *Sac and Fox*, 138; Wallace, "Prelude to Disaster," 283.

58. Ma-ka-tai-me-she-kia-kiak, *Black Hawk*, 133.

59. On the British Band's crossing of the Mississippi and Black Hawk's intentions, see Ibid., 135-38; Atkinson to Kinzie, 10 April 1832, NA, M-1, Reel 30, Frames 75-76; Atkinson to Macomb, 13 April 1832, *BHW*, 2:244-45. On the reaction of federal officials, see Atkinson to Macomb, 10 April 1832, *BHW*, 2:243-44; Clark to Elbert Herring, 10 April 1832, *BHW*, 2:244; Atkinson to Macomb, 13 April 1832, *BHW*, 2:245; Atkinson to Reynolds, 13 April 1832, *BHW*, 2:245-46; Davenport to Atkinson, 13 April 1832, *BHW*, 2:247; Atkinson to Dodge, 14 April 1832, *BHW*, 2:255.

60. Ma-ka-tai-me-she-kia-kiak,*Black Hawk*, 137; Clark to Cass, 6 December 1831, *BHW*, 2:205-6; Street to Clark, 11 January 1832, *BHW*, 2:206-7; Clark to Herring, *BHW*, 2:214-15; F. St. Vrain to Clark, 1 March 1832, *BHW*, 2:216; Elias Langham to Clark, 2 March 1832, *BHW*, 2:216; Andrew S. Hughes to Clark, 13 March 1832, *BHW*, 2:217; Herring to Clark, 15 March 1832, *BHW*, 2:218-19; Macomb to Atkinson, 17 March 1832, *BHW*, 2:219-21; Atkinson to Gaines, 3 April 1832, *BHW*, 2:223-24; Atkinson to Gaines, 3 April 1832, *BHW*, 2:224; Atkinson, Orders, 5 April 1832, *BHW*, 2:225-26; Herring to Kinzie, 6 April 1832, *BHW*, 2:229-30.

61. On the actions of the Rock River Winnebagos and White Crow, see Ma-ka-tai-me-she-kia-kiak,*Black Hawk*, 138-39; Gratiot to Cass, 26 April 1832, *BHW*, 2:314-15; Gratiot, Journal, *BHW*, 2:1302-3; Elihu Washburne, "Col. Henry Gratiot," *WHC*, 10:252-54; A council held at Porters [sic] Grove . . . , 3-4 June 1832, *BHW*, 2:507-12; Minutes of a Talk between Atkinson and Whirling Thunder and White Crow, 28 April 1832, *BHW*, 2:321-24, 323n-324n; Report of Oliver Emmell and White Crow, 27 June 1832, *BHW*, 2:694-96; Minutes of an Examination of Prisoners, 19 August 1832, *BHW*, 2:1028-33; Minutes of an Examination of Prisoners, *BHW*, 2:1034-37; Minutes of an Examination of Prisoners, *BHW*, 2:1055-57; Council with the Rock River Winnebago, 11 September 1832, *BHW*, 2:1133-34. The only Winnebagos with the British Band during this phase of the conflict were those who followed Wabokieshiek, and almost all were of Sauk and Winnebago parentage. See Kinzie to Cass, 28 September 1831, NA, M-234, Reel 696, Frames 345-46; Gratiot to Cass, 24 April 1832, *BHW*, 2:302; Gratiot to Cass, 11 May 1832, NA, M-1, Reel 30, Frames 94-95; A council held at Porters [sic] Grove . . . , 3-4 June 1832, *BHW*, 2:511; Council with the Rock River Winnebago, 11 September 1832, *BHW*, 2:1133-34.

62. Ma-ka-tai-me-she-kia-kiak, *Black Hawk*, 140-41; James Clifton, *The Prairie People: Continuity and Change in Potawatomi Indian Culture, 1665-1965* (Lawrence: The Regents Press of Kansas, 1977), 233-34; Answer of Black Hawk and his Band to Atkinson, 26 April 1832, *BHW*, 2:312-14; A council held at Porters [sic] Grove . . . , 3-4 June 1832, *BHW*, 2:510-11; Owen to the Public, 5 June 1832, *BHW*, 2:527-28; Minutes of an Examination of Prisoners, 19 August 1832, *BHW*, 2:1028-33; Minutes of an Examination of Prisoners, 20 August 1832, *BHW*, 2:1034-37.

63. Ma-ka-tai-me-she-kia-kiak, *Black Hawk*, 140-45; Atkinson to Macomb, 13 April 1832, *BHW*, 2:244-45; Atkinson to Reynolds, 13 April 1832, *BHW*, 2:245-46; Reynolds to Atkinson, 16 April 1832, *BHW*, 2:263; Reynolds to the Militia of the Northwestern Section of the State, 16 April 1832, *BHW*, 2:264-65; Atkinson to the Commanding Officer at Galena, 17 April 1832, *BHW*, 2:268; Reynolds to Cass, 17 April 1832, *BHW*, 2:270; Reynolds, Orders, 20 April 1832, *BHW*, 2:284-85; Reynolds to Thomas Neale, 22 April 1832, *BHW*, 2:296-97; Atkinson to Reynolds, 27 April 1832, *BHW*, 2:320; Reynolds to David Bailey, 30 April 1832, *BHW*, 2:337; Atkinson to Hugh Brady, 8 May 1832, *BHW*, 2:354; Isaiah Stillman to Atkinson, 15 May 1832, *BHW*, 2:372; A Militia Officer's Report on Stillman's Defeat, 18 May 1832, *BHW*, 2:387-88; Wallace, "Prelude to Disaster," 286-88.

64. Ma-ka-tai-me-she-kia-kiak, Black Hawk, 142-44, 146; Atkinson to Dodge, 17 May 1832, *BHW*, 2:377; Samuel Whiteside to Atkinson, 18 May 1832, *BHW*, 2:386; Horatio Newhall to Isaac Newhall, 19 May 1832, *BHW*, 2:393; Reuben Holmes to B. McCary, 23 May 1832, *BHW*, 2:414-15; War News from Galena, *BHW*, 2:377; Albert Johnson, Journal, *BHW*, 2:1311; Nichols, *General Henry Atkinson*, 164-65; Prucha, *Sword of the Republic*, 223.

65. The number of Potawatomis who participated in the Indian Creek Massacre is somewhat speculative. One eyewitness gave estimates of between forty and seventy, while other persons who were not there gave estimates as low as twenty and thirty. See George Walker to Atkinson, 10-11 October 1834, *BHW*, 2:1287, 1291n-1292n; Clark to Cass, 29 May 1832, *BHW*, 2:471; Atkinson to Reynolds, 24 May 1832, *BHW*, 2:430; Minutes of an Examination of Prisoners, 27 August 1832, *BHW*, 2:1055. In arriving at my own estimate of fifty, I have given the most weight to the eyewitness account. For descriptions of the Indian Creek Massacre and the motivations of the anti-American Potawatomis, see Clifton, *Prairie People*, 233; Ma-ka-tai-me-she-kia-kiak, *Black Hawk*, 151; Owen to the Superintendent of Indian Affairs, 24 May 1832, *BHW*, 2:433; Owen to James Stewart, 24 May 1832, *BHW*, 2:433-34; Atkinson to Gratiot, 27 May 1832, *BHW*, 2:457-58; Clark to Cass, 29 May 1832, *BHW*, 2:471; Walker to Atkinson, 10-11 October 1834, *BHW*, 2:1287; Minutes of an Examination of Prisoners, 27 August 1832, *BHW*, 2:1055; Minutes of an Examination of Prisoners, *BHW*, 2:1035.

66. On the Rock River Winnebagos' support of Black Hawk and the Americans, see Ma-ka-tai-me-she-kia-kiak, *Black Hawk*, 153; A council held at Porters [sic] Grove . . . , 3-4 June 1832, *BHW*, 2:508-12; Minutes of an Examination of Prisoners, 19 August 1832, *BHW*, 2:1028-33; Gratiot to G. Porter, 9 June 1832, NA, M-1, Reel 30, Frame 129; E. Brigham to Kinzie, 15 June 1832, NA, M-1, Reel 30, Frame 148; Gratiot, Journal, *BHW*, 2:1303. As with the Potawatomis, the actual number of Rock River Winnebagos who fought with Black Hawk is speculative. The best account cites a prisoner from the British Band who stated that about fifty joined in the depredations. See Minutes of an Examination of Prisoners, 19 August 1832, *BHW*, 2:1028-31. For details on the attacks in the mining district, see Hagan, *Sac and Fox*, 163-64; James Strode to Atkinson, 10 June 1832, *BHW*, 2:566-69; Charles Bracken, "Further Strictures on Ford's Black Hawk War," *WHC*, 2:404; Brigham to Kinzie, 16 June 1832, *BHW*, 2:604-5; William Hamilton to Atkinson, 24 June 1832, *BHW*, 2:663-64, 664n; Kinzie to G. Porter, 9 August 1832, *BHW*, 2:974; Stambaugh to Scott, 11 August 1832, *BHW*, 2:988; Street to Atkinson, 13 August 1832, *BHW*, 2:998; Robert Anderson, Memorandum, 27 August 1832, *BHW*, 2:1057; Stambaugh to George Boyd, 28 August 1832, *BHW*, 2:1074; Council with the Winnebago of the Fort Winnebago Agency, *BHW*, 2:1131-32; Council with the Rock River Winnebagos, 11 September 1832, *BHW*, 2:1133-34; Council with the Rock River Winnebagos, 12 September 1832, *BHW*, 2:1135-36; Atkinson to Jones, 19 November 1832, *BHW*, 2:1212.

67. Ma-ka-tai-me-she-kia-kiak, *Black Hawk*, 153-54; quoted from Minutes of an Examination of Prisoners, *BHW*, 2:1035.

68. Quoted from Stambaugh to Scott, 11 August 1832, *BHW*, 2:988, 989n.

69. Street to Atkinson, 13 August 1832, *BHW*, 2:998; Burnett to Street, 5 June 1832, *BHW*, 2:524, 525n; Council between Atkinson and the Winnebago and Menominee Indians, 6 August 1832, *BHW*, 2:951; Stambaugh to Scott, 13 August 1832, *BHW*, 2:996, 997n; Minutes of an Examination of Prisoners, 19 August 1832, *BHW*, 2:1028-33, 1034n; Stambaugh to Boyd, 28 August 1832, *BHW*, 2:1074; Atkinson to Zachary Taylor, 29 August 1832, *BHW*, 2:1081; Atkinson to Jones, 19 November 1832, *BHW*, 2:1212; Robert Anderson, List of Prisoners aboard the Steamboat *Winnebago*, 5 September 1832, *BHW*, 2:1108-9, 1109n; Kinzie to G. Porter, 26 September 1832, NA, M-1, Reel 31, Frame 157.

70. A. Johnson to Hamilton, 26 May 1832, *BHW*, 2:444; Atkinson to Loomis, 26 May 1832, *BHW*, 2:444; Atkinson to Street, 26 May 1832, *BHW*, 2:445-46; Atkinson to Macomb, 30 May 1830, *BHW*, 2:478; Menominee Indians in United States Service, 4 July 1832, *BHW*, 1:562-63, 563n; Atkinson to Owen, 31 May 1832, *BHW*, 2:491-92; Owen to Atkinson, 3 June 1832, *BHW*, 2:505-6; Street to Dodge, 4 June 1832, *BHW*, 2:520-22; Atkinson to Taylor, 6 June 1832, *BHW*, 2:529-30; Owen to Atkinson, 6 June 1832, *BHW*, 2:534; Street to Atkinson, 6-7 June 1832, *BHW*, 2:535-37; Street to Clark, 7 June 1832, *BHW*, 2:547-48.

71. Hamilton to Atkinson, 13 June 1832, *BHW*, 2:582; Taylor to Atkinson, 13 June 1832, *BHW*, 2:585-86; Atkinson to Dodge, 8 July 1832, *BHW*, 2:751; quoted from Dodge to Atkinson, 18 June 1832, *BHW*, 2:623-25.

72. Lambert, "The Black Hawk War," 457-66; Dodge to Atkinson, 14 July 1832, *BHW*, 2:791; Dodge to Atkinson, 18 July 1832, *BHW*, 2:820; Dodge to Atkinson, 19 July 1832, *BHW*, 2:825-26; Atkinson to Henry and Dodge, 20 July 1832, *BHW*, 2:832; Dodge to Atkinson, 22 July 1832, *BHW*, 2:842-43.

73. Street to Atkinson, 13 May 1832, *BHW*, 2:369; Dodge to Atkinson, 16 May 1832, *BHW*, 2:375; Street to Atkinson, 16 May 1832, *BHW*, 2:376-77; Street to Atkinson, 20 May 1832, *BHW*, 2:397; Atkinson to Macomb and Gaines, 23 May 1832, *BHW*, 2:412; Strode and Reynolds to Atkinson, 23 May 1832, *BHW*, 2:421-22; Atkinson to Macomb, 25 May 1832, *BHW*, 2:435-36; Atkinson to Street, 26 May 1832, *BHW*, 2:445; Atkinson to Joshua Brant, 27 May 1832, *BHW*, 2:457; Stambaugh to G. Porter, 7 June 1832, *BHW*, 2:544-46; Burnett to Street, 5 June 1832, *BHW*, 2:524-35.

74. Street to Dodge, 4 June 1832, *BHW*, 2:521; Stambaugh to G. Porter, 7 June 1832, *BHW*, 2:544-46; Boyd to G. Porter, 3 June 1832, NA, M-234, Reel 315, Frame 649; Boyd to G. Porter, 13 June 1832, *BHW*, 2:581-82; Irwin to G. Porter, 18 June 1832, NA, M-234, Reel 421, Frame 70; Address of Irwin to the Green Bay militia, n.d., GLP MSS, Box 7, Folder 9; G. Porter to Cass, 17 September 1832, *BHW*, 2:1159-60; Stambaugh to G. Porter, 7 June 1832, *BHW*, 2:544-46; Stambaugh to Cass, 10 June 1832, *TPUS*, 12:486-87; Boyd to Atkinson, 23 June 1832, *BHW*, 2:657; Grizzly Bear's Talk, 22 June 1832, *BHW*, 2:650; Atkinson to Boyd, 12 July 1832, *BHW*, 2:770-71; Stambaugh to Augustin Grignon, 4 June 1832, GLP MSS, Box 7, Folder 8; Boyd to Atkinson, 20 July 1832, *BHW*, 2:834; Boyd to G. Porter, 23 July 1832, *WHC*, 12:275-80; Boyd to Daniel Whitney, 21 July 1832, *WHC*, 12:274-75; Roll of Captain Augustin Grignon's Company of Menominee Warriors, 20 July - 28 August 1832, Henry S. Baird

Papers, Box 5, Folder 4, State Historical Society of Wisconsin, Madison, Wisconsin (hereafter cited as Baird MSS); Roll of Captain George Johnston's Company of Menominee Indians, 20 July - 28 August 1832, Baird MSS, Box 5, Folder 4; Boyd to Stambaugh's staff, 24 July 1832, *WIIC*, 12:281; Augustin Grignon, "Augustin Grignon's Recollections," *WHC*, 3:294.

75. Loomis to Atkinson, 31 July 1832, *BHW*, 2:907; Street to Clark, 2 August 1832, *BHW*, 2:917; Milton Alexander to Atkinson, 4 August 1832, *BHW*, 2:928-29; Atkinson to Scott, 9 August 1832, *BHW*, 2:964-66; Taylor to Atkinson, 5 August 1832, *BHW*, 2:942-43; Minutes of an Examination of Prisoners, 19 August 1832, *BHW*, 2:1030; Macomb to Cass, November 1832, War Department, *Annual Report of the Secretary of War for 1832*, 20th Cong., 1st sess., 1832, Ho. Doc. 2 (Serial 233), 60.

76. Atkinson to Scott, 5 August 1832, *BHW*, 2:935-36; Scott to Cass, 10 August 1832, *BHW*, 2:980; Street to Atkinson, 13 August 1832, *BHW*, 2:999; Scott to Cass, 16 August 1832, *BHW*, 2:1012; Minutes of an Examination of Prisoners, 20 August 1832, *BHW*, 2:1037; Street to Scott, 22 August 1832, *BHW*, 2:1042.

77. Stambaugh to Boyd, 2 August 1832, *BHW*, 2:915-16; Stambaugh to Scott, 11 August 1832, *BHW*, 2:987; Stambaugh to Scott, 13 August 1832, *BHW*, 2:996-97; Stambaugh to Boyd, 28 August 1832, *BHW*, 2:1071-73; quoted from Grignon, "Recollections," *WHC*, 3:294-95.

78. The Indians who fought on the side of the United States included 225 Menominee, Santee Dakota, and Winnebago scouts at Prairie du Chien. However, it should be noted that there were many other Indians who acted as scouts during the war whose numbers were not accurately recorded. See Street to Clark, 7 June 1832, *BHW*, 2:547-48; Menominee Indians in United States Service, 4 July 1832, *BHW*, 1:562-63, 563n. On the fifty Potawatomi scouts at Chicago under fur trader Jean Baptiste Beaubien, see Owen to Atkinson, 6 June 1832, *BHW*, 2:534. For the ninety-five Potawatomi scouts with Atkinson, see Potawatomi Indians in United States Service, 22 June - 22 July 1832, *BHW*, 1:560-62. For the 232 Menominee auxiliaries, see Roll of Grignon's Company of Menominee Warriors, 20 July - 28 August 1832, Baird MSS, Box 5, Folder 4; Roll of Johnston's Company of Menominee Indians, 20 July - 28 August 1832, Baird MSS, Box 5, Folder 4. For the 150 Santee Dakotas under Wabasha, see Street to Clark, 2 August 1832, *BHW*, 2:917. The estimates for the Indians who fought with Black Hawk's band are provided earlier in this essay.

79. Mason to Cass, 9 June 1832, NA, M-234, Reel 421, Frames 45-46; Kinzie to G. Porter, 11 June 1832, NA, M-234, Reel 421, Frames 55-56; Cass to Clark, 19 June 1832, *BHW*, 2:630; Cass to George Gibson, 19 June 1832, *BHW*, 2:631; Cass to Owen, 19 June 1832, NA, M-21, Reel 8, vol. 8, pp 460-61; Frame 155; Kinzie to G. Porter, 2 July 1832, NA, M-1, Reel 31, Frame 20; G. Porter to Cass, 13 July 1832, NA, M-234, Reel 421, Frame 79; Clark to Gibson, 16 July 1832, Clark MSS, vol. 4, p. 389; William Marshall to Cass, 26 July 1832, NA, M-1, Reel 31, Frame 75; Owen to G. Porter, 29 July 1832, NA, M-1, Reel 31, Frame 60; Joshua Pilcher to Clark, 18 September 1832, NA, M-234, Reel 728, Frame 234; Helen Tanner, ed., *Atlas of Great Lakes Indian History* (Norman: University of Oklahoma Press, 1987), 152.

80. Ma-ka-tai-me-she-kia-kiak, *Black Hawk*, 160-63; Nancy Lurie, "In Search of Chaetar: New Findings on Black Hawk's Surrender," *Wisconsin Magazine of History* 71 (Spring 1988): 163-83.

81. Ma-ka-tai-me-she-kia-kiak, *Black Hawk*, 180-81.

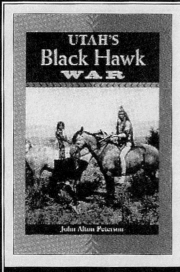

Major General "Mad" Anthony Wayne

William Clark's Journal of
Major-General Anthony Wayne's 1794 Campaign
Against the Indians in Ohio

Introduction by Patrick Bowmaster

F ew men had a more dramatic and varied history of encounters with American Indians as did William Clark. His often romanticized relationship with the Northern Shoshone interpreter Sacagawea on the Lewis and Clark Expedition is well known. Few, however, know that he was one of the first white Americans to fight a skirmish with Indians west of the Mississippi River on that same expedition. Similarly, Clark's participation as an officer in what was perhaps the most decisive campaign against Indians east of the Mississippi is also largely forgotten. Yet Clark left one of the only detailed accounts of that campaign, Anthony Wayne's mission against an Indian alliance in Ohio. This introduction provides the background for Clark's remarkable journal, an account out of print for the past seventy-five years.

The 1783 Treaty of Paris, the peace accord ending the American Revolution, gave the United States title to the Northwest Territory, which encompassed present-day Ohio, Indiana, Illinois, Michigan, Wisconsin, and eastern Minnesota. After the treaty was signed, however, the British refused to uphold that aspect of the agreement and continued to maintain a substantial military presence in the territory. In an attempt to bolster their strength, the British encouraged their Indian allies to forcibly resist any American presence in the Northwest Territory and provided them with muskets and ammunition to help accomplish the task.

The United States desperately needed these new lands. In addition to being a rich fur producing region, it would provide elbow room for a growing nation.

Revenue raised through land sales would also help pay large debts incurred fighting the Revolutionary War.

The American government attempted to pacify the Indians of the territory through diplomatic means. When a treaty failed to materialize, the military was summoned to bring order to the region. On October 22, 1790, a force of 1,500 men under Brig. Gen. Josiah Harmar engaged Miami Chief Michikinikwa (or Little Turtle) and the warriors of several confederated Indian tribes near present-day Fort Wayne, Indiana. The Indians turned back the column in an engagement known as "Harmar's Defeat," which in turn boosted Indian morale and only worsened the overall situation. Thirteen months later the governor of the Northwest Territory, Maj. Gen. Arthur St. Clair, moved out to engage the Indian confederation. St. Clair's column was about the same size as the one Harmar led to defeat the previous year; unfortunately for the Americans, the governor's luck also matched Harmar's. The engagement with Little Turtle's 1,000 Indians, known today as "St. Clair's Defeat," took place on November 4, 1791, once again at the site of present-day Fort Wayne. The casualties suffered by St. Clair's army were so large (when calculated as a percentage of the entire American military force) some historians call it the single greatest defeat in United States military history.[1]

Although St. Clair's disaster merits barely a footnote in today's history books, its ramifications sent a shiver across America. Many people lost confidence in the national government. President Washington's administration suddenly found itself hip deep in a crisis that shook the very foundation of the fledgling republic. The situation in the Northwest Territory had to be resolved.

In 1794, a third military expedition under the command of Maj. Gen. "Mad" Anthony Wayne was organized to try and conquer the territory. Wayne was born in Chester County, Pennsylvania, on January 1, 1745. Before the American Revolution, he had been employed as a surveyor, farmer, and businessman. When war with Britain broke out, Wayne accepted a commission with the Continental Army. By the conclusion of hostilities, he was both a brigadier general and genuine war hero with the appellation "Mad," a nickname born as a result of his quick temper. In 1783, Wayne retired from the army as a brevet major general. His luck outside the service was not as good, however, and he spent the next ten years stumbling through a series of failed business and political ventures.

The old soldier was coaxed out of retirement in 1792 shortly after Congress passed the United States Militia Act on March 5, establishing the creation of a professional standing army called the Legion of the United States. President Washington chose Wayne to command this force. After a period of intensive training, he marched for the Northwest Territory in April 1793.

One of Wayne's subordinates marching with him on the campaign was William Clark, who along with Meriwether Lewis would later win fame as the explorers of the Louisiana Purchase. Clark, a younger brother of Revolutionary War hero George Rodgers Clark, was born in Caroline County, Virginia, on August 1, 1770. While he was a young man, his family relocated to the present-day state of Kentucky. He entered the militia in 1789 and thereafter campaigned against the Ohio Valley Indian tribes. In 1792, Clark accepted a commission in the United States army and as a 1st lieutenant kept a remarkable journal of Wayne's 1794 campaign. Indeed, Clark's journal—which was inadvertently discovered in 1869 by Lyman C. Draper, who was planning to write a history of the campaigns of General George Rogers Clark—is one of the principal sources for this important military expedition.[2]

On August 20, 1794, Wayne's 3,700 men engaged the Indian Confederation and 100 British militiamen from Canada at what became known as the Battle of Fallen Timbers. The action was waged in what is today the Maumee suburb of Toledo, Ohio. Two centuries ago the region was known as "Fallen Timbers" because of a tornado which had swept through the area. The 1,100 Indians who fought against Wayne represented a number of tribes, including the Miamis, Shawnees, Pottawawatomies, Ottawas, Chippewas, Sauk, Fox, and Iroquois. Overall command was wielded by Shawnee Weyapiersenwah (or Blue Jacket), with Little Turtle acting as his second in command.

Blue Jacket was born sometime in the middle of the

William Clark

Independence National Historical Park Collection

1700s. He was a tribal leader when his people participated in the 1774 Lord Dunmore's War battle of Pt. Pleasant, Virginia. His alliance with Great Britain was forged during the American Revolution. Little Turtle was born in the vicinity of Fort Wayne, Indiana, in 1752. In 1780, he helped beat back a French attack against his village. After defeating both Harmar and St. Clair in 1790 and 1791, Little Turtle argued for reconciliation with the Americans, to no avail.

The Battle at Fallen Timbers began when the Indians and British ambushed Wayne's advance guard of 150 Kentucky volunteers. The surprised soldiers quickly fled and were pursued by 300 to 400 braves. The pursuing warriors sent the first organized body of Americans they met, a detachment of regular soldiers, reeling. The attack was finally stalled by several hundred light infantry and riflemen. When Wayne finally had his main line of battle deployed, he launched an attack of his own, driving the enemy back to Fallen Timbers. The experienced Wayne, knowing the battle was all but won, pressed the attack. The Americans swept everything before them and carried the day.

Clark's valuable journal offers a firsthand account of the conditions and morale of Wayne's army. Without it we might never have known of the deep antagonism between the volunteers and regular army soldiers, or how disenchanted some of Wayne's chief subordinate officers were with his leadership and overall management of the campaign.

Wayne prevailed in spite of these difficulties, and Fallen Timbers was exactly the victory President Washington was hoping to achieve. Great Britain agreed to withdraw her military presence from the territory by 1796, and Wayne called for a treaty conference with the Indian tribes of the Northwest Territory. In July 1795, twelve Indian nations met with Wayne at Greenville near Piqua, in what would eventually become the state of Ohio. The resulting and momentous Treaty of Greenville, signed on August 3, 1795, granted United States citizens the right to settle unopposed in a significant portion of the Northwest Territory.

The major participants in the Fallen Timbers Campaign enjoyed futures of varying success. General Wayne remained in the army and presided over the British withdrawal from the Northwest Territory in 1796. He had only a short time left to live, however, and on December 15 of that year died of gout at Fort Presque Isle, Pennsylvania.

William Clark resigned his commission and returned home to the family plantation, which he eventually inherited from his parents. Tilling the soil did not satisfy Clark's restless energy, however, so he sold the land to his brother Jonathan in 1800 and went to live with another brother, George, in the Indiana

Territory. Three years later Clark accepted the offer of his friend and former subordinate Meriwether Lewis (who had served with Clark in the 1795 campaign) to jointly lead an expedition to explore the Louisiana Purchase. The pair set out on their perilous journey into the wilderness on May 14, 1804, and reached the Pacific Ocean in November 1805. They returned the following year, reaching St. Louis on September 23, 1806.

In 1807, Clark became Superintendent of Indian Affairs for the Territory of Upper Louisiana and accepted a territorial militia brigadier general's commission. Early the following year he wed Julia Hancock, a union which produced Meriwether Lewis Clark, a son named after Clark's partner in exploration. Clark's fortunes continued to improve. In 1813, he was appointed governor of the Missouri Territory, a position he held until he ran for the same office (and was defeated) seven years later. In 1814, the journals he and Lewis kept during their expedition were published. Eight years later William Clark moved to St. Louis, where he accepted a position as Superintendent of Indian Affairs. He died there on September 1, 1838.

Blue Jacket, General Wayne's opponent at Fallen Timbers, agreed to the Treaty of Fort Industry in 1805, which further opened up the Northwest Territory to settlement by the United States. His exact fate is unknown, although he probably died in the vicinity of the Detroit River around 1810. Little Turtle counseled his people wisely in the years following the Battle of Fallen Timbers, and in 1797 traveled to Philadelphia and met with George Washington. He died at Fort Wayne, Indiana, on July 14, 1812.

William Clark's Journal*

W[illiam] C[lark]. Greenville,[3] [Ohio], 28th July, 1794: The Federal Army (Viz) 2000 Regulars & 1500 Kentucky Voluntiers, the Latter under the Command of Major Gen. [Charles] Scott[4] and the whole commanded by His Excellency Maj. Gen. Anthony Wayne, marched from Greenville at 8 o'Clock A.M. and proceeded Rapidly with fiew halts to Still Water Creek (12 Miles)

---

* Except for nos. 1-3, the end notes appended to this article were produced by R. C. McGrane, who edited the original transcription in "William Clark's Journal of General Wayne's Campaign," *Mississippi Valley Historical Review*, Vol. I, No. 3 (Dec. 1914).

Where We Encamped for the night our Encampment was secured by falling Trees Which formed Breast Works, abt. 600 yards Square, I shall here only observe as to the order of March.[5] The Voluntiers Marched in reare of the Legion at Supporting distants in Case of an attack.

Fort Recovery 29th July: renewed the March ere the Sun rose, and pushed forward without reguard to Bag or Baggage, as if, not in serch but in actual percuit, of a flying & disorderly Enemy, & passed [Fort] Recovery[6] by Noon under Salute of the Ordinance; after the Troops had well crossed the Creek to [where] the above Garrison [Fort Recovery] stands, *His Excellency* thought proper to order a halt for the coming up of the Baggage and the reare of the army by which time the day was far spent & obliged us to encamp for the night about a mile from the *Fort*. This days march Greatly fatigued the Troops & Worried our Teems and Pack Horses. The Dragoons & Light Troops Sust'd considerable fatigue & Injury from the thickness of the Woods, and Brush thro which they passed on the Flanks.

Beever Creek[7] 30th July 94: The Voluntiers Centinals gave Several alarms during the last night so that our works were man'd the Greater part–Took up the line of March as Soon light without making much Enquiry or Serch by Scout or Spie into the Grounds of the above alarms, but numbers give confidence.[8] Here I Shall take occasion to observe that 900 of the Voluntiers before mentioned had not yet joined the Legion, but are on theire way from F. Washington[9] under the Com'd of Genl. Barbee.

We proceeded with usial Velocity Through Thickets almost impervious, thro Marassies, Defiles & beads of Netles more than waist high & miles in length & on the left flank crossed the water course on Which F. Recovery Stands, more than one Dozen times–but not without Great labor both to men & horses, in plinging through the Muddy bed of Said Creek; notwithstanding all those dificuelties we arrived here early in the Evening and found the Creek, inpassable for waggons, therefore encamped after a March of aboat 12 miles.[10]

Beever Creek 31st July 94: This day Spent throwing a Bridge[11] across the Creek–The Pioniers were sent in advance to cleare the road to *St Maries River*—they were covered by a Company of Voluntiers & our Spies—*observations* on our arrival here, the Troops were Kept under arms for nearly two hours, in which time the creek was to be Bridge, but from this days experiance it was found to be a work of at least 10 hours.

St. Maries River abt the 1st August, 1794 Made an Early move the Troops passed over the Bridge with Lettle confusion, & beat the Traile of the

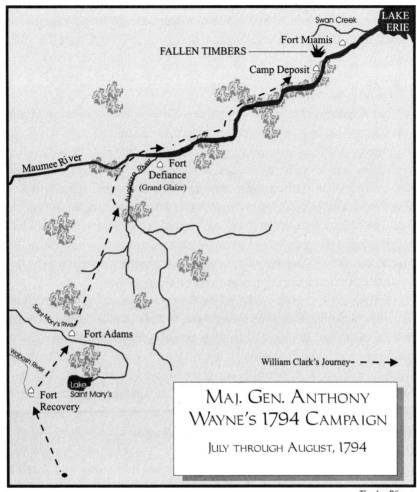

LAKE ERIE

Swan Creek

Fort Miamis △

FALLEN TIMBERS

Camp Deposit △

Maumee River

△ Fort Defiance
(Grand Glaize)

Auglaize River

Saint Mary's River

△ Fort Adams

William Clark's Journey - - - ➤

Wabash River

Lake Saint Mary's

△ Fort Recovery

MAJ. GEN. ANTHONY
WAYNE'S 1794 CAMPAIGN

JULY THROUGH AUGUST, 1794

Theodore P. Savas

Pioniers,-mentioned yesterday, and after a fiew hours march thro low flat Grounds, thick, woods & Much underBrush we emurged Suddenly, into an open extensive and bountiful *Plaine* or *Pararie* which affords an ellegent Sccncry, handsomly intersperced with Small Copse of Trees & abounding in every Species of the Greatest Variety of Herbage, There we at once had a full view of the Legion & as it were, renewed our acquaintants with each other & created a fresh, a laudable degree of Emulation & enspired new animation, but the intence heat of the Sun made our March through this plaine not a little fatiguing, We Soon passed through it—(abt. One mile in weadth) and crossed the River where our Encampment was formed, but a further Examination, of the

Contiguous ground induced his Excellency to recross the River & Incamp on its Banks, in two Columns formed to receve the Enemy in front & reare-This day marched about 12 miles — Crossed Genl. Harmer's [Josiah Harmar's] Trace through the Pararie when on his way to the *Miamis* [Indian] *Village* in Year 1790, Said to be about 30 miles thither.

2nd August 94: The works of a trifling Garrison [the fortification named Fort Adams] began which I recolect to here his Excellency Say would be complete by 8 oClock tomorrow–Wells[12] our Principal Guide & Spy with a small party sent to make discoveries, & Capt. Kibby,[13] with his Columbian Scouters ordered in a Different direction–here Wells Showed Great reluctiance, at ventering with So small a party & declar'd to the Comd. In Chief, that if he would give him 200 Voluntiers he would Engage to take Several Prisoners, but notwithstanding his Excellency had Just offered great rewards for a Prisoner, he paid no attention to this proposition of Wells's & a number of fish taken by the Solds. The Rive affords a Variety as well as a plenty of them.

3rd August 94: The works of the Garrison goes on with Wonderous Slowness in So much that the Commander in Chief request of the Comd's officers of Wings & Corps to lend all possable assitance and give every encouragement to the forwarding of it & all give theire helping hand but time Waited not for us, & night came on e're the work was not yet done–This day fortune in one of her unacountable pranks, (I say unacountable for one will pretend to know why She Should at this juncture, at this critical moment, by an illtimed, prank perturb the minds of Hundreds & create for a moment in theire Breasts such unthought of Sensations & open So large a field for Speculation) had nearly deprived the Legion of its *Leader*, had nearly deprived 'Certain individuals of theire A[nthony] W[ayne] & Particular persons of their concequence-the downfall of some would have been equale to the tumble of our Chief occassion'd by the fall of large Beech Tree which fell about his Marquee, had fortune directed its course a few feet more to the right or left–but (Fav'd Fort'n) His Excellen'cy was more Sceared then hurt, All ended well, tho there was a considerable concorse–Brig. Genl. [Thomas] Barbee arrived brought considerable Stores [supplies]: I ought to have mention'd the return of Wells & Kibby the Last Evening they mad no discovery except the Trace of a Horse & a few men on foot bending towards the Enemey's Settlements, this leads to a belief that a Mr. Newman[14] (in Q Masters Employmt) who had been missing for two days, was taken by the Enemy and were thus carrying him off-A Gen'l order of this day mention the Garrison of F[ort] Randolph [i.e., Fort Adams][15] & Signifying the Comd. in Chiefs intention to move on the Morrow.

4th August Monday of 94: Notwithstanding the Vulnerable, State of the Garrison, by the rising of the Sun, the Beating of the Genl. Was heard to Signify his Excellencys intention to take up the line of march, accordingly the army was conducted over the River, and proceeded through intolerable thick woods & the earth covered with Snagley underwoods & almost impassable Defiles, however we reached a Small durty water a Branch of Glaze [Auglaze] River after a march of Abt. 12 miles, and there took up our Encampment for the night-I can't pass the Situation of Leutenant Underhill[16] unnoticed, the officer was left to the Comd. Of   F. Randolph owing to his being indisposed, and his command consisted of no more than 40 Invalids-thus was he left to finish and Defend this miserable Hold [Fort Adams], in the midst of the Enemys Country, without the Smallest provability of being reinforsed or aided in the Completion of the Works. had this Mode of punishment been authorised by law & Mr. Underhill spoken truths disrespectful of the Comd'r in Chief, I should thought the punishment equal to the crime, but silence proved on that hand.

5th August 94: Renewed the march at 5 o'Clock passed through much such Country as yesterday. Kept down the Creek made about 12 miles.

6th August 94: Commenced the March as yesterday, at 9 miles reached a considerable Stream of Water call'd upper Dellawar [Delaware] Creek, proceeded 3 miles down the Same & there Encamp'd on its Banks–our Spies & about 300 Voluntiers sent in advance, as Supposed neare Some of the Enemys Villagies, which had been Deserted Sence last fall.

7th August 94: Marched at the usial houre continu'd down the Creek 5 miles to the owl town before mentioned halted for an houre, after crossing the Delawar [Delaware] Creek and reached the Glaze [Auglaze] River & after a march of 10 miles we Encamped for the night – From our Spies we had every reason to Suppose the Savages [i.e., the Shawnee Indians] were abandoning theire possissions [positions], and were not in force to resist us. This gave an opening for Enterprise we now were within 12 or 14 miles of theire principal Settlements everybody was flushed with the Idea of Supprising them in the moment of providing for theire Wives & Children the Scheeme was perposed & certain Suckcess insued if attempted – Genl. [James] Wilkinson Suggested the plan to the Comdr in Chief but it was not his plan, nor perhaps his wish to Embrace So probable a means for Ending the War by compelling them to peace[17] – this was not the first occasion or oppertunity, which presented its self to our observent Genl. For Some grand stroke of Enterprise, but the Comdr. in Chief rejected all & every of his plans-This Evening as the Camp was formed, we were alarmed by the Discharge of Several Guns of the Voluntiers Who said seen & wounded an Indian but he was not taken. Had this Alarm been well founded & the Enemy on our Heels, the old gentleman would have been caught sleep for he had already gone to bead to give his ease to his infurmities & was so fast in the arms of Morphous as to give some trouble to wake him understanding the cause of the Bustle.

8th August 94. Renewed the march at the usial time proceeded Down the [Auglaze] River to its confluence with the Miamis [Maumee], about 9 miles, 7 of which thro fields of well cultivated Corn in the most flurishing situation. & found theire [the Maumee Indians] Villages just forsakin[18] Some of the Houses were now burning, they left every appearance of having gorne off with precipation and the greatest consternation, which must afford a mortifying proof of the great advantage we had let slip & the great Enterprise which Seemed to pervade our rules.

This day Set in with a Violent fall of raine, which continued through out & I cannot amit to observe that this was the first only Rainy day sence our departure from Greenville, a Small shower fell a few evenings sence or we should have seen none, never was an army so indebted to fortune, She has certainly been perfuse in her favours – a few days rain, would so impeded our march as to render the Country almost impassable with Waggons &c. &c.

9th August 94: Projected a plan for a Garrison [Fort Defiance] & the work commenced The Dragoons ordered as a covering party for the Fatigue [labor details]. Consequently Kept out, the Light Troops Guarded the Camp and Kept on constant duty – considerable quantites of Corn, was found by the Voluntiers & Sold to the publick for the ennormous Sum of 3 dollers pr. Bushel, this corn might with little or no trouble, have been precurved for the cavelry Horses, which would have been the Salvation of those horses – The Garrison Just mentioned is about to be built directly in the angle of two Rivers [the Auglaze and Maumee rivers], which is very accute, & elegantly Situated commanding a handsome View up & down the Rivers, the Margins of which as far as the Eye can see are covered with the most luxurient growths of Corn, interspurced with Small Log Cabbins arround all of which you observe theire well cultivated gardens, affording almost every Species of prorticultural Vegitables in the greatest abundance.

10th August 94: Resumed our Situation of yesterday the Dragoons Kept out all day. Wells with a fiew of his Spies sent out in order to discover the Situation of our fugetives Enemy & if Possible take a prisoner.

11th August 94: The works of the Garrisson proceeds on but slowly, The Dragoons so Extended as to reach from Glaze River to Miamie [Auglaze River to Maumee River], and entirely Secure the Camp that quater, Volunteers on the north side of Miamie R.

12th August 94. Wells the Spie returned with an Indian & Squar though *he* and one other of his party were wounded *Wells* through the arm & McClalon in the Shoulder neither were Dangerous. This enterprising young man has been almost in reach of the fire from the *British* Garrison, at the foot of the Rapids 50 miles, & in the Camp of the Enemy, and brought off the above mentioned Prisoners from whome we lern the Situation and intention of the Enemey – They are useing every exertion to assemble theire forces, fiew of Potawatams [the Potawatami] have yet come to theire aid, but are expected daily – how much have we to regret that the favourable oppertunity which once presented itself was not embraced, The head of the long talked of Hydra might have been so easily severed from his body, one of his heads at least, which must have greatly wekened him & perhaps saved the effusion of much blood, but this is no consideration with some Folks, I am now lead to a reflection which if indulged, would perhaps give me two great a disgust to a Military life, and embiter my present situation – Were Subalterns of this army, in general, to forego such oppertunities of rendering theire Country a service & absolutely so far neglect theire duty, as do some officers of higher rank, what merit would they find – non.[19]

13th August 94: I should yesterday have mentioned that the Indian prisoner says they lost of their natn 40 warriors Killed and 20 wounded, at F[ort] Recovery on the 30th of June & further that Newman the man Supposed to have been taken by the Savages when St. Maries R. Had Deserted to them and given them Information of the approach, & an exact account of our strength the order of March &c &c – Miller an (tho a white man) & one Prisoner[20] Were this morning Sent with proposals of peace to the Indians, expected to return in 4 days with an answer this mode of Procedure, (to wit) that of sending a flag to the Enemy, Genl. Wilkinson (in a private conversation which I had with him a few evening; Sence) told me he had advised the Comdr in Chief against and shewed me in wrighting his reasons why he said he had given to the commander in Chief – he Strongly recommended a Proclamation Wherein he would Set forth his intention exaggerate his powers & reather threaten then Solicit them to a Treaty &c – at the Same time the Genl. In Confidence shewed me a coppy of a Letter exebiting A.W.

August 14th 1794: Various are the Speculations respecting the Treaty of Peace now on hand – I shall take this occasion to observe that from the time of our first striking the [Auglaze River] (Viz the 6th Inst) The right division crosssed the River & marched on the East side, the Left Division & Baggage on the West side, and at many times the two divisions was not less than 2 or 3 miles of each other So little Support could either wing give the other.

15th August 94: The Beating of Genl. [Orders] Once more prepared us for the move the Line of March was according taken up and after Crossing the Miami River (tho not without the Greatest confusion & disorder for not rule was every laid down, or manner pointed out by which the troops should pass the River & every man seemed to be for himself and I at once saw Dragoons sev'l pices of Artillery Infantry & Riflemen with several waggons nos. of pack horses all huddled together in the river) We proceeded down its Banks on the North Side 9 miles to a considerable Village called *Snake Town* where we Encamped for the night. A Genl. Order yesterday directs all the heavy baggage to be left at Ft. Defiance[21] Maj. Hunt[22] left to the command of Said Garrison all our sick left with him.

16th August 94: Took up the line of March at 5 o'Clock proceeded Slowly by reason of steep reveens which cut the road and made it almost impassible for waggons. Miller returned with a letter from the Inds. (young White Eyes) wherein he thanked the Comdr in Chief for the offer made to the Indians, perticularly for the good wishes, he expressed for theire wives & children, and if the Federal Army would advance no farther then the confluence of the Rivers Miami & Glaze [Maumee and Auglaze] and there Erect no Garrison, they would probably at the Experation of 10 days treat with him, & adds that the Indians were just on theire feet to meet the army as the Comdr in Chiefs letter came to hand – This Letter was generally understood as a Challenge; tho the Genl. had serious intentions of answering it (as they had requested) but I believe Genl. Wilkinson disswaded him from so unnecessary a step – This day marched 10 miles and Encamped on the River bank, the country off from the River thik & wet.

17th August 94: Sunday Took up the line of March at an early hour and proceeded on our way without much difecuelty or interruption except the thickness of the woods which we on the Left had to pass through. The right wing of the army expereanced no inconveneance, but on the contrary enjoyed many pleasing Seans & Prospects afforded from the banks of the [Maumee] River and could but behold with pleasure the gentle gliding of the waters over the Broad Rocky Bead – This day about 11 o'Clock we were overtaken by an Express from Washington with Letters & papers from that quarter &c March 14 miles & reached the head of the Rapids, where we Encamped for the Night – Yesterday put on ½ allowance of Flour.

18th August 94: Our move this morning was not as Early as usual as his Excellency wished to have the vicinity of his camp reconnortered, e'er he left it, this was not less necessary then prudent step, as the Country for at least six miles in our front was a perfect plaine, consequently we had to dread an ambuscade, those precausions were Seldom before this, necessary (I suppose) as I am a witness that our Scouts Seldome left theire camp of a morning e'er the army moved[23] but as this is no business of mine I shall proceed with the army, to *Rocke de Bout* where we arrived after a march of about 9 miles & there threw up our Encampment as usual – *Rocke De Bout* is a small Island of Creggy Rocks of Considerable hight, the top of it is only accessible by one Small point, its Summit is covered with Small groths of Cedar; from the point of land directly opposit this Island on the S. W. Side of the River, we behold one of the most beautiful Landskapes ever painted; the River here is fordable & its bead, entire, of large Fleaks of Black Stone.

19th August 94: Now finding ourselves within 6 or 7 miles off the British Garrison [Fort Miamis], & from what we can discover by our *Spies* the Enemys Encampment. It was deemed expedient to throw up a tempory work as a Deposit for our Baggage &c – which his Excellency called Camp Deposit, in his orders of this day wherein he ordered Capt. Pike[24] to take Command of said Camp; the subLegionary Q. Masters are also ordered to remain here - (Maj. Price, Informed the Comdr in Chief haveing Sencearly promised Genl. Wilkinson to make an alteration in the order of his march that is to say, the Battallion Campanies of Infantry were to march in two Columns and by files from the Right of Companies & being disincumbd of all Baggage, the Dragoons & light Infantry were to move in Center the Riflemen were to Secure the flanks, & the Volunteers, Spies & Scouts, were to be handsomely disposed of. – These things being known throughout Camp, & it being what every man of the Smallest tast for Military disposition or arrangement had long wished for; pleasure seemed perched on every brow, and nothing more appeared to be wanting to ensure us Suckcess, Should the Enemy have the preseumption to give us Battle, but many were yet of oppinion that they could not be brought to a Genl. action – The Dusk of Evening produced a Genl. order, to the astonishment of all, & particullary Genl. Wilkinson, wherein the Comdr in Chief convinced us of his determination to continue the same order of march as hither to practiced,[25] Which to be sure is of all others the most complicated & the orders of Formation Totally impracticable at this time many was full with an Idea of a night Expedition & Supprise the Enemy in theire Camp, which thing was strongly advised by some, and Deemed highly practiable by almost all,– but the abov order told us we were to move at Six o'Clock.

20th August 94 [**Battle of Fallen Timbers**]: A shower of Rain prevented our move at the houre appointed, but we took up the Line of March at 7 o'Clock and found the way extremely bad, much embarrassed by the thickness of the woods on the left and by a number of Steep Reviens [ravines] on the Right, after proceeding about 2 hours our Spies & advance guard Discovered the Enemy and received their fire, but with inconsiderable Loss were driven back[26] and joined the main Body of the Army, by this time the Right division, Comded by Genl. [James] Wilkinson felt the effects of the Enemeys fire, they was immediately formed & returned the fire, at this period Capt. [Robert Mis] Campbell[27] troop made a charge in which he fell & his Troop immediately proceeded through surported by the Infantry's charge which oblidged the enemey to quit theire position and look for more advantagous ground on our Left & they made an exertion to gaine that Flank but Col. [John F.] Hamtramck[28] who commanded in that Quarter was prepared & gave them so warm a reception as made theire Situation here as disagreeable as that on the Right, and the charge both on the Right & left both became Genl. & the Enemy was repulsed with precipation; The charge of the Cavelry closed the seene in front & drove the Enemey 3/4 of a mile[29] at the same instant, The Riflemen & Light Infantry, receved a most heavy fire, We drove the Enemy for about one mile directly out, with the Loss of Lieut. Towl[e]s[30] & a fiew Infantry on our Side, in this quater was Killed 3 white men & several Indians mostly by the Riflemen. The Troops were now refreshed with ½ a gill of Whiskey which they much required as the action continued more then an houre, the greater part of which time they were in full Speed pressing the Enemey – after remaining on this ground a fiew hours Dureing &c we proceeded within about one mile of the British Garrison and there took up our Encampment.

I shall now make a fiew observations or reflections on the Business of this day. Had the Enemey for once forsaken theire long established mode of fighting (Viz) that of extending theire lines so as to gaine the flanks of theire advasary – for by this means they so weakened themselves in all points as not to be able to make but a feable resistance in any one, much less beat & confuse the lines of theire opposers, which in this case they might have easily done, had they kept themselves compact and advanced with Judgement. (I say had the Enemey been formed in tolerable close orders and advanced in the first instance, close on the heals of our retireing Spies & Advanced guard, I am Satisfied they would have made a Breach in any part of our Columns as our Front was so extended as to render the whole in any one part, unequal to the resistants of a well formed body rapidly advancing on them, besides our orders or mode of Formation required very considerable time to preforme the perparitory Evolutions: on the other hand, had the Kentucky Volunters (who composed half of our forces) been so disposed of as to have gained the reare[31] of the Enemy soon after they commenced the attack, Then I am Satisfied we should had the pleasure of seeing every Head of this dreaded *Hydra* at our feet; but from theire Situation or (as some say for the want of orders) they were so far from gaining this grand position, that not more than 300 out of 1500 well mounted Riflemen were ever brought to action, and they but a fiew moments. Cannot but be astonished when the world informed that the Comdr in Chief had been told on the day previous to the action, by an officere of Rank and credebillity "Majr Price of the Volunteers who commd a sort of Independant partizen-corps and had been sent for the Express purpose) that the Enemey were laying in wait *for us* & formed in Such a possition" & also gave His Excellency an exact Discription of the ground I say, the whole world cannot but be surprised that the Comdr in Chief did not availe himself of this advantae & by throwing the Voluntiers in the reare of the Enemey & eventually cut off theire retreat: but so far was his Excel from thus putting an end to this expensive war (I believe that the atack of the Enemey at the time it happined was actually a matter of Surprise to almost every officer in the army – The Bodies of Capt. Campbell & Lieutenant Towles (the only officers killed) were entered immediately after the action. The whole ammount of the Killed on our part were 240[32]   the loss of the Enemey not precisely ascertained but not more than 30 or 40 were found Dead, and a fiew Canadians one33 was taken prisoner, who was a treader amoung the Indians, and says they opposed us with about 900 Indians & 150 Canadians.[34]

21st. August 94: Remained in Camp the whole day, all full with expectation & anxiety, of storming of the British Garrison,[35] which is all the remained for us to do, for the Savage were no more to be found. Says our Scouts

– The evening produced a *flag* from Majr W[illiam]. Campbell Comdr of said Garrison Demanding of the Comdr in Chief by letter[36] the cause of his remaining 24 hours (and his intention) under the Muzzles & nearly in reach of the Cannon of one of his Majisties Posts- His Excellency was not a little displeased at this question & thought it rather impurtenant in the Major & For answer told him he might have been informed of A[nthony] W[ayne]'s business from the Muzzles of his Small arms, yesterday and added that had he been certain the Savages had taken Shelter in the garrison, neither the walls nor Cannon of it would have been an obstruction to his victorious arms &c. This pompious Letter was by Capt. [Henry] DeButts[37] A.D.C. [Wayne's aide-de-camp] & received by a Capt. Spears[,] Bearer of the first Flag, Our Foragers & the Voluntiers, Destroyed & Pilaged the Fields of Corn & gardins, of the Savages & Burnt large stacks of hay within a few hundred yards of the garrison[38] – Lost Several men Sence arrived here by Desertion, a Drummer of the 24th Regiment came over to us this is a regular fortifacation.

22nd August 94: A man who attempted to Desert the Last night, was shot by our Sentinels, which firing caused an Alarm in Camp – His Excellency guarded by the Light Troops, and the Riflemen *they* So posted as to prevent a Surprise from the Savage: proceeded to reconnoiter & Examine the works of the Garrison, and went within Pistol shot of them, & his Excellency declared if he had 10 days Provisions, he would assail it. This reconnoitering Business was not pleasing & deemed improper by Majr Campbell, so that a Flag followed him into Camp and informed (A.W.) That his so near aproach to the garrison could not be again admitted & he would be fired on if he attempted it, this his excellency could but illy Bear & immediately Sent a *flag* & Demanded the Garrison in the name of the United States & ordered Majr Campbell, to move immediately to the next nearest British post. The Majr answered that he should certainly rimain where he was untill he was ordered to evacuate the place, the authority who placed him there, or the fortune of War compelled him to surrender it, this Solderly & Spirited answer, No Doubt raised Ire in the Breast of some, but we could not help our Selves, for spite Burnt all the Indian Hutts throughout the vicinity of the Garrison and put the finishing stroke to the Distruction of the Cornfields, Gardens, Hay Stacks &c &c.

This day got a peep at the return of the killed & wounded, 24 killed & 89 wounded not more then a Dozen. – A party sent to Hunt up & Bury our dead (the wounded officers are Capt. Prier Slough, Van Ranscloagh & Lt. C. Smith[39] – I hate the recolection of the Sufferings of our Wounded, but I am induced here to

Say that no set of men in the like disabled Situation ever expereanced much more want of Conveniancies &c.

23rd August 94: This morning produced a Flurish [drum flourish] & pompious Genl. order which for its novelty &c I shall give a place in this (my note book).

Head Quarters Banks of Miami 23rd Aug. 94: The Commander in Chief takes this oppertunity to Congratulate the Federal Army [on] theire Brilliant suckcess in the Action of the 20th Inst. against the whole Combined forces of the Hostile Savages aided by a Body of Milita of Detroit[40] and countenanced by the British post & Garrison close in theire reare, beyond which the fugitivs fled with disorder, precipation & dismay leaving there Packs, provisions & Plunder in the Encampment in reare of the Post. The Ind's to all appearance haveing totally abandoned there Settlements quite to the Mouth of the River and theire houses & cornfields being destroy'd in every Derection even under the influence of the guns of Fort Miami[s]. Facts which produces a Conviction to the minds of the Savages that the British have neither the power nor Inclination to afford them that protection which they had been taught to expect,[41] but on the Contrary a numerous Garrison well Supply'd with artillery have been compelled to remain tacit Spectators to the Genl. Conflegration around them; & theire Flag Displayed at that Post insulted with impunity, to the Disgrace of the British & honor of the American Arms: The Comdr in Chief therefore request the Army in genl. & every Comd. Officer in particular from the Genl. to the Ensign to accept of his most greatfull thanks, for theire good conduct & unexampled Breavery upon the late glorious & important occasion & which shall be faithfully & particually mentioned in his official communications to the Satisfaction of every officer whose Rank & Situation placed theire conduct in a conspickious point of View & which was observed with pleasure and gratetude by the Genl.[42] Nothing now rem'ns but to pay those Military honors due to the names of the Dead Heroes, who purchased Victory with theire precious Blood, Amongst whom we have to Lament, the early death of that great & gallant officer Captn. Mess Campbell & the Intrepid Lieut. Towles.

Three rounds of shells will be discharged from the Artillery at 12 o'clock as the Funeral Cerimony after a Solemn dirge, performed by the Music. The Troops remaining under Arms in theire present position it will also serve for a Signal for the army to take up the line of march which will be in the Same order but inverted by which we advanced.

NOTES

1. Jerry Keenan, in his *Encyclopedia of American Indian Wars* (ABC-CLIO, 1997), p. 222, writes, "The crushing and stunning defeat was the army's worst in all of the Indian wars: 623 killed and 258 wounded. . . . In fact, no battle of the recently concluded Revolutionary War had produced as many casualties." A Congressional investigation eventually cleared St. Clair, but he lived with the stigma of the defeat for the remainder of his life.

2. In addition to Clark's journal, two other principal sources include Lieutenant Boyer, *A Journal of Wayne's Campaign* (Cinncinnati, 1866) and Thomas Posey, "Journal of an Army Officer, 1792-1800," found in Draper MSS., U16, State Historical Society of Wisconsin. Other important manuscript references on Wayne's campaign include "The Orderly Book of General Robert Todd, 1793-1794," in Draper MSS., U16, and "Memorandum of Occurrences in the Expedition under General Anthony Wayne, 1794," by Nathaniel Hart of Woodford, in Draper MSS., U16.

3. This fort was named after Gen. Nathaniel Green and was situated on the present site of Greenville. According to Hubert, "This was the seventh fortified post in the chain from the Ohio and was located on the south banks of the St. Mary, four miles above Rockford (old Shane's Crossing), Mercer County." A.B. Hulbert, *Military Roads of the Mississippi Basin* (Historic Highways of America, Cleveland, 1904), 207.

4. Born in Cumberland County, Virginia; served as a corporal in a volunteer company of militia in Braddock's defeat; appointed by General Washington as commander of a continental regiment and was with Wayne at Stony Point. At the close of the Revolutionary War he went to Kentucky and settled in Woodford County (1785). He was with St. Clair in the campaign of 1791, and led a force with General Wilkinson against the Indians on the Wabash. In 1808 he was elected governor of Kentucky and continued in office till 1812. He died in 1820. A brief sketch of his life can be found in W.B. Allen, *History of Kentucky* (Louisville, 1872), 77.

5. Especial care was taken to see there should be no unnecessary halts. In case of an accident or break down the following "waggons" were to pass by immediately "so as not to break the line of march" or leave "any opening or interval." Special orders were also issued against disorderly conduct and unnecessary firing "at game for amusement." Draper MSS., U16.

6. This was located in Mercer County, Ohio, and it was the site of the disastrous defeat of General St. Clair. According to a current report of the time it was named Recovery because the cannon lost there were recovered. *Maryland Journal* (Baltimore), February 19, 1794, in Draper, MSS., JJ4.

7. Eleven miles in advance of Fort Recovery. Boyer, *Journal*, 1.

8. Posey's account contradicts the lack of precaution, declaring that "every morning our spy company is ordered out, we have a guard in front and rear of the army, our artillery, military stores, Pack horses and all the baggage goe in the center of the army, on our Right is one company [of] infantry and do Light infantry, one troop of Cavalry and

one Company [of] rifle men, and the same number on the Left of the army." Posey, *Journal*, in Draper MSS., U16.

9. The present site of Cincinnati, Ohio.

10. Boyer under the same date complains of the mosquitoes being very troublesome and "larger than he had every saw." Boyer, *Journal*, 3.

11. This bridge was seventy yards in length. Ibid., 4.

12. Captain William Wells was a member of a famous Kentucky family and brother of Colonel Samuel Wells. He was taken captive by the Miami when a boy of twelve years and was formally adopted into the family of Little Turtle. He fought with the Indians against General Harmar and General St. Clair; but, after duly notifying his adopted kinsmen, he joined Wayne. After the treaty of Greenville, he and his family settled a short distance "from the confluence of the St. Mary and St. Joseph, on the banks of a small stream there, afterward called 'Spy Run' and which still bears that name." He was later granted three hundred and twenty acres by the government and appointed Indian agent at Fort Wayne. During this particular campaign, Wells acted as Indian interpreter. In 1812 he led a band of Indians from Fort Wayne to relieve. Fort Dearborn and was killed in the subsequent massacre. H.C. Knapp,*History of the Maumee Valley* (Toledo, 1872), 95,96; M.M. Quaife,*Chicago and the Old Northwest* (Chicago, 1913), 224.

13. Ephraim Kibby was in charge of spies composed of frontier woodsmen among whom were Millers, McClelland, May, Wells, and Mahaffy. *Michigan Pioneer and Historical Collections*, 34:544, n.

14. Boyer sets the date of Newman's disappearance as August 2. Boyer, *Journal*, 4. Posey was not quite sure whether Newman deserted to the Indians or was taken captive but was sure he gave them the alarm of the approach of the army. Posey, *Journal*, in Draper MSS., U16.

15. Posey refers to the fort only as Fort Adams; Boyer gives no name, calling it simply "the garrison."

16. F. B. Heitman, *Historical Register of the United States Army* (Washington, 1890), 360.

17. This is the beginning of the acrimonious criticism of Wayne's tactics by Clark. From this point throughout the rest of the journal Clark seems to be especially hostile toward Wayne. See introduction on this subject.

18. See n. 14. Posey's explantion of the Indians' flight.

19. Clark is undoubtedly referring to the suggestion of Wilkinson which was rejected by Wayne. See n.17.

20. Posey says an old man was sent to the Indians to tell them Wayne would "rather Treat with them, than meet them in battle, and if they concluded to make peace the old man was to return with an answer, which he promised to doe in two days, at the time appointed the old indian did not return. The next day the General posted of the old squaw with the same message to those head Chiefs, the Old woman promised to return in two days, provided her Tribe wished to make peace, the Old lady failed to return." Posey, *Journal*, in Draper MSS., U16.

21. The spot of encampment was the site of the present city of Defiance, Ohio. Howe says General Wayne after finishing the fort said: "I defy the English, Indians, and all the devils in hell to take it." General Scott standing by said "Then call it Fort Defiance." H. Howe, *Historical Collections of Ohio* (Columbus, 1891), 1:545.

22. Heitman, *Historical Register*, 360.

23. This statement can be disproved by reference to Wayne's Orderly Book. Under date of August 13, the last general orders issued by Wayne before the eve of the battle, Captain Kibby was ordered to advance "in front with his spies and March the best Way." *Michigan Pioneer and Historical Collections, 34: 544.*

24. Heitman, *Historical Register*, 523.

25. However, there was a change in the order of the arrangement as the following illustrates: "The Army will March tomorrow Morning at five Oclock agreeable to the constant order of March, with this difference; That the Columns shall March two deep and in as close Order as Circumstances will permit of, being totally divested of Baggage, the Center will be left free for the Artillery and spare Ammunition." *Michigan Pioneer and Historical Collections,* 34:545.

26. Boyer recounting the same attack says "the front guard, which was composed of mounted volunteers, were fired on by the enemy" and "the guard retreated in the utmost confusion through the front guard of the regulars." (Boyer, *Journal,* 7.)

27. Heitman, *Historical Register,* 169.

28. Ibid., 318.

29. Boyer says the enemy were pursued "with rapidity for nearly two miles." (Boyer, *Journal,* 8). Wayne in his report to Secretary Knox makes a similar statement . *American State Papers, Indian Affairs,* 1:491.

30. Heitman, *Historical Register,* 647.

31. It is worth noting at this point that when the volunteers were ordered to do this at the close of the battle they failed to accomplish their task. (Posey, *Journal,* in Draper MSS., U16.) Yet Wayne in his report to Secretary Knox lauds their bravery. *American State Papers, Indian Affairs,*1:491.

32. Boyer ascertained the lost as thirty killed and one hundred wounded. (Boyer, *Journal,* 8.) Wayne in his report to Knox declared the loss twenty-eight killed and one hundred wounded. *American State Papers, Indian Affairs,* 1:492.

33. Anthony Lassalle by name.Ibid., 494:

34. Wayne in his report put the figure of the enemy at two thousand and his own force a little short of nine hundred. Ibid., 491.

35. Fort Maumee commanded by Major Campbell. Posey, *Journal,* in *Draper, MSS.,* U16.

36. A copy of this letter and the following letters written by Major Campbell and Major General Wayne can be found in *American State Papers; Indian Affairs,* 1:493, 494.

37. Heitman, *Historical Register,* 226.

38. Extract of a letter from an officer in General Wayne's army, dated Grand Glaize, September 21. "Upon the smallest calculation we must have destroyed between

three and found hundred thousand bushels of grain. It will therefore be impossible for the savages to live through the winter, unless their friends the British are remarkably kind to them." *Maryland Journal,* November 15, 1794, in Draper MSS., JJ4.

39. Heitman, *Historical Register, 595.*

40. About seventy of the militia took part in the battle of Fallen Timbers. *American State Papers, Indian Affairs,* 1:494.

41. The Indians sought refuge in the British fort after the battle but were denied admittance. Ibid., 495.

42. This is evidenced in the letter Wayne wrote Knox, August 28, 1794, in which he mentioned by name the various officers deserving praise. Among those favorably commented upon was the young aid-de-camp, William H. Harrison. (*American State Papers; Indian Affairs,* 1:491.) On another occasion Wayne expressed his candid opinion that if Harrison continued a military man he would be a second Washington. Posey, *Journal,* in Draper MSS., U16.

Fighting the Flames of a Merciless War:

SECRETARY OF WAR HENRY KNOX AND THE INDIAN WAR

in the Old Northwest, 1790-1795

Michael D. Carter

"The one side anxiously defend[s] their lands which the other avariciously claim[s]. With mind previously inflamed the slightest offense occasions death, revenge follows which knows no bounds. The flames of a merciless war are thus lighted up. . . ."[1]

With these words, the United States' first secretary of war described the eruption of his country's first major Indian war, the conflict in the "Old Northwest."

Prelude to the War

Secretary of War Henry Knox wrote of the growing conflict with the Indians during a critical transition period for the United States, during the first dozen years following America's independence from Britain. During that time, what came to be known as "Indian Affairs" assumed a high priority. The formation of Indian policy was not only affected by the politics of the time but, in fact, served as one of the driving forces for political change. Under the Articles of Confederation, America's first written form of government, national Indian policy was initially handled by the Confederation Congress. But as the situation between the Indians and frontier whites and between the various tribes and the states rapidly deteriorated, Congress sought to transfer the problem. To underscore the belligerent nature of relations with the Indians, the Congress assigned the responsibility for Indian Affairs to the War Department and thus to Henry Knox.

President George Washington had appointed Knox as secretary of war in 1785. A former bookstore owner from Massachusetts, Knox had served through the Revolutionary War alongside Washington, becoming commander of the Continental Army artillery and rising to the rank of major-general. In addition to operating the War Department, Knox was now burdened by the weak Congress with developing Indian policy.

The constant and unrelenting conflict between whites and Indians on the frontier and a host of other problems demanded that the country create a strong and centralized system of government to deal with the situation. The Constitutional Convention in 1787 designed the foundation for forming such a government under the United States Constitution. When the Constitution took effect, all agreements and contracts made under the older system of government had to be reconfirmed. The implications of this on those involved in Indian Affairs were staggering. Knox, the only high-raking official to carry over in the same post from the old system of government to the new, had to have all of the treaties with the many tribes reratified, renegotiated, or replaced. The awesome prospect of this task was matched, however, by the opportunity that it presented to Knox for formulating new treaties aimed at rectifying the failures of the previous ones. With his friend and former commander, Washington, serving as the first president, Knox was optimistic about his chances for success with the Indians.

Knox's Indian Policy Proposal

Shortly after Washington's inauguration, Knox gave the president a general report on Indian policy as it had existed prior to the newly formed government under the Constitution. He included a much more specific analysis of the situation in the Northwest. Today referred to as the "Old Northwest," this then-frontier area lay north of the Ohio River and west of that river's forks (at modern Pittsburgh). Knox's appraisal of the situation in the region was ominous. He began his report to Washington with the statement that most of the Indian nations in lands claimed by the United States were "discontented, some of them turbulent."[2] Knox summed up the background of the conflict between white settlers and Indian on the northwest frontier as follows:

[Y]our secretary apprehends that the deep rooted prejudices, and malignity of heart, and conduct reciprocally entertained and practiced on all occasions by the Whites and Savages will ever prevent their being good neighbours. The one side anxiously defend[s] their lands which the other avariciously claim[s]. With minds previously inflamed the slightest offense occasions death, revenge follows which knows no bounds. The flames of a merciless war are thus lighted up which involve innocent and helpless with the guilty. Either one or the other party must remove to a greater distance, or Government must keep them both in awe by a strong hand, and compel them to be moderate and just.[3]

Knox recommended that the first step taken by the new government should be to reratify the existing treaties as they stood or renegotiate them. When suggesting the latter, Knox contrasted previous American policy with that of the British, who had avoided conflict by paying full compensation for Indian land.[4]

Knox specifically wanted a new treaty with the Indians around the Wabash River, an Ohio River tributary that today separates the states of Illinois and Indiana. The tribes of the Wabash watershed, which included the Shawnee, Miami, and Delaware, were the most hostile Indian nations of the Northwest towards the United States. According to Brigadier General Josiah Harmar, commander of American forces on the frontier, the Wabash tribes were linked a violent series of murders of white settlers on the Ohio. Secretary Knox believed that these incidents were not authorized or cordoned by the tribal leaders and held out hope for a negotiated truce and peace agreements. He stated, "It is well known how strong the passion for war exists in the mind of a young savage and how easily it may be inflamed so as to disregard every precept of the older and wiser part of the tribes who may have a more just opinion of the force of a treaty."[5]

Secretary of War
Henry Knox

Independence National Historical

Park Collection

The unauthorized raids brought equally horrifying white retaliation. In the panic that ensued after the Wabash attacks along the Ohio, a band of Kentuckians "professing an equal aversion to all bearing the name Indians" attacked an innocent tribe of Indians in the Wabash area, killing many women and children."[6] In this emotionally charged atmosphere, Knox was determined to offer an even-handed and rational assessment of the situation in the Northwest: "[W]hen the impartial mind of the public sits in judgment, it is necessary that the cause of the ignorant Indians should be heard as well as those who are most fortunately circumstanced. It well becomes the public to enquire before it punishes—to be influenced by reasons and the nature of things and not by its resentments."[7]

Knox believed that as matters currently stood in the Northwest, an all-out war was likely. He offered two options to deal with the strife there. One choice was to raise an army and exterminate the Indians, assuming that the country had the manpower to carry out such wholesale destruction. The other option was to make treaties with the Indians and punish whites who violated the treaties.[8] By presenting these two difficult options, Knox made clear the severity of the situation on the frontier. But Knox, in examining the legal, moral, and pragmatic aspects of the options, also expressed his own opinion on national Indian policy.

The conflict in the Northwest was largely a conflict over land and Knox began by addressing the legality of American claims there. Much violence arose from the fact that there were conflicting interpretations of the terms of the 1783 Treaty of Paris, the agreement which concluded the American war for independence from Britain. The United States held that the British had ceded the Northwest to the American government in the treaty. The Indians did not believe that the land had been surrendered, and the British furthered Indian hostilities by agreeing with the Indians that the land was not held by the United States. Knox sidestepped the confusion: he believed that the Indians, as prior occupants of the disputed territory, were the ones who had a right to it by virtue of possession of the soil. This being the case, Indian land could only be legally obtained through their free consent or by the right of a nation's conquest in a "just" war. Knox argued that "to dispossess [the Indians] on any other principle [than free consent or a just war] would be a gross violation of the fundamental Laws of Nature and of that destributive [sic] justice which is the glory of a nation."[9]

To Knox, the United States' choices in the Northwest were simple. The government had to either buy land from the Indians as willing sellers or win it from them in a justifiable conflict of arms. However, Knox saw little excuse for the latter. Both sides had frequently provoked hostilities and committed atrocities, leaving no moral high ground from which to wage a just war. Knox also pointed out that "[i]t is presumable that a nation solicitous of establishing its character on the broad basis of justice, would not only hesitate at, but reject every proposition to benefit itself by the injury of any neighboring community."[10]

Besides the possible immorality of using force to win the land, Knox argued that a war would not be wise economically. There were only six hundred active duty American troops on the entire western frontier, of whom only four hundred could be used in a field expedition. Yet the government did not have the money to pay this small number of existing soldiers. Estimating the total number of warriors among the Wabash tribes at near 2,000, Knox asserted that an expedition designed to destroy and expel those Indians would require a minimum of 2,500 men. He concluded a six-month campaign by that many troops would cost $200,000. He then estimated that the current value of the disputed land was only $16,150.[11]

Knox agreed that if peace and land negotiations with the northwestern Indians failed, punitive force would be required. But Knox believed that time was on the side of the government and advocated patience for now. He based his belief that the northwestern Indians would eventually capitulate on his successful experience with the Creeks [Muskogees] on the southwestern frontier. Experience had also shown Knox that whites could not be prevented from moving into Indian territory. As they encroached, the newcomers drove away and depleted game. The Indians were then left with little alternative but to accommodate to white society or move. It was possible that the Indians might eventually respond to the invasion of settlers by standing and fighting. But Knox believed that by not attacking first, he would have given the government the time needed to better prepare for any future war.[12]

Knox did not advocate the use of offensive force in Indian policy and questioned its morality. He instead wanted negotiation and fair land purchase to become the new government's official policy for settling disputes. Knox felt that with such an approach most of the estimated 75,000 Indians of the various northwestern tribes would willingly allow themselves to be "attached" to the United States. He proposed that the government establish a fund which would yield $15,000 a year for several years to purchase land claims and ensure peace with the frontier Indians. Summing up the moral and pragmatic arguments for his proposal, Knox stated,

> A system of coercion and oppression, pursued from time to time for the same period as the convenience of the United States might dictate, would probably amount to a much greater sum of money [than $15,00 per year] — But the blood and injustice which would stain the character of the nation, would be beyond all pecuniary calculation.[13]

Knox summed up his desire that Washington attempt to first treat with the Wabash tribes. "[O]n examination," he began,

> policy and justice unite in dictating the attempt of treating with the Wabash Indians—for it would be unjust in the present confused state of injuries to make war on those tribes without having previously invited them to a treaty, in order amicably to adjust all difference. . . . If they should afterwards persist in their depredations, the United States may with propriety inflict such punishments as they shall think proper.[14]

The Harmar Expedition

Washington, following Knox's advice, did attempt to reach agreements with the tribes of the Wabash watershed peacefully. But, after a year of continued violence and failed negotiations, the president concluded that he had given Knox's proposals enough time. The southern Indians had, after all, come to terms with the United States within the same length of time. Knox now conceded that the approach that had succeeded in the Southwest had failed in the Northwest. The fighting on the northwestern frontier had become even bloodier.

Arthur St. Clair, the Governor of the Northwest Territories, returned to New York personally confirming all reports of Indian violence and urged a prompt military response to it.[15] St. Clair also indicated that the British were sponsoring or instigating the attacks made by the Indians, a charge denied by the British.[16] Josiah Harmar, who had provided Knox with continuous monitoring reports on the activities of the Northwest Indians over the past several years, supported St. Clair's position. Knox reluctantly agreed with Washington to send a punitive expedition against the Wabash Indians, hoping that a swift victory would bring new negotiations. Brigadier General Josiah Harmar was selected to lead the campaign.

In his report the previous year, Knox had noted the lack of adequate troops for an expedition such as Harmar's. Congress acknowledged Knox's pleas for a larger professional army on April 30, 1790, and authorized raising the ceiling on the number of standing or active troops from 700 to 1,216.[17] However, it would be some time before the additional 500 regular troops could be enlisted and trained, so Harmar's force was to be augmented by state militia called up for the operation. A total of 1,500 men, of whom 1,200 were militia, eventually made up the punitive force.[18] The expedition was to be the largest to date against the Indians on the frontier, and additional appropriations amounting to $100,000 were required to fund the operation.[19]

Harmar's force, mostly composed of predominately untrained, unequipped, and poorly disciplined Pennsylvania and Kentucky militiamen, was hurriedly assembled at Fort Washington (present-day Cincinnati, Ohio). On September 23, 1790, the expedition set out to deliver an ultimatum to the leaders of the Wabash region tribes: immediately conclude a treaty or face

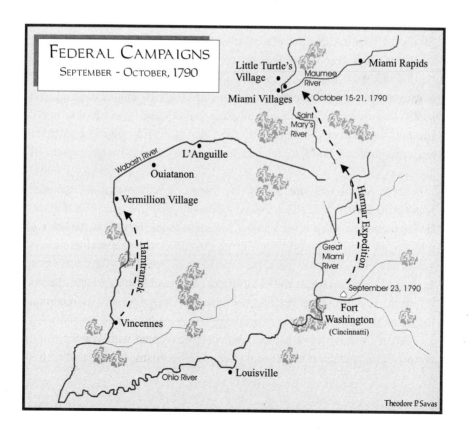

FEDERAL CAMPAIGNS
SEPTEMBER - OCTOBER, 1790

Little Turtle's Village

Miami Rapids

Maumee River

Miami Villages   October 15-21, 1790

Saint Mary's River

L'Anguille

Wabash River

Ouiatanon

Vermillion Village

Harmar Expedition

Hamtramck

Great Miami River

September 23, 1790

Fort Washington
(Cincinnatti)

Vincennes

Ohio River   Louisville

Theodore P. Savas

military action.[20] Knox emphasized to Harmar that the general should take "every possible precaution in the power of human foresight" to prevent being surprised and should also frequently reply upon the "mature experience and judgment of Governor St. Clair."[21]

As Washington had left for vacation during the summer of 1790, he ordered Knox to monitor the Harmar mission and other frontier developments closely.[22] By the time Washington returned to New York (at that time the national capital), Knox still had not heard from Harmar on the progress of the expedition. This was not a good sign as Harmar had been specifically instructed to send frequent reports to the War Department. Two reports from other persons did come in during this time; they did not instill confidence in the outcome of the campaign. From one message, Knox and Washington learned that St. Clair had, perhaps prematurely, informed some British outposts in the Northwest of the expedition. This was done to avoid creating tension with the British, but it meant that the British were provided with an opportunity to warn the Indians. As Harmar and his force had not left their staging area until four days after St. Clair sent word to the British post at Detroit, Harmar's entire mission might have been compromised from its start.[23]

In another report, Washington was informed of rumors that Harmar was a "drunkard." Supposedly, this vice affected Harmar's leadership ability and "no confidence was reposed in him by the people of the Western Country." Washington wrote to Knox, "I gave up all hope of Success [in the expedition], as soon as I heard that there were disputes with [Harmar] about command. The latter information is from report only; but the report of bad news is rarely without foundation. . . . [F]rom the silence which reigns, and other circumstances, [my mind] is prepared for the worst; that is, for expense without honor or profit."[24]

Upset over these reports and the silence from Harmar, Washington prepared to defend the decision to send the expedition in the event of its failure. He instructed Knox to prepare a report for Congress describing why the Harmar mission had been attempted.[25] Washington included Knox's report in his first annual address to Congress, an address that Knox helped write. Knox stressed to Congress the critical nature of Indian affairs and provided several justifications for the mission. However, Washington and Knox were still unable to report on the progress or outcome of the expedition.[26]

When the first news on the campaign was finally received from the northwestern frontier, it was encouraging. Knox was able to report Harmar's initial success in the form of punitive raids against Miami and Shawnee villages in the Maumee River Valley of what is now western Ohio.[27] According to Harmar's estimates,"not less than 100 or 120 warriors were slain, and 300 log-houses or wigwams burned [along with] . . . 20,000 bushels of corn."[28]

But Harmar's early success soon turned to failure and defeat. The overconfident commander proceeded to send detachments of a few hundred troops on smaller raids ahead of the main force. One of these small parties, under the command of Colonel John Hardin of the Kentucky militia, was ambushed by Indians. In the ensuing battle, over thirty American soldiers were killed. Most of the dead were United States regulars, who reportedly stood and fought while the majority of the militia fled. Harmar responded by sending a 360 man force in pursuit of the Indians who had attacked Hardin's group. This force found the guilty Indians, but they fled. The uncontrolled militia pursued the warriors in all directions, abandoning the sixty man contingent of American regulars with them. These regulars were surrounded by a larger group of Indians, who killed fifty of them. All told, 180 men were killed, wounded, or missing, in the two engagements (near modern Fort Wayne, Indiana). A disproportionate number of the casualties were professional soldiers and officers.[29]

Washington gave a full report to Congress of Harmar's expedition at its conclusion, and in it claimed the mission was overall a success in that a show of force had been made towards the Indians. In actuality, the opposite was true. Emboldened by their successes against the Americans, the Northwest tribes became more resolute in their resistance after Harmar's defeat.[30]

Washington's and Knox's candor in reporting the campaign's losses disarmed some congressional criticism. Some hostility may also have been diverted to Alexander Hamilton, who proposed the establishment of a controversial national bank to be supported through a liquor tax during the same session of Congress. The political opposition to Hamilton's plan overshadowed the Harmar fiasco.[31]

When congressional and other critics focused on the mission, they usually blamed Harmar for the outcome. As a result, Knox advised Harmar to demand a court of inquiry to clear his name.[32] Washington agreed to the procedure and ordered Knox to assemble a board of officers to investigate the failure of the expedition.[33] A year later, the board released its findings. The officers found that Harmar's personal conduct was "irreproachable." They ruled that that the tactical employment of the troops under Harmar's command was "perfectly adapted to the country" and that the general's actions actions were either based on "good principles" or justified by circumstances. The investigator's assigned the failure of the expedition to Harmar's subordinates, who had "not properly executed" their commander's orders. It should be noted that the board included several officers who had served on the frontier and were familiar with "Indian fighting" operations and similar combat. Once his name and reputation were cleared, Harmar resigned his commission.[34]

The St. Clair Expedition

Despite Harmar's exoneration, Washington and Knox could not disguise from themselves the extent of his failure. The president, not about to let an American defeat decide the Indian situation in the Northwest, was determined to retaliate against the Wabash tribes. Washington immediately recommissioned Arthur St. Clair, who had served as a commander in the American Revolution, as a major general. The president ordered the general to undertake another punitive expedition. The object was to establish a military post northwest of Fort Washington in the heart of Indian territory, something that Harmar had failed to do. Washington instructed St. Clair to "seek the enemy" and "endeavor by all possible means to strike them with great severity."[35]

Knox authorized a force of three thousand men for St. Clair's mission. These troops were to be composed of regular army soldiers, six month federal levies (i.e., national conscripts), and state militia. The mission began inauspiciously as it took several months to assemble the force, which totaled approximately 2,500 troops. Most of the troops were state militia as many of the requested levies requested of the states by the national government failed to arrive and the existing regular troops on the frontier increasingly failed to reenlist. St. Clair's organizational efforts were further compounded by a severe shortage of supplies and by substandard equipment. These delays held up the expedition throughout the summer campaign season of 1791.

In response to the lateness, Knox wrote St. Clair, "I am commanded to inform you, that [Washington] is by no means satisfied with the long detention of the troops on the upper part of the Ohio, which he considers as unnecessary and improper. And that it is his opinion unless the highest exertions are made by all parts of the army, to repair the loss of the season that the expenses which have been made for the campaign will be altogether lost, and that the measures from which so much has been expected will result in disgrace."[36]

Faced with this pressure to depart, St. Clair, still short of supplies, reluctantly began his expedition into the northwestern Indian territory. On September 1, 1791, Knox wished St. Clair a speedy journey and success for what remained of the season in his operations against the Indians. He instructed St. Clair to first seek to conclude negotiations with the Wabash Indians before beginning any punitive actions.[37]

In spite of the lateness of the season—the expedition did not set out until mid-September—St. Clair unrealistically wrote to Knox that, "All seems now as if it would go well."[38] St. Clair's optimism quickly faded, however, as his force slowly cut a road westward. By mid-October, the expedition had progressed less than seventy miles from Fort Washington. Even more discouraging was the fact that rations were rapidly dwindling and that the expedition's pack horses were dying "so rapidly that nearly every prairie and swamp was littered with their carcasses."[39]

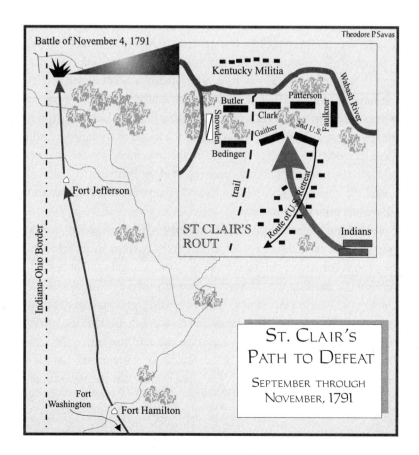

Theodore P. Savas

Battle of November 4, 1791

Kentucky Militia

Butler   Patterson

Clark

Snowden   Gaither   2nd U.S.   Faulkner

Bedinger

Wabash River

Fort Jefferson

trail   Route of U.S. Retreat

Indiana-Ohio Border

ST CLAIR'S ROUT   Indians

Fort Washington   Fort Hamilton

ST. CLAIR'S
PATH TO DEFEAT

SEPTEMBER THROUGH
NOVEMBER, 1791

As October passed to November, the condition of St. Clair's force worsened. The supply situation was so bad that St. Clair had to place his men on half rations, producing outrage on the part of the soldiery, who began to desert in droves. St. Clair was only able to bring the situation under control through the use of corporal and capital punishment.[40] By then, St. Clair's column was down to only around 1,800 men, 300 of his troops having been dispatched to the rear to round up deserters and convey supplies.

As he struggled to regain control over his men and the military situation, St. Clair received intelligence that Indians had been spotted within a few miles of the expedition's main body, which was near what is now the western border of Ohio. The overconfident St. Clair dismissed this information and wrote Knox that "[t]he few Indians that have been seen were hunters only, who we fell upon by accident."[41] The Indians may have indeed been hunters, but St. Clair was oblivious to the fact that he and his dwindling force were the prey.

On the morning of November 4, 1791, St. Clair's force awoke to find itself surrounded by a large force of warriors. A pitched battle was fought, with disastrous results for the Americans. St. Clair's force suffered 900 casualties. In terms of the number of men lost, and even more in terms of the percentage of men lost, the event was one of the worst defeats in American military history.[42]

Word of St. Clair's disaster reached the president before it reached Congress and the public. At the time, Washington was scheduled to give his second annual address in Philadelphia, the new seat of the national government. The president was more vulnerable this time than he had been following Harmar's defeat, as Washington had chosen the leader of the failed expedition. Having learned from the Harmar incident that openness was the best policy, Washington presented a straightforward report of the campaign to Congress. He included the copies of St. Clair's optimistic reports to the War Department, those written prior to the disaster.

Washington's annual address to Congress included a report from Knox to Congress on the current status of Indian Affairs. The secretary included several justifications for having attempted the St. Clair expedition. Knox held that "every pacific measure was previously tried to produce accommodations and avoid expense." He explained that "offers of pacification were held forth to the hostile tribes upon terms of moderation and justice. But these offers, having had no effect, it became necessary to convince the refractory [i.e., the resistant Indians] of the power of the United States to restrain and punish their depredations. Accordingly, offensive operations were directed to be conducted as consistently as possible with humanity." Knox also presented copies of the recent successful treaties with the Creeks [Muskogees] on the southwestern frontier and with the Six Nations [of the Iroquois Confederacy] in New York, and complement this with an appeal to pass more "pointed laws with penalties to restrain our own people."

Knox concluded his report by adding that "[t]he offers of peace are still continued to the deluded tribes, to attach them firmly to the United States [and t]o effect these desireable [sic] objects it seems necessary that the Indians should experience the benefits of an impartial administration of justice." Justice towards the Indians would have to include the conditions that ". . . the mode of alienating their lands, the main source of discontent—should be defined and regulated by such principles as to prevent all controversy. That the advantages of commerce should be extended to them and such national experiments made for imparting on them the blessings of civilization."[43]

As had been the case after Harmar's failure, Washington managed to disarm much criticism of himself by being candid about the extent of St. Clair's defeat.[44] But this time the administration's critics were not diverted by more controversial issues, such as the former national bank debate. Political opponents in Congress demanded an investigation into the St. Clair fiasco. Washington and Knox responded by cooperating fully with Congress during the investigation.

Congress eventually officially absolved St. Clair of blame in the defeat.[45] Insufficient preparation and a lack of supplies were determined to be the culprit in this case. Army contractors became the scapegoats for the disaster.[46] Nonetheless, Congress asked that St. Clair resign his commission.

One positive outcome for Knox of the St. Clair defeat was the passage of the Uniform Militia Act of 1792. The new law reorganized the various state militias and enlarged the federal military. When the administration would again confront the Indian crisis on the frontier, it would have three additional regiments of regular troops. The national government would also the power to draw upon, rather than merely request, the troops of the state militias. Knox now had a much stronger legal foundation from which to fight if negotiations with the northwestern Indians failed.

The Wayne Campaign

As far as the Washington administration was concerned, the defeats of Harmar and St. Clair had to be punished. Knox was accordingly ordered to plan yet another expedition to the Northwest on the very likely chance that the renewed attempts at a peaceful resolution to hostilities failed. On March 9, 1792, Washington called his cabinet together to discuss such the option of a military offensive.

In the cabinet discussion, the question naturally arose as to who would lead another campaign against the western tribes. With St. Clair's forced resignation and the enlargement of the regular Army, the administration considered potential commanders of the newly available forces. Several candidates were considered, including Benjamin Lincoln, Daniel Morgan, Anthony Wayne, James Wilkinson, Henry "Light Horse Harry" Lee, Charles Pinckney, George Weedon, William Moultrie, Baron von Steuben, Charles Scott, and Thomas Sumter.[47] All of these men were Revolutionary War veterans, known to Knox and Washington. Each person was assessed for his potential to carry out the mission, but no one was immediately seen as rising above the others. The decision was put off.

The cabinet members also discussed the issue of enlisting Indians in the fight against their brethren of other tribes. In a rare moment of agreement between the two rivals, both Hamilton and Jefferson were opposed to the idea. Knox, on the other hand, was all for employing as many as 500 "friendly Indians" in the cause on the frontier. Washington was inclined towards Knox's position, as he felt that if Indians were not used "with us," "they would surely be against us." The split among those present resulted in a decision not to invite any of the amicable tribes to join in the campaign against the hostile northwestern tribes. However, the leaders of those potential ally tribes were to be informed that if their young warriors insisted on participating in the fighting, that the United States would gladly accommodate them.

It took one month of deliberations before Washington chose a new commander for the American frontier forces. On April 9, 1792, the president selected Anthony Wayne, who had been initially described by the cabinet as "[b]rave and nothing else. Wayne was commissioned a major general. Daniel Morgan, Marinus Willett, John Brooks, and James Wilkinson received lesser commissions as brigadier generals. The Senate promptly approved these appointments. Two of the appointees, Morgan and Willett, refused to serve under Wayne and were replaced by Rufus Putnam and Otho Williams.[48]

After long consultations with Washington on the nature of the mission, Knox sent Wayne west to receive intelligence from the officers of the Pennsylvania and Kentucky militia. Wayne was to make also contact with as many hostile tribes as possible and extend them offers of a general peace treaty. Wayne was warned not to wantonly attack Indian villages, so as to create a good environment for peace talks. The president added that while he hoped the general would restrain himself from waging a general war against the Indians, so as to promote peace, he approved the "severest punishment" against any Indians who attacked Wayne's force.[49]

As Wayne set out, Secretary Knox dispatched Indian agents and commissioners to open negotiations with the many tribes on the northwestern frontier. Through these representatives, Knox invited tribal leaders to travel to Philadelphia to negotiate treaties with the national government.[50] Special invitations were sent to the leaders of the Miami and other Wabash region tribes, and to those of the Six Nations [of the Iroquois], the latter including Joseph Brant of the Mohawk.[51]

Initially, it seemed as if Knox's renewed efforts to achieve a peaceful resolution to the crisis might work. In March 1792, Major John Hamtramck secured treaties with three of the hostile tribes of the Wabash River watershed.[52] Later that same month, headmen of the Seneca nation of the Six Nations arrived in Philadelphia for peace talks, followed in June by Chief Brant of the Mohawk.[53]

More promising news came in July after Wayne arrived at Pittsburgh. The general reported to Knox that he had no knowledge, nor had he seen any indications, of hostile Indian activity on his journey to the advance base at Fort Jefferson (in what is now southwestern Ohio). As a precaution, however, Wayne told Knox that he ordered the local farmers to fully supply that fort. This was done, Wayne wrote Knox, in case "the Indians prefer the hatchet to the olive branch." Wayne then began to prepare for a possible offensive.

Knox had sent Wayne over seventeen hundred reinforcements from the federalized militias and Wayne proceeded to drill these troops at Fort Jefferson.[54] The general also reported that he and his officers had devised an improved method of firing a musket, which was two to three times as fast as in the past and offered the advantage of giving the soldier a better sight on the enemy. This report reassured Knox that the troops were being well trained for the demanding conditions of frontier warfare. It also instilled confidence in Knox and Washington that they had made a good choice in Wayne. An optimistic Knox wrote to Wayne: "If the hostile Indians can be brought to understand us [it would be best]—it is difficult to conceive of the impediments to a peace—but if they will not listen it will be unfortunate for them."[55]

Wayne consistently kept the secretary of war informed of his situation and progress through a series of reports. By the end of July, these messages indicated that Wayne's situation was becoming less promising. The general reported that some of the reinforcements had already deserted and that the troops left were in great need of uniforms. To make matters worse, smallpox and violent and contagious fever had broken out among his men. Further, a recent raid by hostile "savages" had resulted in the deaths of seven area whites and the loss of several horses. The settlers were begging Wayne to give them military protection. These were not the types of results that Knox wanted in the Northwest. But Wayne was proving himself to be a strong commander. He discouraged further flights by using a brand forming the word "coward" on captured deserters. The desertion rate reportedly dropped off precipitously after this policy was implemented.[56] Knox and Washington could console themselves with the hope that Wayne would be able to overcome other adversities and that their choice in leaders this time was a good one.

Due to the expedition's weakened state, not to mention the political sensitivities in the Northwest, Knox warned Wayne to avoid the British outposts in the region to avoid confrontations with their garrisons. Wayne acknowledged the warning but maintained that he believed that the British were at least indirectly responsible for inciting Indian hostility.[57]

Knox's efforts at peaceful negotiations to solve the frontier crisis took a drastic turn for the worse in August 1792. In that month, two of his representatives, Major Alexander Trueman and Colonel John Hardin, were killed by Indians of the northwestern tribes with whom they were to negotiate treaties. When word of this reached the President, he ominously declared, "If these attempts to disclose the just and pacific disposition of the United States to these people, should also fail, there remains no alternative but the Sword, to decide the difference."[58]

Wayne responded to reports of this blatant resistance to peace overtures by informing Knox that he could begin an all-out offensive against the hostile Indians in the spring of 1793. He wanted to wait until that season to ensure that his men were fully equipped and trained. In the spring, he argued, the Indians were at their weakest, having suffered through the winter.[59] Knox agreed that if war was the only option that a late winter-early spring campaign against the Indians would be "the most efficacious."[60]

After approved a campaign date, however, Knox sent Wayne a hurried and more formal dispatch. Knox stated that "the public requires that peace overtures still must be tried." The secretary of war did not want to engage in a major Indian war just yet. He understood that such an occurrence would arouse the passions of white Americans against all Indians, including those on good terms with the United States. This would endanger and very likely destroy all the hard-won treaties that Knox had made over the past six years. Knox continued to communicate with Wayne and warned him that a majority of Americans were adverse to an Indian war. In addition, the all-out peace initiative by the national government was working at some points along the frontier.[61] General Rufus Putnam, an Indian commissioner and one of Wayne's subordinate officers, successfully negotiated a treaty with the Illinois tribe on September 27, 1792.[62] This achievement and the ongoing negotiations in the Northwest could be jeopardized if Wayne acted hastily.

Shortly after Putnam's diplomatic success, Knox informed the president of British overtures to mediate a broad settlement between the United States and the northwestern tribes. Neither Washington nor Knox trusted the British or liked the idea of their becoming officially involved in the ongoing Indian negotiations. After consultation with the rest of the cabinet on December 10, 1792, the British offer was rejected. However, Washington allowed that if the American military met with another defeat in battle with the Indians the idea should be reexplored.[63]

Indian affairs were one of the main issues of Washington's 1793 annual address to Congress. Through that address, Knox provided an in-depth account of all present negotiations and treaties with the Indians. Ironically, Knox's report of the diplomatic efforts was so thorough that it encouraged their replacement with a military solution. Congress was convinced that the government, and the War Department in particular, was doing everything in its power to peacefully contain the Indian situation. If this was the case, it left no solution but warfare to deal with Indian hostilities of the type Wayne was experiencing. The stage was thus set for "Wayne's legion" to begin offensive operations, and the spring campaign season was only a few months away.[64]

Washington was sensitive to Knox's concerns for a peaceful solution to the Indian crisis and realized that fair and humane treatment of the Indians was preferable to coercion. The president was also aware that an Indian war could become genocidal. The destruction many tribes would inevitably follow as the war expanded and the fragile system of treaties crumbled. Washington wanted to avoid this by every possible means. Aware of how future generations might judge their decision for war, Washington wrote to Knox that "the honor and future reputation of the Country was more intimately blended therewith than was generally supposed."[65]

Washington and Knox had left the final decision to begin a military campaign to Wayne, should treaty negotiations be futile. Knox tried again to impress on Wayne both the unpopularity of a potential Indian war and his own concerns for America's future reputation: "If our modes of population and war destroy the tribes, the disinterested part of mankind and posterity will be apt to class the effects of our conduct and that of the Spaniards in Mexico and Peru together."[66] But while he made his preference for diplomacy quite clear to Wayne, Knox made it clear that Wayne could rely upon his and the nation's support if war were unavoidable. Knox concluded that if peace can only "be obtained but at the price of a sacrifice of national character, it is presumed the citizens at large will unite as one Man in prosecuting the war with the highest degree of vigor until it shall be advantageously terminated in all respects."[67]

In a last, desperate effort to resolve the crisis in the Northwest, Knox announced plans on February 16, 1793, for a major peace conference with the hostile tribes. The basis of this conference was to be the 1789 Treaty of Fort Harmar, a general treaty which had not been agreed to by all of the concerned tribes. Knox instructed his commissioners to invite all the Indian leaders of tribes that not yet treated with the federal government to present their territorial claims. The commissioners would then, under Knox's authority, employ a liberal system of compensation to gain all lands disputed with whites through purchase. The sanctity of all lands left to the Indians was to be guaranteed by the national government, and a $10,000 annuity was to be paid to the tribes that signed the new treaty.[68]

In authoring the negotiations, Knox optimistically hoped that the new agreement would reaffirm the favorable boundaries defined in the Fort Harmar treaty. If that should fail, he ordered his commissioners to negotiate a boundary that came as close as possible to those in the 1789 agreement. With Washington's support and Senate approval, Knox indicated that the proposed new treaty would become official one year from the signing. He called for a truce with the western tribes in the interim. If an agreement could not be reached in a timely fashion, Secretary Knox urged his representatives to secure a truce of from three to seven years, during which time it was hoped a lasting treaty could be arranged. Knox did insist on stipulation during these last ditch negotiations: the United States would have preemption rights to any territory ceded to the Indians, meaning that if they chose to sell it they could only sell it to the national government.[69]

By March, Knox had arranged a formal date for what was to become known as the Lower Sandusky [River] Peace Conference. Negotiations were to begin on June 1, 1793. To further facilitate the negotiations and demonstrate the administration's good faith, Knox approved of a plan to distributed copies of a presidential proclamation entitled the "Letter of Protection for Friendly Indians." This document gave a presidential guarantee of protection for the property and rights of Indians that would agree to a treaty with the federal government, as well as support of punishment for those whites violating the same.[70]

Unfortunately for Knox, it was already too late for any treaty to resolve the disputes on the frontier. American Indian commissioner General William Hull was to arrange the conference. But British authorities in Canada refused to allow Hull to purchase or transport provisions for the meeting within the portions of the Northwest that they still occupied. Knox also learned that the Indians invited to the conference were insisting upon setting the Ohio River as a southern boundary, which would drastically affect or nullify claims there by the federal government and private land companies. The prospect of successful negotiations now looked very doubtful. But the cabinet agreed that they should nevertheless continue diplomatic efforts in order to placate the opponents of an Indian war.[71]

As negotiations in the Northwest looked more and more unlikely, Knox changed his tone in his communication with Wayne. The secretary now acknowledged that "under the present circumstances, the [treaties] will be a work of complicated difficulty." Nevertheless, Knox cautioned Wayne that the commissioners were still out among the unprotected in Indian territory and that any hostile actions on Wayne's part might jeopardize the mand their mission. Knox's caution delayed an escalation of hostilities that lasted through the entire spring and summer of 1793.[72]

While Wayne continued to report an increase in Indian violence on the frontier, Knox still halfheartedly hoped for a miracle. The secretary continued to send Wayne instructions for the upcoming peace conference.[73] But Knox now began to calculate the odds in the event of conflict. The secretary of war needed from Wayne an accurate count of the number of warriors who would be accountable to any treaties signed by their leaders. He also suggested to Wayne that "some faithful Indians be present at the treaty to inform you of the numbers for you ought to be acquainted with the numbers you have to combat."[74]

By September 1793, it was clear that diplomacy had failed. Knox had tried everything in his power to prevent war and had been stymied. He felt frustrated and betrayed. His own honor had been slighted, and Knox was prepared to sacrifice that of the nation if necessary. He wrote Wayne, "The Indians have refused to treat. You are now the judge whether your force will be adequate to make those audacious savages feel our superiority in Arms."[75]

By now, however, the 1793 spring-summer campaign season was almost over. Wayne held to his belief that spring was the best time to attack the Indians. As summer proceeded into autumn, the commander stockpiled ammunition, requested more artillery, and continued training his troops. The troops also passed the fall fighting very small and limited engagements with the Indians. As winter came, Wayne's men settled into their encampments and awaited the spring. Knox kept in contact with Wayne over the winter. He relayed tactical advice from Washington, including the assurance that when spring did arrive the war would begin. The general who had been known as "Mad" Anthony Wayne since the American Revolution was to be unleashed. Knox's only hope for a peaceful future lay in the war's being over quickly.[76]

As the 1794 campaign season approached, Knox and the rest of the administration were filled with anticipation and anxiety. Detailed maps of the theater of operations had been sent to the War Department by Wayne's second-in-command, Brigadier General James Wilkinson. Both Washington and Knox were immensely pleased by this, as such mapmaking stood in marked contrast to the noticeable lack of reporting, communication, and preparation during the earlier punitive expedition.[77]

Washington wanted nothing to derail Wayne's preparations for the upcoming mission. Aware of the potential problems that could be caused by tribes that lay outside the campaign area, Washington told Knox to maintain good relations with the Six Nations at any cost. Knox was authorized to offer of an additional annuity to Chief Brant of the Mohawk if his people would remain neutral during the upcoming campaign. The president then ordered Knox to check all existing current treaties with the many "Tribes of Indians now in amity with us" to see if the United States still had any outstanding obligations towards them and, if so, to promptly fulfill them.

Wayne had used the two years during Knox's protracted attempts at negotiation to prepare for war. Determined not to suffer from the weaknesses of his predecessors, he insisted on adequate supplies and logistical support and emphasized vigorous discipline and training of his soldiers. He had also used the time to cut a road from Fort Washington far to the north, into Indian country, and had established many blockhouses and fortified positions along the way. Thus, when he embarked on his operation in the spring of 1794, the first leg of his route would be already prepared and his men would be seasoned road-builders.[80] When the campaign season finally began, Knox sent Wayne reinforcements to replace the numerous deserters. These fresh troops were mounted militia from Kentucky, who brought Wayne's force up to approximately 3000 men.

Wayne made his goal for the summer of 1791 Fort Miamis, a newly established British post near present-day Maumee and Toledo, Ohio. Wayne believed, as did Washington, that the British were attempting to "keep this Country in a state of disquietude with the Indian Nations and also to alter the Boundary between them and us, if, by any means they can effect it." To counter such agitation, Wayne audaciously led his legion to within a few miles of the post.[81] From this position, Wayne wrote Knox on August 14, 1794,

> Thus, sir we have gained possession of the grand Emporium of the hostile Indians of the West, without loss of blood. The very extensive and highly cultivated fields and gardens, show the work of many hands. The margins of those beautiful rivers, the Miami of the Lakes, and the Auglaize, appear like one continued village for a number of miles, both above and below this place; nor have I ever before beheld such immense fields of corn, in any parts of America, from Canada to Florida."[82]

It was obvious from these crops that the Indians were well acquainted with what Knox called the "blessings of agriculture." The secretary of war, oblivious to the fact that Indians had been cultivating crops for centuries, believed that farming would "civilize" the Indians by turning them from a hunting and gathering lifestyle.[83] However, it would be obvious in a few days that the adoption of an agricultural way of life did not mean the end of the warrior lifestyle.

On August 20, 1794, an allied Indian force of Shawnee, Miami, Ottawa and other warriors attacked Wayne's legion from the cover of a cluster of trees felled by a tornado. This feature would give to the engagement the title the "Battle of Fallen Timbers." This time an American frontier expedition, under Wayne's firm command, held its ground. Employing a forceful bayonet charge, born of cold discipline and months of training, Wayne's men counterattacked and drove the Indians out of the timber and into the open. In this environment, the American cavalry, dragoons, and mounted militia could operate at will. They exacted a terrible toll on the Indians. The defeat of the warriors was made complete when they were chased to the gates of Fort Miami, but refused admittance and refuge by the British.[84]

In the following days, Wayne destroyed all the corn and several villages along the Miami River that he had described earlier. He reported his intention to do the same along the Auglaize River.[85] The destruction was carried out despite the appeals of the British. When nothing was left to be burned, Wayne, satisfied that he had showed the Indians that the British would not or could not protect them, returned with his force to Cincinnati on the Ohio River.[86]

The Treaty of Greenville

The American victory at the Battle of Fallen Timbers vindicated Knox's and Washington's strategy and choice of commanders. Wayne's success in battle and his brutally efficient destruction of Indian crops and villages, along with news that the British were going to abandon their frontier posts in compliance with the recent Jay Treaty, brought the defeated northwestern tribes to the peace table.[87] On August 3, 1795, the Treaty of Greenville was dictated by Wayne to the representatives of twelve tribes, with 1100 Indians present. The treaty established the sought-after peace agreement with the Indians. It also secured for the United States most of what is now the state of Ohio and 300,000 additional acres in the Northwest and made it possible to establish an American fort at the key location of Detroit.[88] For its part, the United States relinquished claim on all Indian lands north of the upper reaches of the Mississippi River, west of the Great Lakes. According to the fifth article of the treaty, the Indians could use their lands as they wished, but could only sell to the federal government. In return, the partially relocated northwestern Indians received a promise of protection from the United States government.[89]

Conclusion

Secretary of War Henry Knox had a firm understanding of the many factors and delicate problems in Indian Affairs. This grasp included a knowledge of the long history of reciprocal hostilities on the part of both Indians and whites. During the early years of the United States under the Constitution, Knox's understanding enabled him to adopt a course of action, out of both a sense of justice and military necessity, that favored negotiation and treaties over armed invasion. The secretary's influence undoubtedly curbed Washington's natural tendency to immediately fight the Indians, and Knox must be credited with persuading the president to exhaust what they saw as all other realistic alternatives before deciding on war. In the end, however, not even Knox could not prevent a major Indian war.

Through vigorous lobbying in the aftermath of the disastrous defeats of Harmar and St. Clair, Knox was able to strengthen the nation's military resources. The result was that when Wayne met the Indians, he had been prepared with a large enough force. The resulting victory at Fallen Timbers and the advantageous provisions of the Treaty of Greenville were due as much to the efforts and policies of Knox as to Wayne's tactical brilliance.[90]

The victory at Fallen Timbers and the Treaty of Greenville gained the United States an enormous region and forged a peace that lasted for five years, a relatively long time for the strife-ridden Northwest. The cost, however, had been high. Countless lives and national honor had been sacrificed to achieve the temporary settlement. Furthermore, American Indian policy in its true essence did not change during Knox's tenure. Previously, white North Americans had usually dictated land cessions to the Indians on the basis of force. The new American government continued to conduct its Indian policy on the premise of the right to territory through military victory. Although it took a decade of negotiations and punitive actions to overcome them, once the Indians in the Northwest were finally defeated militarily the Treaty of Greenville was dictated to them as conquered nations. The concept of the Indians' natural right of possession of the soil, which Knox had argued so vehemently and which had been acknowledged in Congressional legislation, was only heeded when convenient and when not supplanted by the so-called right of conquest.

Ultimately, Knox realized that the two cultures, Indian and white, were incompatible. The population explosion and territorial expansion of whites signaled that conflict would only be a matter of time. In his policies, Knox hoped to convert the Indians into citizens whenever possible, so that when the inevitable competition came, the Indians would at least have some basic rights and freedoms established. Knox might be criticized today for failing to understand the Indians' own sense of rights and values. But Knox demonstrated and provided a sense of justice and propriety in a history of Indian relations that has involved much dishonor.

NOTES

This article was based upon a paper originally presented the Twenty-Ninth Annual History Forum at Duquesne University in Pittsburgh, Pennsylvania in October 1995. The author wishes to acknowledge professors Mary Lou Lustig, Helen Bannan, Jack Hammersmith, and Joe Hagan of West Virginia University and Holly Mayer of Duquesne University for their advice and useful criticism.

1. Knox to Congress, July 10, 1787, *The Journals of the Continental Congress,* vol. 32 (Washington, D.C.: Government Printing Office, 1905), 328.

2. Francis S. Drake, ed., "Life and Correspondence of Major-General Henry Knox," in *Memorials of the Society of the Cincinnati of Massachusetts* (Boston: Press of John Wilson and Son, 1873), 488-495.

3. Knox to Congress, July 10, 1787, *Continental Congress,* vol. 32, 328.

4. W. W. Abbot, ed., *The Papers of George Washington, Presidential Series,* vol. 2, (Charlottesville, Virginia: University Press of Virginia, 1983), 370-374.

5. Report to the President, Indian Department Number 1: The Wabash Tribes, 1789, Henry Knox Papers II, Box 3, vols. 2 and 3, Massachusetts Historical Society.

6. Ibid., Knox lists the unfortunate Indian victims as "Piankeshaws, who prided themselves in their attachments to the United States." Retaliatory attacks by frontier whites upon innocent Indians was epidemic during the early republic period and some of the incidents caught the attention of the country's chief executive. After relaying information regarding atrocities committed against two Seneca Indians to Knox, Washington in a show of respect for the Six Nations, promptly dispatched Colonel Timothy Pickering to meet the headmen of the Seneca. Pickering assured them that the actions were neither authorized nor condoned by the government, and that a reward was being offered for the capture of the attackers, who once in custody would be duly punished. Compensation to the families of the victims was also offered by the U.S.

government. Washington to Knox, Sept. 20, 1790, John C. Fitzpatrick, ed., *The Writings of George Washington from the Original Manuscript Sources 1745 - 1799, George Washington Bicentennial Edition*, vol. 31 (Washington, D.C.: United States Government Printing Office, 1938), 124.

7. Henry Knox Papers II, Box 3, vol. 7.

8. Henry Knox Papers II, Box 3, vols. 2 and 4.

9. Henry Knox Papers II, Box 3, vols. 2 and 4-6.

10. Abbot, *Papers of George Washington*, vol. 2, 491.

11. Henry Knox Papers II, Box 3, vols. 2 and 4-6.

12. Henry Knox Papers II, Box 3, vols. 12-13; Abbot, *Papers of George Washington*, vol. 2, 491.

13. Henry Knox Papers II, Box 3, vols. 11-12; Abbot, *Papers of George Washington*, vol. 2, 493-494.

14. Henry Knox Papers II, Box 3, Vols. 2 and 8.

15. St. Clair to Knox, August 23, 1790, *American State Papers, Indian Affairs*, vol. 1, 92-94. St. Clair also brought word that the Indians were acting in concert with the British commander as Detroit, whom they referred to as "their father at Detroit." St. Clair had negotiated a treaty with chiefs from the Seneca, Wyandot, Delaware and other nations at Fort Harmar on January 9, 1780. The treaty, subsequently named the "Treaty of Fort Harmar," reacknowledged the land boundaries defined in the 1784 Treaty of Fort Stanwix and the 1785 Treaty of Fort McIntosh, but accomplished little else and hostilities soon resumed. James R. Jacobs, *The Beginning of the U. S. Army, 1783-1812* (Princeton: Princeton University Press, 1947), 48-49.

16. Harold C. Syrett, ed., *The Papers of Alexander Hamilton*, vol. 6 (New York: Columbia University Press, 1961), 550-551. The British diplomat George Beckwith was the individual who strongly denied such charges on behalf of his government. See in Syrett the record of Hamilton's dialogue with Beckwith of August 8-12, 1790, concerning incidents on the northwestern frontier.

17. J. F. Callan, *Military Laws of the United States*, rev. ed., 87-90, cited in Jacobs, *U. S. Army*, 50-51.

18. Knox to St. Clair, August 23, 1790, *American State Papers: Documents, Legislative and Executive, 1789-1831, Class II, Indian Affairs, 1789-1827*, vol. 1 (Washington: Gale and Seaton, 1832), 98-99.

19. Syrett, *Hamilton Papers*, vol. 6, 563 and vol. 7, 416; *American State Papers, Indian Affairs*, vol. 1, 98. War Department expenditures for the year totaled over $200,000 exclusive of the expedition.

20. Jacobs, *U. S. Army*, 52-53. A second, smaller operation was conducted by Major John F. Hamtramck prior to Harmar's main expedition. Hamtramck's operation ended in dismal failure when his force was unable to make contact with any of the hostile Indians and returned prematurely to Fort Washington.

21. Knox to Harmar, August 24, 1790, *American State Papers, Indian Affairs*, vol. 1, 99.

22. Douglas Southall Freeman, *George Washington: A Biography*, vol. 6, (New York: Charles Scribner's Sons, 1954), 277.

23. Washington to Knox, November 4, 1790, John C. Fitzpatrick, ed., *The Writings of George Washington from the Original Manuscript Sources, 1745-1799*, George Washington Bicentennial ed., vol. 31 (Washington: Government Printing Office, 1938), 144; J. P. Boyd, ed., *The Papers of Thomas Jefferson*, vol. 17 (Princeton, New Jersey: Princeton University Press, 1983), 133.

24. Washington to Knox, November 19, 1790, Fitzpatrick, *Writings of Washington*, vol. 31, 156-157.

25. Ibid., vol. 31, 143; Freeman, *Washington*, vol. 6, 285.

26. "Second Annual Address to Congress," Fitzpatrick, *Writings of Washington*, vol. 31, 164-167.

27. William B. Skelton, "Social Roots of the American Military Profession: The Officer Corps of America's First Peacetime Army, 1784-1789," in *The Journal of Military History*, vol. 54, no. 4, October, 1990, 445.

28. Harmar to Knox, November 4, 1790, American State Papers, Indian Affairs, vol. 1, 104. Harmar's search-and-destroy raid against the Miami Indian village occurred in October. The estimates given for enemy dead on the raid are questionable, as a conflicting damage estimate is given in *American State Papers, Indian Affairs*, vol. 1, 20-30. The latter, while it also gives the estimate of 20,000 bushels of corn destroyed, lists the destruction of only 184 "cabins" and gives no mention of Indians killed.

29. *American State Papers, Indian Affairs*, vol. 1, 20-30; Jacobs, *U. S. Army*, 56-59.

30. Ibid. Jacobs adds in *The Beginning of the U. S. Army* that not only were the United States forces defeated, but no significant physical gains were made (in terms of the establishment of forts of the construction of serviceable roads) in return for the cost in lives and treasure.

31. Freeman, Washington, vol. 6, 288-289.

32. Knox to Harmar, January 31, 1791, cited in Jacobs, *U. S. Army*, 62n.

33. Washington to Knox, June 19, 1791, Fitzpatrick, Writings of Washington, vol. 31, 299.

34. American State Papers, *American State Papers: Documents, Legislative and Executive, 1789-1831, Class III, Military Affairs, 1789-1831*, vol. 1 (Washington: Gale and Seaton, 1832), 20-30. The report of the board of officers conducting the investigation was dated September 24, 1791. A copy of the findings was sent to St. Clair who, at the time, had his hands full with a situation as difficult as the one that had faced Harmar. On the qualifications of the investigating officers, see Jacobs, *U. S. Army*, 60-65.

35. Freeman, *Washington*, vol. 6, 60-65.

36. Knox to St. Clair, August 25, 1791, Knox Papers, Massachusetts Historical Society.

37. Knox to St. Clair, September 1, 1791, Knox Papers, Massachusetts Historical Society.

38. St. Clair to Knox, September 23, 1791, Knox Papers, Massachusetts Historical Society.

39. Wiley Sword, *President Washington's Indian War: The Struggle for the Old Northwest, 1790-1795* (Norman, Oklahoma: University of Oklahoma Press, 1985), 162-163.

40. Ibid., 164.

41. St. Clair to Knox, October 21, 1791, Knox Papers, Massachusetts Historical Society.

42. Freeman, *Washington*, vol. 6, 336-340; Leroy V. Eid, "American Indian Leadership: St. Clair's 1791 Defeat," *The Journal of Military History*, vol. 57, no. 1, January, 1993, 71. To place the magnitude of the disaster in perspective, Eid notes that St. Clair's losses during his three-hour defeat were three times greater than those suffered by George A. Custer's command at the Battle of the Little Bighorn in 1876 and greater than the combined American losses at the battles of Long Island and Camden, two of the bloodiest contests of the American Revolution. See also Emory Upton, *The Military Policy of the United States*, 4th ed. (Washington: Government Printing Office, 1917), 80. St. Clair's defeat in 1791, following on the heels of Harmar's defeat the year before, made life as an officer in the United States Army during this period rather hazardous. As William B. Skelton indicates in his study of the officer corps of the early American republic, a higher percentage of American officers became casualties in combat during the Indian wars in the Northwest (with 12.1% killed) than at any other time in United States history. The percentage of casualties was even higher than that among officers who were on active duty in 1860 and served through the American Civil War of 1861-1865 (of whom 8.0% were killed). See Skelton, "Social Roots of the American Military Profession: The Officer Corps of America's First Peacetime Army, 1784-1789," *The Journal of Military History*, vol. 3, no. 4, October, 1990, 447-448.

43. Hamilton to Knox, October 17, 1791, vol. 29, 149, Knox Papers, Massachusetts Historical Society; Syrett, *Hamilton Papers*, vol. 9, 401-402; "Minister for the President's Speech," October 24, 1791, Knox Papers, vol. 29, 161, Massachusetts Historical Society.

44. Freeman, *Washington*, vol. 6, 336-340. Word of St. Clair's defeat did not reach Philadelphia until December 8, 1791, with Washington officially notifying Congress on December 12, 1791.

45. Cullen, ed., *Papers of Jefferson*, vol. 23, 189n-190n. St. Clair remained the governor of the Northwest Territory for several years thereafter.

46. Jacobs, *U. S. Army*, 120.

47. "Notes from March 9, 1792, Cabinet Meeting," Cullen, *Jefferson Papers*, vol. 23, 240-243; Sparks, *Writings of Washington*, vol. 12, 506-512; Sword, *Washington's Indian War*, 205. The comments regarding the qualities of the prospective candidates include such remarks as "Morgan No head. Health gone. Speculator. Wilkinson. Brave, enterprising to excess, but many unapprovable [sic] points in his character. Lee. A better had and more resource than any of them. But no economy, and being a junior officer, we should lose benefit of good seniors who would not serve under him. Pinckney. Sensible.

Tactician. But immersed in business. Has refused other appointments and probably will refuse this or accept with reluctance."

48. Cullen, *Jefferson Papers*, vol. 1, 240-243; Syrett, *Hamilton Papers*, vol. 11, 363; Richard H. Kohn, *Eagle and Sword: The Federalists and the Creation of the Military Establishment in America, 1783-1802* (New York: The Free Press, 1975), 125-126.

49. Richard C. Knopf, ed., *Campaign Into the Wilderness: The Wayne-Knox-Pickering-McHenry Correspondence* (Columbus, Ohio: Anthony Wayne Parkway Board, Ohio State Museum, 1955, vol. 1, 4 and 7.

50. Syrett, *Hamilton Papers*, vol. 11, 372 and 377; Knox to Captain Peter Pond and William Steedman, January 9, 1792, and Knox to Major Alexander Trueman, April 3, 1792, *American State Papers, Indian Affairs*, vol. 1, 226-227. One of the first individuals contacted by Knox to renew negotiations with the northwestern tribes after St. Clair's defeat was Samuel Kirkland, a missionary who later founded Hamilton College. Knox contacted him on December 20, 1791, to ask him to meet with the Five Nations [of the Iroquois Confederacy].

51. Knox to Brant, February 25, 1792, and Knox to the "Senacas," January 7, 1792, and February 10, 1792, *American State Papers, Indian Affairs*, vol. 1, 225-228; Cullen, *Jefferson Papers*, vol. 23, 147 and 243; Washington to Knox, February 25, 1792, Fitzpatrick, *Writings of Washington*, vol. 31, 484-485; Kohn, *Eagle and Sword*, 143-146. It is suspected that Brant may have been the commander of the Indian forces that fought against St. Clair. See Larry V. Eid, "American Indian Leadership and the St. Clair's Defeat," *The Journal of Military History*, vol. 57, no. 1, January, 1993, 71-76, and also Warren W. Hassler, *With Shield and Sword* (Ames: Iowa State University Press, 1982), 55.

52. Syrett, *Hamilton Papers*, vol. 11, 448.

53. Cullen, *Jefferson Papers*, vol. 23, 243.

54. Knopf, *Campaign into the Wilderness*, vol. 1, 7, 15, and 17-18.

55. Ibid., vol. 1, 17-18.

56. Ibid., vol. 1, 17-18, 30, 46, 52, and 60.

57. Ibid., vol. 1, 46, 52, and 60.

58. Washington to Jefferson, J. Catanzariti, ed, *The Papers of Thomas Jefferson*, vol. 24 (Princeton, New Jersey: Princeton University Press, 1983), 316; Knopf, *Campaign into the Wilderness*, vol. 1, 54.

59. Knopf, *Campaign into the Wilderness*, vol. 1, 60.

60. Catanzariti, *Jefferson Papers*, vol. 25, 272.

61. Knopf, *Campaign into the Wilderness*, vol. 1, 75, and vol. 2, 5.

62. Catanzariti, *Jefferson Papers*, vol. 25, 118; Freeman, *Washington*, vol. 6, 377. After the treaty was signed, the Indian leaders journeyed to Philadelphia to discuss the agreement and their complaints with Knox and other United States officials. The leaders remained from December, 1792, to May, 1793. The treaty was referred to the Senate for approval on February 13, 1793, but was rejected in January, 1794, because it did not give

the United States the right of preemption of Wabash River and Illinois River land. See *American State Papers, Indian Affairs*, vol. 1, 319-329 and 338-340.

63. Catanzariti, *Jefferson Papers*, vol. 24, 719-721.

64. Freeman, *Washington*, vol. 6, 377.

65. Knopf, *Campaign into the Wilderness*, vol. 2, 5.

66. Ibid.

67. Ibid.

68. Catanzariti, *Jefferson Papers*, vol. 2, 5.

69. Ibid.

70. Ibid., vol. 25, 258-259 and 424-425.

71. The cabinet was also unanimously of the opinion that the Senate was not be consulted prior to the conclusion of any treaty, but was to be consulted afterwards for its approval, if necessary. Knox had been ill just prior to Washington's March 25, 1793, departure for his annual vacation to Mount Vernon and had been unable to attend a cabinet meeting with the president to discuss the Indian situation. On Knox's recovery, he, Hamilton, and Jefferson met on April 2, 1793, and the three sent a report on their conclusion to Washington.

72. Knopf, *Campaign into the Wilderness*, vol. 2, 42 and 61.

73. *American Military History* (Washington: United States Army Center of Military History, 1989), 113.

74. Addendum to Knox to Wayne at Fort Washington, April 20, 1793, Guild Collection, Massachusetts Historical Society.

75. Knopf, *Campaign into the Wilderness*, vol. 2, 127.

76. Ibid.

77. Fitzpatrick, *Writings of Washington*, vol. 33, 313.

78. Washington to Knox, April 4, 1794, April 5, 1794, and April 9, 1794, Fitzpatrick, *Writings of Washington*, vol. 33, 313-314 and 321.

79. American Military History, 113.

80. Harold L. Nelson, "Military Roads for War and Peace, 1791-1836," *Military Affairs*, vol. XIX, no. 1, Spring, 1955, 1; A. B. Hulbert, *Historic Highways of America* (Cleveland: n.p., 1904), vol. 7, 200 and 217-218. According to Nelson, "the record of no pioneer army in America equals the marching records of Wayne (whom the Indians named 'The Whirlwind' because of his marching speed) and his legion."

81. Washington to Knox, April 4, 1794, Fitzpatrick, *Writings of Washington*, vol. 33, 313-314; *American Military History*, 113.

82. Wayne to Knox, August 14, 1794, *American State Papers, Indian Affairs*, vol. 1, 490, and Helen Carr, *Inventing the American Primitive: Politics, Gender, and Representation of Native American Literary Traditions, 1789-1936* (New York: NYU Press, 1996), 48.

83. Carr, *Inventing the American Primitive*, 46-50.

84. *American Military History*, 113.

85. Wayne to Knox, August 28, 1794, *American State Papers, Indian Affairs*, vol. 1, 490; Carr, *Inventing the American Primitive*, 48.

86. *American Military History*, 113.

87. Ibid ; Robert M. Taylor, Jr., ed., *The Northwest Ordinance, 1787: A Bicentennial Handbook* (Indianapolis: Indiana Historical Society, 1987), xix. Knox had similar military success on the southern frontier late in 1793, when John Sevier led a force of citizen soldiers from what was then the Tennessee district of North Carolina to a smashing victory over the Creeks and Chickamauga band Cherokees at the September 13, 1794, Battle of Nickojack,Tennessee. See John K. Mahon, *The American Militia: Decade of Decision, 1789-1800*, University of Florida Monographs, Social Sciences, no. 6, Spring, 1960 (Gainesville, Florida: University of Florida Press, 1960), 25.

88. Drake, ed., "Life . . . of . . . Knox" from *Society of the Cincinnati*, 189.

89. George Dewey Harmon, Sixty Years of Indian Affairs: Political, Economic and Diplomatic, 1789-1850 (Chapel Hill, North Carolina: The University of North Carolina Press, 1941), 36-38. There were a few exceptions to granting all land north of the Mississippi River and west of the Great Lakes to the Indians. Some 150,000 acres on the north side of the Falls of the Ohio River (across the river from Louisville, Kentucky), the post of Vincennes on the Wabash River, Fort Massac (in modern Illinois), and lands already in the possession of the French-descent and other white settlers were to remain the property of the United States and its citizens.

90. Stanley Elkins and Eric McKitrick, *The Age of Federalism* (New York: Oxford University Press, 1993), 436.

THE BATTLE OF
FALLEN TIMBERS

An Historical Perspective*

G. Michael Pratt

T wo hundred years ago the United States, a confederation of Indian tribes, and Great Britain all sought control of the land known as the Northwest Territory, a vast area north of the Ohio and east of the Mississippi rivers. For the young United States, the control of this area was vital to its survival. The addition of the Northwest Territory would permit the U.S. to grow beyond its original thirteen colonies. Monies gained through the sale of this land would pay the Revolutionary War debts that threatened to bankrupt the national government. For the United States, there was also an issue of military credibility. During the previous four years, the U.S. army had been severely beaten twice by the Indian tribes of the Ohio River watershed, and the army was ridiculed at home and abroad. In 1794, its newly reorganized army prepared to face the Ohio tribes for the last time. If the campaign ended in defeat, the U.S. would reconsider proposals for an Indian Buffer State in the lands north of the Ohio River.

For Great Britain, the loss of the Northwest Territory meant a loss of fur trade profits and a further reduction of her empire. The English had left their Indian allies out in the cold by the treaty that ended the American Revolution

---

* Editor's Note: Dr. Pratt delivered the keynote address for the bicentennial commemoration of the Battle of Fallen Timbers in August 1994. The ceremony took place at the Fallen Timbers State Memorial, along the banks of the Maumee River. This article is adapted from that speech. An interview with Dr. Pratt follows this article.

and secretly feared that angry Indians might turn on the Canadian frontier. Great Britain voiced support for continued war and hoped to regain control of the Northwest Territory following an Indian victory. In the spring of 1794, the British-built Fort Miamis in a show of strength and solidarity with their Indian allies, but no one knew if these British actions were more than just a show.

For the Indian peoples of the area, there was only one issue. They faced the loss of their lands and their lives in the continuation of a long and bloody war with the frontier settlers. It was a war that had been fought almost constantly for fifty years and by three generations. It was a war fueled by hatred and intolerance of cultural and racial differences. It was a war in which no quarter was expected or given by either side.

Because the issues were vital to all concerned, the outcome was destined to be significant. Fallen Timbers was not an event that burst on the scene suddenly, leaving an indelible memory. It was not like the modern-day explosion of the space shuttle *Challenger*. Rather, a significant outcome was anticipated, but none could be certain of what that outcome would be. Fallen Timbers was more like the Apollo moon landing. Many of the participants realized they would be a part of history and therefore recorded the events leading to the battle and its aftermath. These accounts tell us of the course of the Battle of Fallen Timbers.

About 8:00 am. the 150 mounted Kentucky volunteers that were leading Gen. Anthony Wayne's army (or legion) downstream bumped into the center of an ambush line of about 1,100 Indian warriors and 100 British volunteers. These warriors included members of the Shawnee, Miami, Wyandot and other allied tribes, under chiefs like Blue Jacket and Little Turtle. Overwhelmed by a heavy fire, the Kentuckians fled towards the main army some 500 yards in their rear. They were pursued by 300-400 warriors who, anticipating a quick victory, gave up their prepared positions and rushed forward. A front guard of army regulars was also overwhelmed, but the Indian attack was stopped when it encountered a stiff skirmish line of several hundred light infantry and riflemen that were covering the deployment of the main body of the Legion infantry.

Here, in a jumble of trees felled by a tornado, the warriors and the Legion skirmishers traded gunfire for fifteen to twenty minutes while the main army finished deploying its line of battle and then opened fire with its light cannon. Once in position, the Legion battle line charged into the fallen timber, supported by its dragoons and some militia. The 400 or so warriors who had become thinly dispersed across a broad front were overwhelmed by over 1,000 infantry and cavalry. In this instant the tide of battle was reversed. Driven back to their

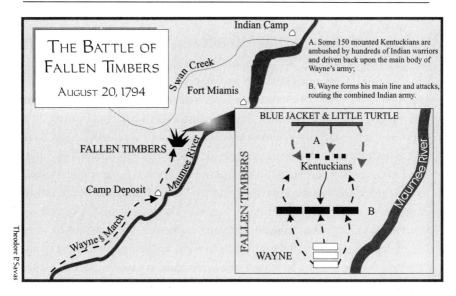

THE BATTLE OF FALLEN TIMBERS

AUGUST 20, 1794

Indian Camp

Swan Creek

Fort Miamis

A. Some 150 mounted Kentuckians are ambushed by hundreds of Indian warriors and driven back upon the main body of Wayne's army;

B. Wayne forms his main line and attacks, routing the combined Indian army.

FALLEN TIMBERS

Camp Deposit

Maumee River

Wayne's March

BLUE JACKET & LITTLE TURTLE

A

Kentuckians

B

WAYNE

FALLEN TIMBERS

Maumee River

Theodore P. Savas

original position, the retreating warriors created disorganization and panic among the Indians who had remained behind.

Only on the extreme right of the battlefield, out near present-day Monclova Road, was there an organized attempt to defeat the Legion's charge. There, 100 Wyandots led by Chief Tarhe, 100 British militia, and some Odawas retreated slowly and fired rapidly into the left side of the advancing army. Lieutenant Henry Towles and Little Otter, an Odawa Chief, met their deaths during this portion of the fight. Outnumbered and driven from the battlefield, the warriors fled downstream past Fort Miamis, whose silent cannon loudly proclaimed that the British had once again failed their Indian allies. The battle left everyone wondering where the events of the day would lead.

Fallen Timbers gained for the United States what is today Ohio, Indiana, Illinois, Wisconsin and Michigan. Today, the United States stretches across an entire continent and is the richest and most powerful nation in the world. Much of the size, population and wealth of our country developed from the resources and industrial might of the territory that was won two centuries ago. For two hundred years, Canada has been overshadowed by that same population and industrial power that developed in areas that were once under the control of British Canada. For two hundred years, the descendants of the warriors who fought there have been viewed as a beaten and captive people by the majority of later Americans. They have been moved from reservation to reservation in response to the desires of their conquerors. Only recently have the voices of these original Americans again been heard in their homeland. Viewed from the perspective of history, the Fallen Timbers Campaign was a turning point in the development of not only the United States, but all of North America.

Because of the significance of its outcome, the Battle of Fallen Timbers passed into the realm of myth and legend. Today the events loom larger than life. For the United States Army, the engagement was something from the final scene of the movie *Rocky*—almost knocked out twice but refusing to yield. Or, as the legend goes, the Army rose from the mat and marched into glory under Mad Anthony Wayne. But in reality, General Wayne was ill, he was ambushed, and his orders went unheeded. Captain Robert Mis Campbell, just before he was killed, said of the battle, "all is confusion." The Indians of the legend are described as savages blocking the course of civilization; but in reality, the dead they left on the Fallen Timbers battlefield were scalped and mutilated by the "civilized" Americans. The British role in the battle is usually ignored, but the British participants were all volunteers. They were some of the last to retreat and their unit suffered a greater percentage of dead than either Wayne's Legion or the Indian Confederacy. The final irony of the legend of Fallen Timbers surrounds Chief Turkeyfoot. The Indian leader is said to be the only individual from either side to have his own monument, Turkeyfoot Rock. However, the story of Turkeyfoot exhorting his warriors from the rock appears to be a total fiction.

Viewed from the perspective of history, the Battle of Fallen Timbers, like all other battles, was a messy and desperate affair. Like all other battles, it was a gamble among political leaders that was wagered with human lives. For those whose lives were bet, this battle, like all battles, had personal significance. On August 20, 1794, Sgt. Eli Edmonson of the 4th Sub-Legion laid his life on the line. Edmonson fought for nearly two hours until he was struck down by a bullet near the end of the battle. Too badly wounded to move, he lay suffering alone on the field for two days and two nights. During that time, General Wayne did not issue any orders to search for the wounded or bury the dead. On August 22, Eli Edmonson died just minutes before his body was found by the first burial detail. Like all of the individual Indian warriors and all of the British militia who were killed there—and like at least thirteen of his fellow Legionnaries—Sergeant Eli Edmonson was buried in an unmarked grave, and his name appears on no monument.

INTERVIEW

A Conversation With Archaeologist G. Michael Pratt

Interviewed by Michael A. Hughes

Dr. G. Michael Pratt discovered the "lost" (i.e., mislocated) battlefield of Fallen Timbers [1794] and is one of the handful of authorities who specialize in military historical archaeology. He has worked at some of the most important Civil War and Indian wars sites in the United States. Dr. Pratt completed his Bachelor's degree in anthropology at Miami University and his Master's and Doctorate at Case Western Reserve University. He has been active for over twenty years in advising his native state of Ohio on historic preservation.

Currently, Dr. Pratt is professor of anthropology and Director of Archaeology at Heidelberg College in Miami, Ohio. Dr. Pratt's address, "The Battle of Fallen Timbers: An Historical Perspective," is one of the features in this issue of *JIW*. According to Dr. Pratt, the American victory over the Shawnee, Ottawa, and other Indian nations defending their land at Fallen Timbers was decisive in the growth of the United States.

* * *

MAH: You are best known for finding the "lost" site of the battle of Fallen Timbers [1794]. How did you go about finding it, and how did you feel when you realized that you had located the actual site of that important engagement?

GMP: We had done considerable historical research beforehand and had read as many British, American, and Indian accounts as I could find. We tried to use to these accounts to determine the troop positions and felt I knew where they were even before we began the archaeological work. I was very confident in predicting the locations, but everyone was certain that the battlefield was elsewhere. We found the first bullet within a half hour and the first [Anthony] Wayne button within an hour. I felt not so much a sense of discovery as of relief—"yes, I'm right; nobody's going to think I'm a fool now!" There was no excuse for so many artifacts being where we surveyed unless it was the battlefield.

Finding it so quickly also allowed us the opportunity to examine more of the battlefield, since we did not have to waste substantial time trying to locate it first.

MAH: How did you become involved in military historical archaeology?

GMP: I was always interested in Ohio history and military history, and also in historical archaeology. Ohio is big on prehistoric archaeology, though. What turned me towards the subject was work on Fort Miamis, a 1790s British fort connected with the Battle of Fallen Timbers and the Dudley Massacre. That work made me aware of how many significant historical areas there were in northwest Ohio. That led to Fallen Timbers and other projects.

MAH: There are so many locations in your area suitable for further investigation. . .

GMP: We conducted several field studies to determine which areas to look at in northern Ohio and soon realized we had opportunities to work at several sites. The growing recognition of the importance and potential of these areas suggested the need for a field program in history and archaeology. Heidelberg College agreed and responded by creating its Center for Historical and Military Archaeology. Since its creation, opportunities to dig have come up at several locations. We're positioned to go to these thanks to the background research we performed. The "Old Northwest," including lower Michigan and Ohio, was the location of both the western theater of the War of 1812 and several important Indian conflicts. A number of sites relating to these events are clustered closely and are an easy drive from the college. However, our most recent survey site,

Buffington Island battlefield [Civil War, 1863], is a five-hour drive, so that we had to get additional funding to work there. We've also been doing preliminary testing at the location of Fort Adams, one of the first fortifications built in Anthony Wayne's 1794 campaign against the northwestern Indians and a fort that was architecturally unique. It's one of the reasons we're looking for a way to develop a more sustained archaeological program. There is great local interest in the fort, but the location is one hundred miles from us.

MAH: Did anything else motivate you to work in this field?

GMP: I was inspired to work in military historical archaeology by my longtime friend and colleague Dave Bush, who was working out the University of Pittsburgh. He excavated the site of the Johnson Island [Ohio] Civil War prison camp. [For an update on Bush's work at Johnson's Island, see the July/August 1999 issue of *Archaeology* Magazine.] He now works for Heidelberg College as director of the Center and is doing an extensive survey covering prisoner life at the camp.

MAH: What other projects have you worked on recently?

GMP: We've done preliminary work on the site of the 1782 Battle of Sandusky, between Tiffin and Upper Sandusky, Ohio. That's where Col. William Crawford was captured by Delaware and Shawnee Indians before being burned at the stake, an event recorded by several witnesses. The battle was part of a major series of events in the American Revolution in the West. We did a metal detector survey there in awful weather.

MAH: I also recall you worked in the past year or two at the site of the War of 1812 Battle of Frenchtown or River Raisin. [An American force organized to recapture Detroit, which had been surrendered to the British in 1812, was attacked in its encampment at Frenchtown by the British garrison of Detroit and its Indian allies on January 22, 1813.] Are the results of that excavation published?

GMP: We did that survey for Midwest Environmental consultants. The report is not published but has been given to the city of Monroe, Michigan, the site of Frenchtown.

MAH: Can you elaborate a bit on that action for us?

GMP: During the War of 1812, the town of Frenchtown built a stockade or puncheon fence around the back of the town. A British detachment encamped there after the British captured Detroit in 1812. When the Americans retook Frenchtown the next year, Kentucky militiamen used the stockade to fortify their position. When the American right wing was crushed by the British and Indians in a counterattack on January 22, 1813, the left wing, at the stockade, was not defeated but was surrendered by their commander, James Winchester. The massacre of the surrendered American wounded by the Indians following the battle also took place at the stockade.

MAH: What remains of the site?

GMP: The major elements of the site of Frenchtown and the battlefield were later destroyed in a major way by the construction of two paper mills. However, we did find the left portion of the stockade. I think that there are other traces of the stockade between industrial plants, roads, and so on in Monroe. We may also be able to find more of the north-south wall of the stockade. It would also be nice to find out the site of the east-west wall. We're planning additional fieldwork.

MAH: Many of our readers are interested in the American Civil War as well as the Indian Wars. You're currently involved in an exploration of the July 19, 1863 Buffington Island, Ohio, battlefield, where Confederate cavalryman John Hunt Morgan was cut off from escape to Kentucky while being pursued on his disastrous 1863 raid north into Ohio. As I recall, the project is being supported by the American Battlefield Protection Program (ABPP) of the National Park Service. What does the current exploration involve?

GMP: The ABPP is helping finance the project. The battlefield is on the west bank of the Ohio River. We are conducting a survey of part of the Buffington Island battlefield that is in privately owned areas, not those in the area of a large gravel pit; we're working north and south of the pit. The project was decided on after the U.S. Army Corps of Engineers had already granted a permit allowing the gravel digging and the litigation by historic preservationists that resulted. Our project avoids that controversy. The gravel works have destroyed part of the battlefield but we will be surveying unaffected areas to tie down what events happened where. To some degree we need the results from Buffington to demonstrate the value of the surviving battlefield area as an archaeological site. An argument has been made against doing work at Buffington on the grounds that everything was destroyed in the dump zone.

Our work will be similar to that carried out at the Fallen Timbers battlefield, and during the metal detector survey conducted at the Little Bighorn battlefield [1876] under Richard Fox and Douglas Scott. We worked a little over two weeks at Fallen Timbers. At Buffington Island we'll have two weeks, but we will be working over a much larger area.

MAH: What is the value of archaeological evidence as opposed to documentary evidence? What is unique about the discoveries made through archaeological research?

GMP: That's a good question. Take Buffington Island as an example. Basil Duke, Morgan's subordinate, believed the Confederates kept up a sustained firefight at Buffington Island. He later claimed that the Confederates in the rear had formed several successive lines, each time forcing the Union cavalry to dismount. He felt that this had helped hold the line while Morgan and the rest escaped northward through the Ohio River bottoms. The Union troops, though, claimed there were only a few moments of resistance before their heroic advance. Archaeological evidence will support one side or the other by the concentration of bullets—either no lines or sustained skirmish lines will be shown by mapping.

MAH: So one value of archaeological work is that it can confirm or deny opposing records?

GMP: Yes. The Battle of Frenchtown is another example. It's natural to record events from one's own perspective. The British said they found a formidable stockade on the American left, with the Kentucky militia there well fortified. The militia said that the stockade was flimsy and that only their fortitude and sharp marksmanship held the British in check. Archaeology demonstrated the stockade was indeed not very substantial.

MAH: Can you provide us another case?

GMP: The recent survey by Scott and Fox at the Little Bighorn battlefield provides another good illustration of how archaeology helps settle historical questions. There has been a big dispute as to what happened there. Was there a heroic defense by George Custer's troops, or were they driven off by the Indians? The clumping of cartridges can now be used to trace the collapse of Custer's skirmish lines and the evidence of troops not firing is a sign of panic. The survey there had a lot to say about how Custer was defeated.

When doing surveys like those at Little Bighorn and Fallen Timbers, the first step is to recover evidence and the second is to get an overall idea that will support the reconstructed troop positions. But, later, the evidence can be used to develop information about the emotional and physical conditions of troops and of how they react under the stress of combat. There are several different layers of information available through archaeology that are not readily available in the historical record.

MAH: You're a former chairman of the Ohio Historic Preservation Advisory Board. Why do you think it is important to preserve battlefields?

GMP: As an archaeologist, I've always felt a special relationship with the archaeological sites. Being able to touch or see an object gives a direct connection with the historical past. Being able to stand on a site, to visualize what happened there, provides a connection to history that watching a movie or television program or reading a book cannot give you. The physical battlefield furnishes a connection—physical, emotional, and intellectual—with history. The land helps us understand that the historical past is a part of us.

My mentor, Dr. Larry Nelson, the director of Fort Meigs park, says that history is to a country what memory is for a person. We use it to make decisions now or to project alternatives into the future. A country's lack of knowledge of its history leads to a lack of national direction. Perhaps current events demonstrate such a deficiency of direction, or a lack of foresight due to a lack of knowledge of the past. We will lose our ability to stick to an informed course if we lose our connection to the past.

You can't get this sense of connection through other attempts. Living history does well at creating this sense among professionals or experienced researchers, and it may also come to them through literature, but this is not true for the general public. The possibility of making a connection to history by visiting a site is important to the public as a whole, even if the public doesn't always realize it.

MAH: Thank you for taking time to speak with me today for JIW. You've certainly had some interesting experiences and I think our readers will feel the same way.

Jerry L. Russell, Founder and National Chairman

THE STUDY OF THE MILITARY HISTORY of the early settlement of North America, and the continuing conflicts between Indian and Indian, Indian and settler, Indian and soldier, has long been a subject that has fascinated succeeding generations of Americans.

In the early decades of this century, an organization known as **The Order of Indian Wars of the United States**, made up primarily of retired military men, actual veterans of the Indian Wars, devoted its attention to the study of the U.S. military establishment's role in the development and settlement of this country's westward-moving frontier. That organization became an affiliate of the American Military Institute in 1947, and is once again active for descendants.

IN 1979, WE FOUNDED A **NEW** ORGANIZATION, inspired by that other group--a "spiritual descendant," if you will--but having no connection, official or otherwise with the predecessor. Our purpose, however, is similar--but broader: the in-depth study and dissemination of information on America's frontier conflicts. We are as interested in the "Indian side" as in the "Army/settlers side," although this organization, and its Assemblies, are not to be a forum for political or sociological crusades or guilt trips---our interest is in **military history**.

An additional purpose, equally important, we believe, is our concern for the historic preservation of those important sites associated with the history of the Indian Wars in America. Citizens' groups **must** become more involved in historic preservation, or much of our past will be irretrievably lost, in the name of 'progress'. Historic military sites are an important part of our national heritage, and the preservation/protection of these sites will be a major, continuing, concern of our organization--hence our motto: WE WHO STUDY MUST ALSO STRIVE TO SAVE! HERITAGEPAC is the national lobbying organization established in 1989 to work for preservation of battlesites. Our main publication is the *OIW Communique*.
DUES ARE $20 A YEAR.

Our 21st Annual National Assembly, Focusing on the 125th Anniversary of The Red River War, will be held September 16-18, 1999, in Amarillo, Texas, With Tours Led By Neil C. Mangum, Superintendent, Little Bighorn Battlefield, to Adobe Walls, Palo Duro Canyon & The Washita Battlefield, Plus 12 Speakers.
WRITE FOR INFORMATION.
Order of the Indian Wars
P. O. Box 7401, Little Rock AR 72217
501-225-3996   > indianwars@aristotle.net <

CAPTAIN ALBERT BARNITZ
AND THE BATTLE OF THE WASHITA
New Documents, New Insights

S. Matthew Despain

O ver the last twelve years, archeologists have discovered physical evidence that challenges conventional interpretations of the major Indian wars engagements at the Washita and Little Bighorn. [Ed. Note: See "Archaeological Evidence: The Attack on Black Kettle's Village on the Washita River," *Journal of the Indian Wars*, Vol. 1, No. 1]. On occasion, researchers find documentary evidence that has a similar impact on Indian wars history. The author was fortunate enough to be one of those researchers.

In my case, the "find" was additional material by and about Capt. Albert Barnitz, discovered in the Walter Mason Camp Collection and other collections at Brigham Young University. The documents provide important new information on the 1868 Battle of the Washita. Surprisingly, the materials had not been located and utilized by either Stan Hoig or Robert Utley, two leading authorities on that battle.

Hoig's *The Battle of the Washita* is the most popular work on the battle or massacre on the Washita River, as reflected in its continued reprintings. The work is a narrative history that is well written but does not closely examine the fight's intricacies or controverted points. For some reason, the diaries and letters of Barnitz, one of George A. Custer's officers at Washita, were not used in Hoig's research. For readers wanting detailed and often differing information on Barnitz and the Washita, Robert Utley's *Life in Custer's Cavalry: Diaries and Letters of Albert and Jennie Barnitz, 1867-1868* is essential. However, the Brigham Young University material on Bartnitz was not discovered until after the publication of Utley's work.

The documents found in the Camp Collection are valuable for several reasons. First, they confirm many of Utley's conclusions about the Battle of the Washita and fill in some of the missing parts in Utley's work that Utley himself noted were absent. Second, Barnitz's writings remind us that battles are, after all, fought by individuals, whose observations of events are digested from their narrow and personal perspective. This article is about the experience of one individual, Capt. Albert Barnitz, whose personal account of the Battle of the Washita is priceless.[1]

* * *

The events and issues leading to the 1868 winter campaigns and the Washita fight of November 27, 1868, have been recounted well elsewhere and will not be reexamined here. [Ed. Note: See "Custer at the Washita and Little Bighorn," *Journal of the Indian Wars*, Vol. One, No. 1].

Amid heavy snow the Seventh Cavalry pushed south out of the winter campaign base camp at Fort Supply on November 23, 1868. By forced march the cavalry made the Antelope Hills two days later. The next morning Custer divided his command into two groups. The first group, which consisted of Company M under First Lt. Owen Hale, Company H under Frederick Benteen, and Company G under Captain Barnitz, all under Maj. Joel Elliott's command, was to proceed up the north side of the Canadian River to find Indians. The remaining group, meanwhile, encamped and awaited news from Elliott.[2]

After ten miles Elliott's scouts found what they were seeking, a recent trail. Elliott's Osage Scouts identified it as a war party trail since there were no dog tracks.[3] News was sent back to Custer, and by 9:00 a.m. Custer's and Elliott's forces were reunited. With only an hour's rest, the entire command was on the trail again until about 2:00 or 3:00 a.m. in the morning, when the Osage scouts discovered what turned out to be Black Kettle's Cheyenne camp on the Washita River.[4]

The Seventh Cavalry waited as Custer and his officers crept to the crest of the ridge that separated the soldiers from the Cheyenne village. Custer was satisfied that the river bottom actually contained a village when he heard "the distant cry of an infant" and a "tinkling of a little bell."[5]

Custer's battle plan divided the regiment into four battalions in order to encircle the village and attack it at dawn. The first battalion, under Major Elliott, was comprised of Companies M and H and Captain Barnitz's Company G.[6]

Elliott's force was to take up a position downriver on the northeastern end of the village along the wooded river bottoms. En route, the column crossed several trails indicating the way to the village. Fearing the command's noise might cost the element of surprise, Elliott moved his force behind a set of large bluffs further downstream. There, Elliott halted his troops while he and Barnitz ascended a "very steep conical hill" later known as Sugar Loaf Butte.[7] The two reached the crest where, in order to avoid silhouetting themselves against the skyline, they kept low next to the crusted snow. Peering down through the darkness of the timber-choked river bottom was, as Barnitz put it ". . . like looking down into a well."[8] Barnitz could not see anything, although the yelping of several Indian dogs confirmed the village's position.[9]

Satisfied, Elliott and Barnitz climbed down to the waiting command. On reaching the foot of the bluff, however, the two were beset by a half-dozen bawling fox hounds which had wandered from the cavalry pack train and followed the regiment's trail. These dogs appear to have been Custer's own prized Scottish fox hounds, which he brought along on the campaign. Fearful the animals would foil the surprise attack, Elliott ordered his men to kill the dogs by strangulation or with their knives. This little-known episode is not found in Hoig's *The Battle of the Washita*. Thus, Barnitz's testimony reveals a previously little-known incident that could have jeopardized the outcome of the campaign.[10]

Soon after silencing the hounds, Elliott's command began descending with some difficulty a deep and narrow canyon leading toward the village. The troopers made their way out through another dangerously steep side ravine in single file, holding onto their horses' manes so as not to fall off. The cavalrymen continued on to the Washita River three-quarters of a mile downstream from the village.[11]

With dawn approaching, the three companies moved upriver to be in position east of the village before the band struck the tune "Garry Owen," the signal to attack. Barnitz and Company G dismounted and crossed the icy Washita to form the left flank of Elliott's command. This movement meant that Barnitz's Company G would fight on the south side of the river, with the company's right flank against the waterway. Most of G Troop remained on foot after the river crossing, but ten remounted men were placed on the far left to stop any Indians attempting to escape between Barnitz's position and Capt. William Thompson's F Troop, which was positioned on the south side of the village.[12]

According to Barnitz's account, the placement of companies under Elliott's command could not be what Hoig maintains in *The Battle of the Washita*. Hoig has Elliott's entire command on the north side of the river, with Barnitz's company covering Elliott's right flank. This was not the case, according to Barnitz, who clearly stated that G Troop crossed to the south bank of the Washita to hold Elliott's left flank.[13] Barnitz's account of the initial deployment of G Troop is further supported by the fact that he was wounded well south of the river.[14]

Moving west toward the village, Barnitz's troop passed a large Indian pony herd downstream from the village. The fact that these soldiers passed the herd substantiates Barnitz's recollection that Company G established the southeastern line of Elliott's flank, since the pony herds were below the village along the river, where Custer later exterminated them.[15]

With daylight approaching that bitter cold morning, Barnitz's men advanced as swiftly as possible upriver to the village and came across a smaller pony herd. Unseen by the troopers was an Indian wrapped in a blanket who, when the troopers moved close to the herd, sprang up and raced toward the village with others running behind him. Some of the men raised their carbines, but Barnitz ordered them to hold their fire so as not to alarm the village until the last possible moment. The fact that these Indians ran toward the village without firing any warning shots may indicate they were boys (who rarely carried guns) tending the herds.[16] Barnitz's men moved ahead more rapidly before news of their presence reached the village. As the soldiers reached a shallow ravine at the wooded edge of the village, a shot rang out, the band struck "Garry Owen," and the fight was on.

Just how the Cheyenne discovered the troopers is another issue upon which the Barnitz papers shed some light. In Hoig's account, a young Indian who had come out to investigate the barking of a dog fired a warning shot after seeing a soldier moving close to the camp. This may be partially true, but the discovery of Barnitz's men by the youth tending the ponies and the subsequent flight of both Indians and soldiers toward the village was what alerted the village to the Seventh Cavalry's presence. According to Barnitz, by the time the shot was fired from the village, his troops were already at its edge, meaning the Indian youth had already reached the encampment and sounded the alarm. In all probability, the excitement generated by the running boys provoked the dogs and roused the unnamed Indian, who either saw the soldiers approaching or was told of their presence by the frightened youngsters.[17]

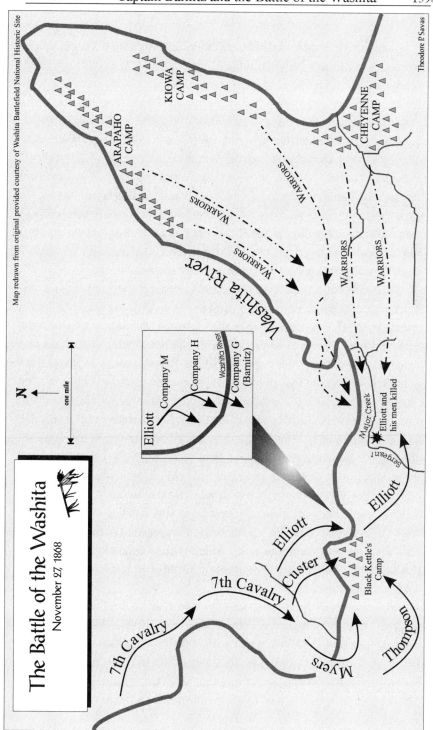

The Battle of the Washita
November 27, 1868

Map redrawn from original provided courtesy of Washita Battlefield National Historic Site

Theodore P. Savas

N

one mile

Washita River

KIOWA CAMP

ARAPAHO CAMP

CHEYENNE CAMP

WARRIORS

WARRIORS

WARRIORS

WARRIORS

WARRIORS

WARRIORS

Elliott
Company M
Company H
Washita River
Company G (Barnitz)

Major Creek

Elliott and his men killed

Sergeant

Elliott

Elliott

Custer

7th Cavalry

7th Cavalry

7th Cavalry

Myers

Thompson

Black Kettle's Camp

As fighting commenced that frozen morning, Major Elliott's forces moved in from the northeast with his still-dismounted Company G advancing through the eastern end of the encampment in a skirmish line. The mounted charge by the rest of Custer's command (excepting the band and sharpshooters) drove many of the Indians eastward downstream toward Elliott's G Troop. This push, along with the fact that many of the Cheyenne were fleeing toward other villages downstream, placed a good portion of the escaping Indians in G Troop's line of fire.[18] As the Cheyenne made a run for it through the timbered river bottom, Barnitz's men, as he put it, "just lit into them and piled them up."[19] Some Indians dug in behind logs and stumps, returning fire for a time, but to no avail.[20] There, in the bottomlands below the village, was where the heaviest fighting continued to occur. The fact that nearly one-third of all the battle's wounded soldiers were from G Troop bears out that assessment.[21]

As the fighting continued, Barnitz discovered a group of women and children fleeing south and moved to force them back toward Thompson's command, which was attacking from the southwest. Turning back to the fight, Barnitz glimpsed yet another group fleeing southeast, although this one was composed of warriors. Riding up from behind, Barnitz shot down two of them and watched as a third took aim at him. The cavalryman turned his horse and charged. He galloped past the Indian, turned and charged again, and then a third time. Both he and the warrior were holding their fire for a clean shot. Suddenly, the warrior threw up a buffalo robe to frighten Barnitz's horse and throw his aim off. Both fired simultaneously. A ball from a Lancaster rifle entered Barnitz's left abdomen and exited three and a half inches left of his spine, fracturing two ribs in the process.[22] Barnitz, who somehow remained mounted, gazed through the smoke of both guns and saw the warrior still standing. The Cheyenne, however, had dropped the butt of his gun to the ground and with his left hand was using the weapon for support, while his right hand clutched the chest wound Barnitz had inflicted. Barnitz drew his revolver and killed the warrior with a second shot.[23]

Hoig mistakenly notes in his work that the Indian Barnitz fought was called Magpie, who later in life recounted being charged by a man similar in description to Barnitz.[24] This cannot be the case for four reasons. First, Barnitz killed the warrior he faced, whereas Magpie survived. Second, in Charles Brill's interview of Magpie, the warrior claimed he carried with him his father's cap and ball revolver; Barnitz, however, unequivocally states the warrior was armed with a Lancaster muzzleloader rifle. Third, Magpie was only wounded in his calf, while Barnitz inflicted two serious wounds, one deadly, on the warrior he faced. Fourth, Magpie and his companions took the weapons and the horse from the soldier they shot; Barnitz lost neither. Instead, the wounded cavalryman turned his mount and rode toward the village.[25]

The documents in the Camp Collection corroborate earlier accounts by Barnitz in Utley's work and attest to Barnitz's faculties of recollection. The remainder of this article will describe in greater detail than had previously been available what became of Barnitz after he was wounded.

In pain and unable to utter a sound, Barnitz rode slowly toward the village for a few hundred yards, down a slightly descending plain. Because of the fighting, the deep snow, and possibly the scent of blood, Barnitz's horse "was on tiptoes, so to speak, snorting and prancing."[26] Barnitz later recalled that a number of stray shots from the fight passed overhead and he heard yelling and shooting from the same direction. As the captain continued toward the village, he sensed death drawing near. Barnitz came upon a ring of large boulders, into which he rode.[27] After dismounting, he took the horse's reins, passed his arms through them, placed his hands in his overcoat, and laid down to die. He could only hope that if he died, his horse's presence would attract some of the troops so his body would not become food for the wolves.[28]

After a time, however, the horse became restless. Snorting and stomping its feet, it tried climbing out of the ring of stones, dragging Barnitz from one side to the other across the rocks and snow. Luckily for the wounded captain, in a matter of minutes two men from his own company discovered him. The joyousness Barnitz felt as a result of the reunion was cut short when Indians from the lower villages were seen moving upstream toward the captured village. One of the troopers turned to Barnitz and said, "Captain, the Indians are charging down upon us, what shall we do?" At that moment, some of Captain Thompson's troopers arrived. The men unsaddled their horses, turned them loose, and were instructed to "throw their saddles into the enclosure and get in and fight." The Indians, however, took to the ridges above the village and no fighting took place.[29]

Barnitz and his small detachment remained behind the boulders until the fight in the valley was nearly decided. The wounded officer was placed on a buffalo robe and carried down the hill a few hundred yards to a secure area, where Doctors Henry Lippincott and William Renicke examined him. After seeing his wounds, both doctors agreed that Barnitz was mortally injured. The captain was taken down to the captured village, where everything possible was done to make him comfortable.

Later that day, Lieutenant Godfrey found his friend Barnitz in the village under a pile of buffalo robes and blankets. Godfrey told Barnitz about his condition, to which Barnitz exclaimed, "Oh Hell! They think because my extremities are cold I am going to die, but if I could get warm I'm sure I'll be alright. These blankets and robes are so heavy I can hardly breathe." Godfrey ordered a fire to be built for his friend and the weighty coverings removed.[30]

Of course, Barnitz's case was not terminal, at least immediately. He lived 44 years after the battle, but the wound forced his retirement from the Army within two years. He died July 18, 1912. An autopsy revealed that a growth which had formed around the old wound caused his death. A piece of his overcoat was also discovered in his body, driven there by the slug the Cheyenne fired.[31]

The precious years between the day an unnamed Cheyenne shot Barnitz and the day he eventually died of that wound gave him time to leave an invaluable set of papers, documents which contribute greatly to our understanding of the Battle of the Washita.

NOTES

1. The Walter Mason Camp Collection at Brigham Young University contains only part of the interviews and correspondences Camp conducted with members of the Seventh Cavalry around the turn of the century in his preparation to write a history of the Seventh. Unfortunately, the book was never completed. This is the same collection Kenneth Hammer used for his *Custer in '76* (Provo, Utah: Brigham Young University Press, 1976), a well known piece of Custerania. The other works referenced above and throughout this paper are Stan Hoig, *The Battle of the Washita* (Lincoln: University of Nebraska Press, 1979); and Robert M. Utley, *Life in Custer's Cavalry: Diaries and Letters of Albert and Jennie Barnitz, 1867-1868* (Lincoln: University of Nebraska Press, 1977).

2. Walter M. Camp Notes concerning the Battle of the Washita, TMS, Kenneth M. Hammer Collection, MSS 1473, Box 3 Folder 4, Archives and Manuscripts, Harold B. Lee Library, Brigham Young University, Provo; First Lieutenant Edward G. Mathey to Walter M. Camp, 18 May 1910, ALS, Walter Mason Camp Papers, MSS 57, Box 1 Folder 13, Archives and Manuscripts, Harold B. Lee Library, Brigham Young University, Provo; Brigadier General E.S. Godfrey, "Some Reminiscences, including

the Washita Battle, November 27, 1868," *The Cavalry Journal*, vol. 37 (October, 1928), pp. 7-8.

3. Utley, *Life in Custer's Cavalry*, p. 216. Customarily dogs accompanied hunting parties; however, their use during raiding was unknown since the dogs' actions could reveal a party's presence.

4. Godfrey, "Reminiscences," p. 8; Utley, *Life in Custer's Cavalry*, p. 216; Hoig, *The Battle of the Washita*, pp. 119-21.

5. Captain Francis M. Gibson, personal narrative of the Battle of the Washita, TD, Charles Kuhlamn Collection, MSS 1401, Box 3 Folder 8, Archives and Manuscripts, Harold B. Lee Library, Brigham Young University, Provo, p. 16; Utley, *Life in Custer's Cavalry*, p. 219.

6. Albert Barnitz to Walter M. Camp, January 12, 1910, ALS, Walter Camp Papers, MSS 57, Box 1 Folder 11. See also Utley, *Life in Custer's Cavalry*, p. 219.

7. Albert Barnitz to Walter M. Camp, January 12, 1910; Albert Barnitz to Walter M. Camp, 18 November 1910, ALS, Walter Camp Papers, MSS 51, Box 1 Folder 14. See also Utley, *Life in Custer's Cavalry*, p. 220.

8. Albert Barnitz to Walter M. Camp, November 18, 1910.

9. Ibid. Barnitz indicates that the barking of Indian dogs was distinguishable from that of coyotes because the dogs remained in the low ground of the village while the coyotes stayed on the elevated plains.

10. Ibid. See also Utley, *Life in Custer's Cavalry*, pp. 198, 220, 223.

11. Ibid.

12. Listing of officers of the Seventh Cavalry in November, 1868, Walter Mason Camp Papers, MSS 57, Box 1, Folder 12. See also Utley, *Life in Custer's Cavalry*, pp. 224-225.

13. Hoig, *The Battle of the Washita*, pp. 124, 128, and Battlefield map. Hoig's book places Elliott's entire detachment on the north side of the river. His map also indicates this, but then places Company G on the far right. See also Utley, *Life in Custer's Cavalry*, pp. 224-225.

14. Albert Barnitz, interviewed by Walter Mason Camp, May 7, 1910, TMs, Kenneth M. Hammer Collection, MSS 1473, Box 3 Folder 4.

15. Utley, *Life in Custer's Cavalry*, p. 221.

16. Ibid., p. 225; Godfrey, "Reminiscences," p. 9.

17. Hoig, *The Battle of the Washita*, p. 128; Albert Barnitz to Walter M. Camp, November 18, 1910, ALS, Walter Mason Camp Papers, MSS 57, Box 1, Folder 14; See also Utley, *Life in Custer's Cavalry*, p. 225.

18. Interview of Ben Clark by Walter M. Camp, October 22, 1910, TMS, Kenneth Hammer Collection, MSS 1473, Box 3, Folder 4.

19. Interview of Albert Barnitz by Walter M. Camp, May 7, 1910, TMS, Kenneth Hammer Collection, MSS 1473, Box 3, Folder 4; See also Utley, *Life in Custer's Cavalry*, p. 225.

20. Albert Barnitz to Walter M. Camp, November 29, 1910, ALS, Walter Mason Camp Papers, MSS 57, Box 1, Folder 14.

21. Gibson, personal narrative, Charles Kuhlamn Collection, Brigham Young University, p. 25.

22. Interview of Albert Barnitz by Walter M. Camp, May 7, 1910, TMS, Kenneth Hammer Collection, Box 3, Folder 4; Interview of Ben Clark by Walter M. Camp, October 22, 1910, TMS, Kenneth Hammer Collection, Box 3, Folder 4; Records of the Adjutant General's Office, Medical Records, Report of Diseases and Individual Cases, File F, 421, National Archives; Utley, *Life in Custer's Cavalry*, p. 226.

23. Ibid., p. 227.

24. Hoig, *The Battle of the Washita*, pp. 132-133.

25. Charles Brill, "The Men Whom Custer Forgot," TMS, Robert Spurrier Ellison Collection, MSS 782, Box 9, Folder 11, Archives and Manuscripts, Harold B. Lee Library, Brigham Young University, Provo.

26. Albert Barnitz to Walter M. Camp, November 29, 1910, Walter Mason Camp Papers, MSS 57, Box 1, Folder 14.

27. The only group of rocks that match Barnitz's description is directly north of the location of the old state visitor's pavilion, which was on high ground on the north side of an abandoned railway (the modern visitor pavilion is on the south side of the old railray). The rocks are today obscured by trees and brush.

28. Albert Barnitz to Walter M. Camp, November 29, 1910, Walter Mason Camp Papers, MSS 57, Box 1, Folder 14.

29. Interview of Albert Barnitz by Walter M. Camp, AMS, Walter Mason Camp Papers, MSS 57, Box 3, Folder 4. As noted earlier, this part of the article is based on a portion of Barnitz's account that Robert Utley found missing from the captain's journal and from another, later and briefer, account by Barnitz written in 1889. See Utley, *Life in Custer's Cavalry*, pp. 220, 227.

30. Godfrey, "Reminiscences," p. 12.

31. Utley, *Life in Custer's Cavalry*, pp. 243-247.

FEATURES

A Decisive Two Hours and Twenty Minutes
The Battle of Tippecanoe and the
Tippecanoe Battlefield Museum

Cindy Bedell

T he fierce battle fought between the United States and the warriors of the Prophetstown Confederacy near the Tippecanoe River produced a major setback to Indian unity and a slogan so striking that it produced a president. The Tippecanoe Battlefield is today a National Historic Landmark, preserved so that everyone may remember the conflict that took place there on November 7, 1811. Visitors walking the battlefield will today discover a serene and beautifully wooded area where over 200 soldiers and Indians fell dead and wounded. This article briefly describes the chief personalities, events, and features of Tippecanoe.

Tecumseh and the Prophet: The Shawnee brothers Tecumseh and Tenskwatawa, the Prophet, were charismatic leaders in the Indian resistance to American settlement in the Indiana Territory. An outstanding orator, Tecumseh imagined a strong pan-Indian confederacy, a uniting of the tribes under a common goal of resistance to white expansion. At the same time, the Prophet preached a return to the old ways, rooting his ideology in traditional tribal values.

Prophetstown: After the American Revolution, the native peoples of the eastern North American woodlands had been forced to adapt at an accelerating pace. Westward migration of white settlers across the Appalachian Mountains intruded into traditional Indian territories. The Indians were increasingly subjected to disease, alcoholism, and social disintegration as a result. Prophetstown, founded near the junction of the Wabash and Tippecanoe rivers, emerged out of the Prophet's ideas. Representing a symbolic boundary line between settlers and Indians, Prophetstown beckoned the Woodland Indians with a vision inspired by their traditional lifestyle. Prophetstown, a true historical intersection, would become an archetypal last stand culturally and militarily.

William Henry Harrison: The United States government, prompted by letters from William Henry Harrison, governor of the Indiana Territory, was concerned about the ideas and strength emanating from Prophetstown. Of Tecumseh, Harrison wrote: "He is one of those uncommon geniuses, which spring up occasionally to produce revolutions and overturn the established order of things." In September of 1811, taking advantage of Tecumseh's absence from Prophetstown, Harrison organized an army of about 1,000 men and marched north from Vincennes, Indiana, the capital of the Indiana Territory. His regiment arrived at the Tippecanoe River on November 6, 1811. Harrison's goal was to disperse the Indians living at Prophetstown and thwart the goals of the pan-Indian confederacy.

The Prophet was duly concerned with the U.S. military presence only one and one-half miles from his village, and confederacy warriors prepared to engage Harrison's troops. Unfortunately, the Prophet disregarded Tecumseh's order of restraint and patience and decided to engage Harrison without waiting for reinforcements. Indian warriors, primarily Shawnee, invaded the American encampment on the rainy morning of November 7, 1811.

John Tipton, one of the soldiers serving with Harrison's column, left a rare firsthand account of the Battle of Tippecanoe which, with the original spelling and punctuation, is reproduced below:

> [T]hirsday the 7 agreeable to their Promise Last night we ware answered by the firring of guns and the Shawnies Brakeng into our tents a blood Combat Took Plaice at Precisely 15 minutes Before five in the morning which Lasted 2 hours and 20 minuts of a Continewel firing while maney times mixd among the indians So that we Could not tell them indians and our men apart they kept up a firing on three sides of us took our tent from the gueard fire our men fought brave and By the timely help of Capt Cook with a Company of infantry We maid a Charge and Drove them out of our timber across the Prairie our Losst in killed and wounded was 179 and thiers graiter than ours among the Dead was our Capt Spier Spencer and first Lieut Mcmahan and Capt Berrey that had Been attatchd to our Company an 5 more killd Dead and 15 wounded after the indians gave ground we Burried our Dead among the kentucians was killd mayj Davis badly wounded and a number of others in all killd and wounded was 179 but no Company suffered like ours we then held an Election for officers I was elected Capt.[1]

Initially, it appeared as though the Indian confederacy would emerge victorious. After two hours of intense fighting, however, Harrison's regiment held its ground and the Prophet's warriors retreated. On November 8, Harrison's men invaded nearby Prophetstown and burned it to the ground.

The Aftermath: The Battle of Tippecanoe had serious consequences. The Prophet lost his power base and moved to Kansas. Tecumseh's plan of a strong pan-Indian confederacy was dashed. Believing it was his destiny to wage war against the encroaching American settlers, Tecumseh joined with the British and fought in the War of 1812. He was killed fighting alongside the British at the Battle of the Thames in Ontario on October 5, 1813. Harrison parlayed the Battle of Tippecanoe into a political rallying cry, "Tippecanoe and Tyler, Too!" He was elected the ninth president and died shortly after taking office.

The Tippecanoe Battlefield Museum and Grounds: The museum contains informative exhibits on the battle. A fiber-optic map with a 10-minute narrative illustrates and explains the movement of troops on November 7, 1811. The museum exhibits aim to weave a story, encouraging visitors to draw their own conclusions about the Battle of Tippecanoe.

The museum also houses a variety of artifacts related to various inhabitants of Prophetstown and American soldiers. A particularly interesting artifact on display is a bowl from Prophetstown. This beautiful vessel, worn smooth with use, is thought provoking. A Captain Park took the bowl from Prophetstown on the day after the battle, before Harrison burned the village. The hat, sword, and Masonic emblems of another officer, Colonel White, reflect his wealth. A common soldier's possessions, however, show the contrast in lifestyle between the mounted cavalry and those men on foot. The museum also has copies of excerpts from Lydia Bacon's journal. Bacon's husband, Josiah, was the quartermaster for the U.S. Military. Lydia traveled with Josiah and kept a journal of her trip through the Indiana wilderness. Her writing reflects her amazing personality and deep religious faith. Her entries are engaging and open a window onto a little-known past.

Visitors will also not want to miss the November 7, 1911, photograph depicting the Centennial Battle Commemoration. This wonderful picture captures the emotion a former generation of people felt about the battle. Every

---

[1] John Tipton Papers, Volume 1, 1809-1827 (Indiana Historical Bureau, Indianapolis, 1942), 77-78.]

exhibit is a must-see for any visitor who wants to grapple with the meaning of the Battle of Tippecanoe.

John Tipton purchased the 16-acre battlefield and deeded it to the state of Indiana on November 7, 1836, the 25th anniversary of the battle. In 1873 an iron fence, which survives today, was built around the battlefield. Starting in 1892, the Tippecanoe Battlefield Monument Association spearheaded the funding and construction of a commemorative obelisk and also smaller monuments marking where officers fell. On November 7, 1908, people gathered at the battlefield to hear patriotic speeches and participate in memorializing the Battle of Tippecanoe.

Visitor Information: The Tippecanoe County Historical Association operates the Tippecanoe Battlefield Museum and Museum Store. The battlefield and museum is located in Battleground, IN, northwest of Indianapolis. The museum is handicapped accessible. Foreign language brochures in French, German, Japanese, and Spanish are available. Hours are seasonal. If you have any questions, please call (765) 567-2147. Visiting days and hours are as follows: January through May, Tuesday–Sunday, noon–5:00 p.m.; June through December, Monday–Saturday, 10:00 a.m.–5:00 p.m., and Sunday from noon–5:00 p.m. Admission is $3.00 for adults, $2.00 for children, students, seniors & AAA. Group tour rates are available (please schedule in advance).

The Tippecanoe County Parks and Recreation Department maintains the 102-acre Tippecanoe Battlefield Park, which includes picnic areas, the 13-mile Wabash Heritage Trail, and Wah-ba-shik-a Nature Center. Readers of *JIW* are encouraged to spend a day at the Tippecanoe Battlefield. Don't forget to pack your lunch.

THE INDIAN WARS

Organizational, Tribal, and Museum News

P lans to protect the Fallen Timbers battlefield [see related articles in this issue of *JIW*] within the National Park System are finally progressing. Two other important sites associated with Anthony Wayne's 1794 campaign against the tribes of the "Old Northwest," Fort Miamis and Fort Meigs, are also involved. If current plans are approved, Fallen Timbers will be the first "affiliated status" battlefield in the system and the first under local versus federal control. However, acquisition of the battlefield is contingent on the city of Maumee (the location of the battlefield) being able to negotiate a purchase price with the site's owner, the city of Toledo.

Among the major proponents on behalf of a battlefield park are the Maumee Valley Heritage Corridor, Inc., Congressman Marcy Kaptur, and archaeologist Mike Pratt. The key player seems to be Stephen J. Pauken, mayor of Maumee. Pauken was the only person called on to give testimony on the park bill, S. 548, before the U.S. Senate Subcommittee on Energy and Natural Resources. In addition, Pauken has worked hard to explain to his constituents the economic benefits of preserving the battlefield as a park.

The 19th annual meeting of the Order of the Indian Wars on September 16-18, 1999. *Journal of the Indian Wars* was begun with the inspiration and cooperation of this worthwhile study, tour, and preservation group. The annual meeting will be held in Amarillo, Texas, and will focus on the Red River War [southern Plains] of 1874. There will be a dozen lectures on white and Comanche combatants. Neil Mangum of Little Bighorn National Battlefield and Brett Cruise of the Texas Historical Commission will lead tours of the battlefields of Adobe Walls and Palo Duro Canyon, and there will be an optional tour to the new Washita Battlefield National Historical Site in Oklahoma on September 19. The pre-August 10th cost for the meeting (including lectures, meals and tours through September 18) is only $310 for OIW members, and $335 for non-OIW members. For more information, contact OIW Assembly, Box 7401, Little Rock, AR 72217. Those wishing to stay at the meeting place, Radisson Inn Amarillo Airport, should contact the hotel directly: 7909 I-40 East Lakeside, Amarillo, TX 79118; (800) 333-3333 or (806) 373-3303. The group hotel rate is $62.00 plus tax per room.

The public is invited to participate in the development of Washita Battlefield National Historic Site [1868] by commenting on the park's proposed General Management Plan. To date, the suggested interpretive themes for the park are A) that Washita was a clash between two incompatible cultures; B) that the attack was the first implementation of a "total war" strategy on the southern Plains; C) that the attack at Washita has always been controversial; D) that Black Kettle, a proponent of peace, was, ironically, the subject of two attacks; E) that the battle brought George A. Custer to prominence as an Indian fighter; F) that the attack at Washita was a pivotal event in Cheyenne history and in Indian relations; and G) that "the hallowed ground of Washita provides opportunities to understand the resiliency of the human spirit and the struggle of societies to maintain cultural identity." More information may be found on the Internet at www.nps.govplanning/waba/news/, or you may write Washita Battlefield National Historic Site, P.O. Box 890, Cheyenne, OK 73828.

The most important autumn event in Indian wars history will be the long awaited groundbreaking ceremony of the National Museum of the American Indian (Smithsonian Institute), which will take place on September 28, 1999. The museum will be placed on the National Mall in Washington, D.C., between the National Air and Space Museum and the U.S. Capitol, on the last open site on the mall. It is scheduled to open in 2002. The museum "is dedicated to the preservation, study, and exhibition of the life, languages, literature, and arts of Native Americans." Its collection will be drawn from that of the former Heye Foundation in New York City. This collection, comprising over a million objects, had outgrown its former building when the new National Museum of the American Indian was authorized by an act of the U.S. Congress in 1989.

Since that time, part of the collection has been displayed through special exhibits at the Heye Center of the National Museum of the American Indian, located in the old U.S. Custom House in Manhattan. Updates on the progress of the Washington museum can be found on the internet at www.si.edu/organiza/museums/amerind/whatsnew.htm.

Organizations, tribes, parks, and museums are invited to submit relevant news for publication in *JIW*. Our mailing address is Michael A. Hughes, Editor, *Journal of the Indian Wars*, 834 East Sixth St., Box E, Ada, OK 74820. News submissions should include a brief, abstracted version of any information and are subject to editing for length and content. The submission of news automatically grants *JIW* the right to publish the information and/or post the information on our web site.

THOMAS ONLINE

A Beginner's Guide to Researching the Indian Wars on the Web

Rodney G. Thomas

Within the last four years, the ability to conduct historical research using the Internet has dramatically expanded. For those with access to the Web, it has been a welcome tool. The Indian wars of the United States is one subject area that has kept pace with the overall growth of resources as reflected in the hundreds of web sites available on this topic.

This initial discussion of those sites is broken down into three main themes. The first deals with a basic understanding of Internet terminology, techniques, and aids in web-based research. The second identifies some of the better sites and assesses their appropriateness (and accuracy) to as it relates to Indian wars research. Finally, I shall make some recommendations for further study and use.

It is not my intent to provide a detailed guide to PC-based computing in this column, but we need to have some common understanding of basic terms and procedures. I am assuming that a large percentage of our readers have some experience on the Internet, and seek their indulgence. For those who have infrequent or no exposure to researching web-based resources, it is my hope that this column will spur your interest and help you get started. A one-hour class in any setting will give the most inexperienced researcher the skills and techniques necessary to begin researching online.

The first term that needs to be explained is "browser." Programs or applications that permit access to other computers on the Internet are called "browsers." The most common include "Netscape," "Internet Explorer," "Opera," etc. These browsers are reached by simply "signing on" to an "internet service provider" (ISP), such as America Online (AOL), Microsoft Network (MSN), Prodigy, or some local internet service provider of lesser fame but with equal access to the Internet. Once signed on, the browser can be used to access websites you have already visited and saved (known as "bookmarking" a site) or to use a program known as the "search engine" to find additional or new sites. Some of the more popular search engines are Infoseek, Alta Vista, Yahoo, and Excite. These search engines are tremendous aids in locating information on the Internet, and some are much better or preferred over others. Search results are returned in some order, normally with the website address "hyper-texted," a coded shortcut to the website you can access simply by clicking on it. Hyper-linked text is usually blue in color and underlined. When the site opens up, you can "browse" or "surf" through all the information it contains by clicking onto other "page" links within each website. It is this linking of different page and websites that makes researching extremely gratifying—or totally perplexing. The next several paragraphs refers to some of these terms and processes, especially regarding accuracy, ease of use, and so on.

What is on the Web about the Indian wars? I used AOL as my ISP and Infoseek as my search engine, and typed in a simple query: "Wounded Knee." These two words returned 4,226 "hits" (references to web sites or lines on web sites with information on the subject.). Another query, "The Battle of the Little Bighorn" (MSN using Alta Vista) returned 385 sites. "Indian Campaigns" (MSN using Yahoo) yielded only 408 sites, while "Indian Wars" (Netscape using Excite) found 9,685 hits! Even more interesting is that the word "Apache" did not return a single hit, while "Comanche" returned over 100, with most of them dealing with Captain Keogh's horse at the Little Bighorn fight in 1876. What does all this mean? The answer is not simple, but it is necessary if we are to understand good researching techniques that will not waste a lot of valuable time and effort.

All browsers are not created equal, and neither are the search engines. Thus, the result of your search has much to do with which browser and search engine you employ. I used to think that these programs actually went and "searched" the entire Internet. This is not so. The "engines" find what the search engine companies have been paid to find. Search engines conduct their task by organizing data warehouses full of URLs filed by key words for that particular search engine. In other words, when the user hits the "go" button on your search engine, it usually only searches the data warehouse for that engine. Efforts are now underway to make these warehouses more readily available to each other, and there are some programs (often called "spiders," "moles," "ferrets," etc.) that access many different data banks.

Each browser also views the same file or information site differently, so what appears as a very clear and well organized site in Netscape may show up poorly in Explorer (or visa versa), and not at all in other browsers. This is usually a matter of poor website construction by the designer, a unsophisticated web host, or a combination of the two. In any case, this performance and display will affect the user's research effort, so be prepared to use more than one browser. Good searching techniques take into account this inequity and capitalize on the strengths of each search program and browser.

What do all the numbers or "hits" represent? The 9,685 hits about "Indian Wars," for example, included over 5,000 references to India, Great Britain, England, and Russia. If time is of the essence on the Web (and when isn't it?), wading through unproductive sites to locate those dealing with "US Indian Wars" is a tremendous waste of time. Thus, the more specific the search, the better the results. The trick is to use quotation marks to frame a query. For example, a search for Little Big Horn will return everything with the words "little," "big," "horn," "little big horn," and "little bighorn" found on the Internet. However, if your search is "framed" with quotation marks, the search engine only returns those entries with the specific verbiage inside the marks. Thus, "Little Bighorn" produced only 385 hits, as opposed to more than 3,000,000 without the quotation marks!

Lastly, some search engines list the same site a number of times, depending on how that particular site was placed in the data bank and with what "key words." This is why over 4,000 results show up on a topic like "Wounded Knee." The same three sites were being registered over 400 times each. Even if the results parameter of an engine is set at twenty sites per page, the amount of time required to research these results is staggering. And the older your computer (modem speed, processor speed, memory of both the computer and viewer, and so on), the longer this process becomes. Web business advertising and search engine parameters are built on the premise that any sites listed after page three of the search results are not going to be examined by the searcher. My experience tells me the same thing applies to research as well.

As useful as the Internet can be, it is unfortunately a repository for misinformation, which can be posted and perpetuated with impunity. Only the host or the webmaster can change a website, and requests to correct improperly posted material often fall on deaf ears. Inaccuracy is often the result of some well-intentioned effort to provide the "truth" and thus becomes "fact" by its mere existence. Many sites provide little or no academically acceptable citation or source information. Several sites are nothing more than a platform for political purposes wrapped in the guise of history. In short, researchers must exercise some discernment when using information from the net.

Many websites are placed on the larger ISPs, such as AOL, CompuServe, etc. These websites are usually free but often are not very well done or routinely maintained. A lack of documentation of the material posted on these sites compounds these problems. "Serious" sites can also suffer from the same lack of attention and detail. Unfortunately, it is impossible to assess a site's value until you review it. In the past few years, large numbers of sites are being individually hosted and well maintained. Since websites stay "on the web" until the owner or the host removes them, the earlier efforts clutter searches and make it more difficult to find professional efforts.

A good place to begin looking for quality web pages is on the "mega-sites." These list large numbers of other sites on a particular subject. Some of the web masters of these mega-sites took the time and effort to organize their pages in some rational basis, but by and large they are simply huge repositories of web site addresses. They can be easily located with simple queries, such as "Native American, Indian," etc.

Let me recommend five excellent sites. Glenn Welker compiled a great site (http://www.indians.org) which offers ten pages of single-spaced listings of organizations dealing with American Indian subjects. It is a gold mine of information. Karen Strom's effort (http://www.hanksville.org/NAresources), with its superb topical organization, should also be at the top of any list. J. S. Dill's creation (http://www.dickshovel.com) and its "First Nations" segment of Native American literature, history, and art is very well respected by Native American organizations. I also habitually check "The Native American Navigator" (http://www.ilu.columbia.edu/k12/naha/naproj.htm), another well respected and information-packed educational site, and Jim Janke's "Old West" (http://www.homepages.dsu.edu/jankej/oldwest/oldwest.htm) always has new places to investigate. Each of these sites is well maintained, frequently updated, monitored, and well constructed for research. There is the occasional political message, but these are not overly intrusive. These five addresses are a great starting point for finding and bookmarking sites for future referencing and researching. Each contains hundreds of potential researching opportunities.

Any researcher worth his or her salt must bookmark three additional sites: http://www.lbha.org, http://www.cbhma.org, and a relative newcomer, http://www.garreyowen.com. The first and foremost website to view when beginning online research, especially of the western United States, is Jay

Kanitz's Little Bighorn Associates site (www.lbha.org). Kanitz's website is top notch in terms of both site construction and the information packed into its contents. One visit is not enough to reveal everything it offers. Jay has dedicated a large amount of time constructing an easily navigable, quick loading site that is constantly maintained and updated. The second site, Custer Battlefield Historical and Museum Association site (www.cbhma.org), is solidly produced but does not offer the Kanitz's content. Still, it is a quality production and deserves frequent visits. The last of the three, www.garryowen.com, is about one year old and growing in content and quality. If your time is limited, however, head straight to Kanitz (www.lbha.org).

The refined search locations described below should be bookmarked for convenient routine return visits. The home page for H-AMINDIAN (http://www.asu.edu/clas/history/h-amindian), a member of the H-Net, is an on-line discussion site and electronic forum for issues related to American Indians. I highly recommend this site, especially for serious researchers and in-depth reference study. Lisa Mitten's "New Indian Books" (http://www2.pitt.edu/~lmitten/indbks.htm) has been on the web since 1994, and it is the only site I am aware of that provides a monthly list of new books. "The Archives of the West" (http://www3.pbs.org/weta/thewest/) provides a superb collection of art, photos, and references about the West and Indian wars history. Most museums now have at least an overall introductory website, and one example that has expanded research possibilities is the Heard Museum at www.heard.org.

For the beginner, I recommend starting at the some of the mega-sites and refining research efforts from them. Using the search engines is an important technique, and focusing a search item is a learned skill. Knowing how to save time in wading through search results is paramount for saving resources. Hopefully, I have provided some research sites even the experienced web user has not yet visited. I intend to continue searching for new and different sites useful for researching the Indian wars. The sites set forth in this column are more than enough to keep you busy for some time to come.

I encourage readers of *Journal of the Indian Wars* to E-mail me additional sites related to the Indian wars (ppaladin@pacificwest.com), and I will publish them in this column.

Fine Books on Frontier Military, Northern Plains Indians, and General Custer

Custer and the Cheyenne, by Louis Kraft. Excellent reconstruction of Custer's winter campaign on the southern plains. Includes detailed information on the origins, fighting, and conclusion of the Battle of the Washita. According to historian Robert M. Utley, "This is a beautifully designed book, well written, ground in deep research and thoughtful analysis." Vol. 5 of the Custer Trails Series. 224pp., photos, maps, notes, biblio., index, d.j., cloth. 1st. ed. ISBN 0-912783-24-9. $65.00

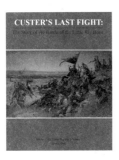

NEW! *Custer's Last Fight: The Battle of the Little Big Horn,* by David C. Evans. Vol. 1 in a new Battle of the Little Big Horn series. You think it has been done before? Not this way! Evans has synthesized the voluminous LBH literature and arrived at provocative conclusions that will give pause even to the most seasoned Custer student. 604pp. photos, notes, index, bibliography, rosters, official documents, maps. ISBN 0-912783-30-3. $85.00. Limited Signed and Numbered Edition: $175.00

NEW! *Custer Battle Casualties II: The Dead, The Missing and a Few Survivors,* by Richard G. Hardorff. Sequel to 1991 Vol. I. New material on the Custer and Reno casualties: the unidentified on Greasy Grass Hill, Deep Ravine, the River Dead, Garryowen Burial in 1926, more. Includes photo essay by James Brust of then and now views of the Custer battlefield, including the earliest known view (1877). "A significant contribution to our knowledge and understanding of what happened." Historian Robert M. Utley. 213pp., maps, index, bibliography. ISBN 0-912783-26-5. $42.50. Limited (50 copies) Signed and Numbered Edition: $150.00

NEW! *"Exactly in the Right Place": A History of Fort C. F. Smith, Montana Territory, 1866-1868,* by Barry J. Hagan, C.S.C. A spellbinding, comprehensive history of a famous fort on the Bozeman Trail, based on letters, diaries, and official reports. The most sophisticated Indian Wars scholar will admit Father Hagen has written the definitive work on this subject. Vol. 12 in the *Montana and the West* series. 300pp., endpaper maps, photos, notes and biblio., index. ISBN 0-912783-31-1. $65.00. Limited Signed and Numbered Edition: $150.00

UPTON AND SONS, PUBLISHERS
917 Hillcrest Street, El Segundo, California 90245
Web Site: www.uptonbooks.com / E-Mail: richardupton@worldnet.att.net
FREE CATALOG / ORDER: 800-959-1876 / Fax: 310-322-4739

REVIEWS

A Guide to the Indian Wars of the West, by John D. McDermott (Lincoln: University of Nebraska Press, 1998), 205pp. Illustrations, maps, notes, bibliography. Paper. $16.95

Outside of a few well known sites, many historic locations in the United States go unnoticed. Hundreds of these are associated with the Indian wars. Sadly, few battlefield tour guides cover the Indian wars beyond George A. Custer's escapades. A similarly small number of texts examine how the Indian wars were fought by both sides. John D. McDermott's new book is unique because it combines a traveler's and historical guide into a book targeted to the general reader.

The first part of McDermott's *Guide* is a primer of sorts on the Indian wars, split into sections on their causes, the opponents, the campaigns and their tactics and strategy, the Indian way of life, and even the Indian wars in literature and the arts. Although McDermott doesn't break any new ground, he uses historical and reference texts effectively in creating his chapters and backs up his conclusions with tables and solid reasoning. His presentation of the historical background of the Indian wars is concise and readable, though a bit on the thin side.

The latter half of the *Guide* covers one hundred and nineteen battlefields, including state parks and national monuments, grave sites, forts, and museums. Each description typically comprises one to three paragraphs. These narratives are organized state by state into geographical areas, such as California and the Northwest, the Southwest, the Southern Plains, the Northern Plains, and so on. An overview of the campaigns and battles waged within these geographical zones is also included.

Each entry provides contact information on touring the site and often includes specific local directions, visiting hours and, occasionally, phone numbers. Some of the guide's entries are not as helpful as others. For example, a few of the battlefields are on private property, and the *Guide* does not always indicate when this is the case or whether such battlefields are accessible to the public. Similarly, the *Guide* does not always indicate which battlefields require an admission fee to gain entry. No effort was made to include state/federal park or driving maps, which would have increased the book's value.

McDermott seems to have based his entries on the National Park Service's excellent but now dated book *Solder and Brave: Historic Places Associated with Indian Affairs and the Indian Wars in the Trans-Mississippi West* (1971).

As a result, his own *A Guide to the Indian Wars of the West* shares the strengths and weaknesses of that earlier book, including its vague and generalized directions. Thus, when *Soldier and Brave* incorrectly claims Nebraska's Blue Water Battlefield can be seen from an overlook in the Ash Hollow Historical State Park, McDermott repeats the error. Although the state of Nebraska does own land for a still-undeveloped overlook of the Blue Water Battlefield, that land is miles away from the Ash Hollow State Park, and the battlefield cannot be seen by visitors at the state park. McDermott makes a few mistakes of his own as well. For example, he lists the Quanah Parker Star House under Kansas sites rather than Oklahoma sites.

Despite its brief length and its shortcomings, *A Guide to the Indian Wars* is still the most extensive traveler's guide published to date on the western Indian wars, and as such is a good resource on the subject for general readers.

Allan Dunkin   Richardson, Texas

Frontier Soldier: An Enlisted Man's Journal of the Sioux and Nez Perce Campaigns, 1877, by Private William F. Zimmer, edited and annotated by Jerome A. Greene (Helena, MT: Montana Historical Society Press, 1998). 171pp. Illustrations, maps, notes, index. Paper. $15.95

A well worn adage holds that appearance is everything. Few would dispute that popular perceptions influence our judgment of people, places and events. Our concept of the post-Civil War Indian-fighting Army is a good case in point. The image of that institution created by the 19th-century dime novel and dramatized by the 20th-century Hollywood screenwriter has become difficult to distinguish from reality. How many of us have been captured by the image of the rugged cavalry unit, whose rapid pursuit of Indians on the warpath results in the interception and defeat of its quarry? Or of the perfect order in which the disciplined horsemen in blue charge to glory? Or of the successful return of the "hostiles" to the reservation? The general public at large remains under the influence of such Western film classics as John Ford's *She Wore a Yellow Ribbon* and *Rio Grande*.

These images intrigued this reviewer as he read Jerome Greene's exemplary edition of Private William Zimmer's journal for the year 1877. Zimmer was in some ways representative of the men who served in the ranks in the late 1800s. A native of Germany, Zimmer's family had emigrated to Canada and the United States, and he had briefly served in the 191st Ohio Volunteer Infantry at the close of the Civil War. After working ten years as a carpenter and farmer, Zimmer enlisted in the Army in 1876 and was assigned to Company F,

Second Cavalry, then stationed at Fort Ellis, Montana Territory. Yet in one important respect, Zimmer was an exception to the norm. While serving with Col. Nelson A. Miles against the Sioux and Nez Perce in 1877, Zimmer kept a diary. He was one of the few enlisted men who did so during the Indian wars. His rare and valuable journal provides a rare and candid view of the common soldier; it also serves to create a more realistic impression of the Indian-fighting Army.

To be sure, Zimmer's graphic accounts of the Lame Deer Fight and the Battle of Bear Paw Mountains perpetuate the legendary image of the 19th century military, since he describes the invariable cavalry charge and defeat of the enemy. Yet his diary goes beyond these occasional glimpses of glory and valor and provides a clear impression of the daily routine of the enlisted man on campaign. In between the rare engagements with hostile Indians, the frontier soldier endured monotony, regimentation, and hardships, which led many to question why they joined the service in the first place.

A constant theme coursing through Zimmer's journal is the boredom of Army life which, combined with alcohol and gambling, invariably produced the same results. Zimmer recorded on April 2, 1877, that two men of his company "had a skirmish all to themselves, & several of the other boys got into difficulty, all on account of the sutler arriving here with some whiskey." Tempers had not improved by July, when he noted that after one of the companies had received four months' pay, a man was seriously wounded "in a drunken brawl." As the troops returned to Fort Ellis in October after the defeat of the Nez Perce, two soldiers "while under the influence of liquor, got in a quarrel & one shot the other not seriously." Even after their resettlement at the post, Zimmer observed that "[g]ambling & drinking is going quite lively." Added to this pattern were a succession of self-inflicted gunshot wounds ("it's strange that so many trigger fingers get shot off & always accidental"), giving the impression that such episodes accounted for more casualties than the heat of battle!

If such observations do not completely dispel the romantic view of the frontier army, Zimmer's portrayal of troops on campaign trail should. He captured the essence of Indian fighting as he described the fruitless efforts of the Second Cavalry to pursue the survivors of the Lame Deer fight. The enlisted man's attitude towards campaigning becomes clear as Zimmer describes what he regards as an aimless march over inhospitable terrain. The realities of frontier war become vividly clear to the reader when Zimmer describes his column's approach to the Little Big Horn Valley nearly a year after the Custer fight: "We spent a miserable night, it raining all the time, and at daylight, still raining, we saddled up and were soon on our way where God only knows. On [and] on and on we went & the rain fell faster. About 10 A.M. we got lost & went circling around & came back to our own trail. . . . We found a ravine. . . .

here we waited for it to clear off, but night came & it [is] still raining." The next day's march was no better and the rain continued to fall. Zimmer later recorded his skepticism about the battalion's vain pursuit as it again followed a disappearing trail. "You might as well hunt a needle in a haystack," he concluded. After eight months of campaigning, only fifty-eight of the ninety men in Zimmer's column's returned to Fort Ellis "sound & well." The horses had fared no better. So much, Zimmer discovered, for the glory of Indian fighting.

Comprehensive annotations by veteran National Park historian Jerome Greene compliment this rare insight into the enlisted man's world of the 1870s. The editor's authoritative comments allow even the uninformed reader to follow Zimmer's story with ease. Greene notes that the journal entries are not always contemporary; several which contain information on subsequent events were added when Zimmer apparently transcribed the original diary into its present form. However, these later additions do not detract from the unique value of this firsthand account of life in the frontier Army. As such, it belongs in the library of every serious student of the 19th century Indian wars next to such seminal studies as Don Rickey's *Forty Miles a Day on Beans and Hay* and Sherry Smith's *Sagebrush Soldier*.

C. Lee Noyes   Morrisonville, New York

Tecumseh: A Life, by John Sugden. Henry Holt, 115 West 18th Street, New York, NY 10011. Photos, maps, d.j. 512pp. Cloth. $34.95.

A plethora of books have been written about a variety of Indian leaders. Until now, however, very few have succeeded in capturing his subject as completely and capably as John Sugden in *Tecumseh: A Life*. A biographer's task when writing about someone who over the passage of nearly two centuries has morphed from man to myth is to utilize original source materials. Only by mining archival data can a biographer hope to reclothe his subject in a patina of flesh, to demythologize him and present, as far as possible, the reality of the man or woman and their times. Sugden has accomplished this herculean task magnificently and in the process establishes accurate (and thereby meaningful) historical context to the Shawnee chief's remarkable life. Until Sugden's opus, it was difficult to get a solid grip on exactly who Tecumseh really was, for most of the writings purporting to document his life are either unreliable or largely fictional.

Tecumseh (Tekamthi) was born in what is today Ohio. Soon after the conclusion of the American Revolution, Tecumseh schemed of a way to fuse the diverse and often warring North American tribes into a confederation powerful enough to halt the natural westward expansion of American settlers. His dream was to coalesce Indians from Canada to the Gulf of Mexico and create an obstacle through which the white man could not penetrate. In order to have a chance for success, the Shawnee leader needed not only his charisma and good luck, but military, political, and oratorical skills, all of which he possessed in abundance. He also had the assistance of his brother Tenskwatawa, or the Prophet, who shared Tecumseh's dream. Through years of hard work and difficult journeys, Tecumseh managed to create a relatively powerful pan-Indian federation, a natural by-product of which was reduced intertribal warfare and apathy toward the encroaching white settlers. Unfortunately and against the wishes of Tecumseh, the Prophet confronted William Henry Harrison in battle at Tippecanoe in 1811 and suffered a significant defeat. Joining forces with the British during the War of 1812, Tecumseh and his confederation worked tirelessly to block American thrusts into Canada. Tecumseh himself led joint British-Indian forces in engagements across much of the American-Canadian frontier. Unfortunately for the alliance, the fearless chief and quasi-empire builder was killed on October 5, 1813, at the Battle of Moraviantown. Exactly how he died remains an unsettled question.

Although Tecumseh accomplished a great deal, his multi-tribal confederation did not stand a chance of defeating American westward expansion. The various Indian tribes had been waging war against one another for centuries, and the deep distrust and hate such bloodshed naturally fostered stained relations and broke apart Tecumseh's always unstable system of alliances. Logistical problems, differences in cultures and languages between the Indians themselves, the uneasy nature of the British-Indian alliance, and the sheer superiority of American military might and technology doomed the warrior's best efforts from the outset. Yet the outcome is clear only in hindsight; the historical importance of Tecumseh the man was not the result of his efforts but the endeavor to stand for something greater than just himself or the Shawnee. "All people need heroes," writes Sugden, "their Lincolns, Nelsons, and Joan of Arcs, people who embody ideals and aspirations and about whom a national identity can be hung" (390).

But the value of Sugden's effort is not just that it is a good story, but a good *believable* story. So much written today, especially about Native American and minority history, is simply unreliable because it is penned from a clearly biased perspective. Reality and history often take a back seat to fantasy and mythology. The sheer volume of manuscript material upon which *Tecumseh: A Life* is based is staggering and forecloses that possibility. This archival foundation, together with the author's own expansive and acknowledged expertise on the subject, adds an imprimatur of scholarly reliability seldom found elsewhere in any field.

The author's claim of having worked on this subject for thirty years is thus readily believed and fully appreciated. In addition, he supports his efforts with outstanding explanatory end notes jammed with tantalizing additional bits of information, and his publisher added excellent illustrations and several good maps.

Sugden has taken a difficult subject teeming with political, historical, and sociological pitfalls and produced a book brimming with analysis, fresh revelations, and credibility. In so doing he has managed to accomplish something every good biographer must strive to do: cloak his subject in human attire and push aside the legend.

Theodore P. Savas   Mason City, IA.

Lakota Warrior, translated and edited by James H. Howard, with an Introduction by Raymond Bucko (University of Nebraska Press, Bison Books Edition, Lincoln, 1998). 84pp. Thirty-nine plate illustrations (sixteen in color), bibliographical references. Paper. $15.00.

To aficionados of the Plains Indian wars as well as Native American art, the wartime exploits of Lakota warrior White Bull, as represented in an old business ledger book, is a classic. James H. Howard's famous analysis of the White Bull ledger artwork and writings, now republished, was first printed in 1968 under the title *The Warrior Who Killed Custer*. To new readers and students of this genre or time period, *Lakota Warrior* will become one of your favorites as well.

In 1934, Walter S. Campbell, under the pen name Stanley Vestal, published his biography of White Bull *entitled Warpath: The True Story of the Fighting Sioux Told in a Biography of Chief White* Bull. As readers enjoy this republication of *Lakota Warrior*, I suggest they make use of Vestal's book as a supplement to understanding the ledger itself.

White Bull's fame was cemented by his exploits well before Vestal's book appeared. The warrior was selected as the symbolic head of the Indian delegation to the 1926 celebration of the battle at the Little Big Horn. He led the entourage in its meeting with Brig. Gen. E. S. Godfrey in a peace ceremony on the battlefield. Vestal increased White Bull's visibility after the Indian's death by asserting that White Bull was the one who killed Custer.

The value of this reprint resides in Raymond Bucko's introduction and his work in correcting some of the mistakes made by Howard in translating the notes that accompany each drawing by White Bull. White Bull learned to write his native tongue in the late 1870s, and this personal touch helps define the exceptional nature of his work. *Lakota Warrior* is White Bull's life in his own words and art. Included in this warrior's tale are stories and drawings of the Wagon Box fight, the Fetterman fight, and, of course, the Little Big Horn, where he counted seven coups. He adds events of his youth and Lakota culture to present probably the most complete story of an American Indian warrior of the times. Bucko's explanation of the Custer killing story is very interesting and brings together the thinking of authors Vestal and Howard, and of Dr. Raymond DeMaille, who first pointed out the difficulties in Vestal's assertion that White Bull had killed Custer.

Howard's work on the White Bull ledger book has been too long out of print, and this republication brings it back to the general public in fine fashion. Additional publications of this genre of American Indian art are not only warranted but should be anticipated. Already a classic in many circles, *Lakota Warrior* should be in every library of those even moderately interested in the history of the American West or American Indian artwork. It is a true warrior's story and one well told.

Col. Rodney G. Thomas, U.S.A. (Ret)   Morrisville, NC

Tecumseh and the Shawnee Confederation, by Rebecca Stefoff. New York: Facts On File, Inc., 1998, 138pp. contents, illustrations, maps, notes, chronology, index. Cloth. $19.95

Reaping the Whirlwind: The Apache Wars, by Peter Aleshire (New York: Facts On File, Inc., 1998), viii, 152pp. Photographs, maps, notes, index. Cloth. Contact publisher for price.

These two books are the first two of six projected titles for juvenile or young adult readers in the Library of American Indian History series. Rebecca Stefoff's *Tecumseh and the Shawnee Confederation* attempts to educate younger readers about the esteemed Shawnee leader and his efforts to unite Indian tribes against the whites, while Peter Aleshire's *Reaping the Whirlwind* sheds new light about the lengthy and costly Apache wars.

Tecumseh was born in the present-day state of Ohio in 1768. He grew up to be brave, respected, intelligent, strong, a natural leader, a spellbinding orator, astute politician, and skilled war chief. He rose to prominence arguing an inflexible opposition to both the encroachment of white settlers on Indian land and the ceding of Indian territory. He steadily gained supporters and became a top-level war chief in 1794 and an admired political leader soon after. In 1805, he joined with his shaman brother Tenskwatawa, the Shawnee Prophet, to start a movement that would eventually gain an enormous Indian following from many tribes of his brother's native Old Northwest and beyond.

The movement called for all Indian peoples to return to their traditional ways, to reject all things white, and to deal with whites as a unified force. It also held that all Indian land should be considered jointly owned by every tribe and that no Indian land could be given up unless all Indians supported such an act. Finally, the dispossession of the Indians from their land would be checked, even if it meant war. Three years later, in present-day Indiana, Tecumseh and Tenskwatawa founded Prophetstown, which was to be the political seat of the Indian confederation. In 1811 Prophetstown and Tecumseh's dream were destroyed by American forces at the Battle of Tippecanoe. Tecumseh, who was absent at the time of the fight, continued to resist the whites in the aftermath of the defeat. He and his allies sided with the British at the outbreak of the War of 1812, but Tecumseh lost his life at the 1813 Battle of the Thames.

Stefoff's narrative relies on a synthesis of secondary sources, and quotations from published primary sources are sprinkled throughout the text. Her style will appeal to younger readers, and the endnotes will be easily understood by those interested in tracking down primary sources.

Tecumseh and the Shawnee Confederation is better than many other current books on Indians for younger readers, but still has some weaknesses. Stefoff lists two works with a significant degree of fictionalization in her Selected Further Reading list. This will make it more difficult for young readers to distinguish what is fact and what is not. Military history is given short shrift, in spite of the fact that warfare and the warrior tradition played a key role throughout most of Tecumseh's life. The slighting of military history by writers today is a common trend and one that must be reversed if balance and perspective and are to achieved. Perhaps the most notable weakness is that the book contains too much superfluous material that in no way helps the reader understand Tecumseh and his cherished confederation.

Peter Aleshire, who unlike Stefoff is a known authority on his subject, has produced a worthy history of the Apache Wars for young readers. *Reaping the Whirlwind* seeks to solve the "lethal puzzle" (vi) of why the Apache Wars continued for so many costly years in spite of the fact that during the entire period there were many on both sides who understood the conflict and were ardent advocates of peace.

Aleshire's answer to the puzzle is thorough, balanced, and convincing. He lists several reasons for white-Apache conflict. American policy makers, for example, failed to set aside reservations for the various Apache bands that conformed to their homelands and allowed bands hostile to one another to live apart. The Indians were not fairly paid for land taken from them, and adequate rations were not provided to Indians who had given up their traditional life style.

Important Apache leaders chose to fight to the death for what they knew to be a lost cause rather than accept peace on terms they considered unacceptable. Some whites, military suppliers for example, sought to keep the war going for their own financial benefit. The Apache's reliance on hunting and raiding for subsistence and the penchant for white prospectors to invade Apache land guaranteed ongoing hostile encounters. Both sides believed they were racially superior and their enemy subhuman. Apaches and whites conducted the war with an inhumanity that maintained the cycle of violence. War was central to the Apache culture. The Indians had adapted remarkably to the harsh land in which they lived and fought, and the Apache war leaders possessed immense skill. All of these factors helped to ensure that the end of the conflict would be long in coming. In solving the "puzzle" of the Apache Wars, *Reaping the Whirlwind* offers what is for all intents and purposes a balanced account of the subject that only occasionally shows a pro-Apache bias.

Peter Aleshire's narrative relies on a synthesis of published secondary sources. He uses quotes from published primary sources to enliven his text, and he writes in a style easily understood by younger readers and yet in no way condescending to them. *Reaping the Whirlwind* contains a considerable amount of well-chosen and quality-reproduced illustrations, each accompanied by informative captions. Several clear and concise maps will prove helpful to young people unfamiliar with the Southwest. This work also utilizes numerous short essays that exist independent of the narrative and serve to break up the text. Most of these offer biographical sketches of important figures on both sides and will certainly be welcomed by younger readers. End notes follow each chapter and provide the road map necessary to entice youthful readers to have their first personal experience with primary sources.

Reaping the Whirlwind's flaws are few but worth noting. Aleshire quoted from secondary sources rather then paraphrase the words of other writers. His text is in some places repetitious, and this reviewer believes that his listing of two novels in his "Selected Further Reading List" only confuses truth with imagination. Another irksome inclination in today's literature, and one Aleshire falls prey to, is to vaguely refer to United States Army units as "soldiers" or "troops" rather than identifying them by unit. Similarly, Aleshire often foregoes stating fully the rank of United States army officers mentioned in the text. These last two omissions are especially curious since the author is careful to designate the specific band of all Apaches to whom he refers.

Nonetheless, *Reaping the Whirlwind* is a worthy and even strong addition to grade school and public libraries. Parents wishing to nurture a love of history in their children would also do well to purchase it.

Patrick A. Bowmaster   South Farmingdale, NY

Books Received for Review

The following books have been received since the publication of *Journal of the Indian Wars* (vol. 1, no.1) and have not yet been reviewed, though some may be under consideration for review. *JIW* welcomes qualified book and video reviewers. If you are interested, please contact the managing editor at the address on the back of this issue's title page. Please include information on your qualifications, your areas of knowledge, and any specific titles or types of works in which you have an interest.

Here They Once Stood: The Tragic End of the Apalachee Missions, by Mark F. Boyd (University Press of Florida, 1951; first paper printing 1999.)

The Plains Indians, by Paul H. Carlson (Texas A & M Press, 1998.)

The Indian Southwest, 1580-1830: Ethnogenesis and Reinvention, by Gary Clayton Anderson (University of Oklahoma Press, 1999.)

The Invasion of Indian Country in the Twentieth Century: American Capitalism and Tribal Natural Resources, by Donald L. Fixico (University Press of Colorado, 1998.)

Space and Time Perspective in Northern St. Johns Archeology, Florida, by John M. Goggin (University Press of Florida, 1952, 1998.)

A Face in the Rock: The Tale of a Grand Island Chippewa, by Loren R. Graham (University of California Press, 1995; first paper printing 1998.)

Indians in the Making: Ethnic Relations and Indian Identities Around Puget Sound, by Alexander Harmon (University of California Press, 1998.)

The Conquest of the Karankawas and the Tonkawas, 1821-1859, by Kelly F. Himmel (Texas A & M Press, 1999.)

The Encyclopedia of Native American Biography: Six Hundred Life Stories of Important People, from Powhatan to Wilma Mankiller, by Bruce E. Johansen and Donald A. Grinde, Jr. (Da Capo Press, 1997; first Da Capo paper printing 1998.)

Custer and Company: Walter Camp's Notes on the Custer Fight, edited by Bruce R. Liddic and Paul Harbaugh (University of Nebraska Press, 1995; first Bison paper printing 1998.)

Wild Justice: The People of Geronimo vs. the United States, by Michael Lieder and Jake Page, (University of Oklahoma Press, 1997; first paper printing 1999.)

American Indian Biographies, edited by Harvey Markowitz (Salem Press, Inc., 1999.)

Ready Reference, American Indians (three vols.), edited by Harvey Markowitz (Salem Press, Inc., 1995.)

Red Jacket, Seneca Chief, by Arthur Caswell Parker (University of Nebraska Press, 1998.)

Indian War Sites: A Guidebook to Battlefields, Monuments, and Memorials, by Steve Rajtar (McFarland & Company, Inc., 1999.)

Massacre at the Yuma Crossing: Spanish Relations with the Quechans, 1779-1782, by Mark Santiago (University of Arizona Press, 1998.)

Early History of the Creek Indians and Their Neighbors, by John R. Swanton (University Press of Florida, 1998; reprint of 1922 publication.)

Custer and the Great Controversy: The Origin and Development of a Legend, by Robert M. Utley (University of Nebraska Press, 1992; first Bison paper printing, 1998.)

Unconquered People: Florida's Seminole and Miccosukee Indians, by Brent Richards Weisman (University Press of Florida, 1999.)

The Only Land They Knew: American Indians in the Old South, by J. Leitch Wright, Jr. (University of Nebraska Press, 1981; first Bison paper printing 1999.)

Book Notes

Although it does not yet rival the multi-decade flood of Civil War books, the pace of publication in Indian wars and related subjects has picked up considerably in recent years. This mini-deluge includes excellent new books as well as reprints of old classics. *Journal of the Indian Wars* offers full reviews of selected titles elsewhere. "Book Notes" is an attempt to keep pace with this bonanza of offerings by presenting timely capsule reviews and other pertinent information that will be of use and interest to our readers.

The first book for consideration is *Indians in the United States and Canada: A Comparative History*, by Roger Nichols (University of Nebraska Press, 312 North 14th Street, Box 880484, Lincoln, NE 68588-0484, 472pp., 12 photos, 5 maps, notes, biblio., index, hardcover, ISBN 0-8032-3341-8. $60.00). This deeply researched and competently written study explores Indian-white relations in the United States and Canada. The author, a professor of history at the University of Arizona, contends that, although the Indian cultures in both regions suffered similar hardships, the course and extent of the changes were substantially different at times. This divergence of experiences, he continues, shaped the present living conditions and opportunities for native peoples in both countries.

Indians in the United States and Canada draws upon a vast array of primary and secondary sources in order to outline and discuss the evolving relationships between Indians and whites, from colonial times through today. The author neatly breaks down the history of these relations in five segments and methodically compares and contrasts the effects of each stage on native peoples in both countries. This approach makes it easier to appreciate the complexity and range of experiences of both sides. The photos are interesting and well selected and the maps, gathered together at the front of the study, are excellent. Unfortunately, the price tag will likely limit the circulation of this fine work to institutional purchases and a few private readers.

Across the Wide Missouri, Bernard DeVoto's Pulitzer prize-winning study of the decline of the fur trade in the 1830s, is back in print in this attractive paper edition (Houghton Mifflin Company, 222 Berkeley Street, Boston, MA 02116, 454pp, 2 maps, appendices, notes, biblio., index, paper, ISBN 0-395-92497-9. $15.00). Originally published in 1947, *Across the Wide Missouri* won widespread critical acclaim for its sweeping, saga-like tale of the trials and tribulations of the Rocky Mountain fur trade. As the author readily admits, his study is not a complete general history but a discussion of the fur trade's climax and decline. DeVoto's approach is unique. Instead of dryly relating the facts of the fur trade, he describes it as a business, a way of life. Each trapper and trader felt and lived through similar characteristic experiences, and by relating these, DeVoto explains how the fur trapping episode shaped the development of our westward expansion as well as our ultimate heritage. It is unfortunate that illustrations were not added to this edition, and the two maps at the end of the book are detailed yet difficult to utilize quickly and easily. Still, *Across the Wide Missouri* offers a slice of Americana that will never be experienced anywhere else again.

Timucuan Chiefdoms in Spanish Florida, 2 vols., by John E. Worth (University Press of Florida, 15 NW 15th Street, Gainesville, FL 32611, 280pp., 18 tables, 11 b&w photos, 10 line drawings, notes biblio., index, d.j., cloth. ISBN: 0-8130-1574-X (vol. 1), and ISBN 0-8130-1575-8 (vol. 2). $49.95 ea.). These two volumes (subtitled *Assimilation*, and *Resistance and Destruction*) offer the latest in both archaeological and archival research on an overlooked aspect of Spanish Florida Indians: the assimilation and eventual destruction of the indigenous Timucuan socieites of interior Spanish Florida near St. Augustine. In addition to field work and standard research sources, Worth utilizes previously unknown or infrequently-used Spanish documents, which help expain the integration of the culture into the colonial system, and by extension, much of the rest of America. The author is an anthropologist at the Fernbank Museum of Natural History in Atlanta and specializes in the archaeology of the southeastern Indians during the Spanish colonial era. Detailed, meticulously written, and with useful and informative tables and charts, *Timucuan Chiefdoms in Spanish Florida* adds greatly to our knowledge of the history of the period.

Here They Once Stood: The Tragic End of the Apalachee Missions, by Mark F. Boyd, Hale G. Smith, and John W. Griffin (University Press of Florida, 15 NW 15th Street, Gainesville, FL 32611, 189pp., maps, illus., b&w plates, appendices, notes biblio., index. Paper. ISBN: 0-8130-1725-4. $14.95.) A paper fascimile reprint of a study that first appeared in 1951, *Here They Once Stood* examines the final years of the "Mission era" of northern Florida. The authors' work has been described as "an historical-archaeological case study" of a pair of Spanish missions and area around them (today's Leon and Jefferson counties). These missions were run by Franciscans, who established simply, often crude outposts among a most inhospitable people. *Here They Once Stood* offers a totally different picture than the one so many of us have of the Spanish missionary following conquering armies into little-explored territories. This study, both useful and interesting, fills a narrow specialty niche in the genre.

Journal of the Indians Wars staff

INDEX

Did he save the balance of the 7th Cavalry from annihilation, or were his actions responsible for the death of George Armstrong Custer and 267 others? It would be his destiny to be forever –

In Custer's Shadow: Major Marcus Reno

by
Ronald H. Nichols
Introduction by
Brian Pohanka

Volume 15 in the Source Custeriana Series

1000 copy printing with more than 400 pages, over 60 photographs, and 11 maps, Ron Nichols has given us the definitive look at Custer's controversial second in command.
Available in a blue and white three piece binding, 250 copy authors' autographed edition
ISBN 0-88342-069-4 . . . .$50.00

Regular edition in gold stamped, blue binding
ISBN 0-88342-068-6 . . . .$35.00

Available from:
The Old Army Press
P.O. Box 2243
Fort Collins, CO 80522
or order toll free 1-800-627-0079

CIVIL WAR REGIMENTS:
A JOURNAL OF THE AMERICAN CIVIL WAR

DO YOU HAVE ALL THE BACK ISSUES?
(OTHERS ARE LISTED ON THE BACK COVER)

CIVIL WAR REGIMENTS:
A Journal of the American Civil War

BACK ISSUES (CONTINUED)

Early issues of CWR are listed below. Unfortunately, some are sold out or in very low quantity. If you want an issue listed as "sold out," let us know; occasionally our distributor will get one back or we will run across one. If we do not have one, one of the book search sites on the internet may be able to locate one for you.

VOLUME THREE:

No. 1: "The 10th Louisiana Infantry Battalion," by Arthur Bergeron; "The 20th Massachusetts Volunteer Infantry," by Anthony J. Milano; "The 1st Florida Special Battalion," by Don Hillhouse. Columns, book reviews. $8.00 LOW STOCK.

No. 2: The Sumter Artillery: The 11th Battalion, Georgia Light Artillery," by James Speicher; "Wilderness to Petersburg: Unpublished Reports of the Sumter Artillery"; Midnight Engagement: John Geary's White Star Division at Wauhatchie," by Doug Cubbison. Columns, book reviews. $8.00. SOLD OUT

No 3: "The 96th Pennsylvania Infantry," by David A. Ward; "To Rescue Gibraltar: John G. Walker's Division and the Relief of Fortress Vicksburg," by Terrence J. Winschel; "Colonel Holden Putnam and the 93rd Illinois Infantry," by John W. Huelskamp. Columns, book reviews. $8.00 SOLD OUT

No. 4: "All that Brave Men Could Do: Joseph Finegan's Florida Brigade at Cold Harbor," by Zack C. Waters; "The Battle of Belmont and the Citizen Soldiers of the 27th Illinois Infantry," by Peter Ellertsen. Columns, book reviews, and Volume Index. $8.00 LOW STOCK

VOLUME TWO:

No. 1: **VICKSBURG**. "Vicksburg Revisited," by Edwin C. Bearss; The First Honor at Vicksburg; The 1st Battalion, 13th U.S. Infantry," by Terrence J. Winschel; Into the Breach: The 22nd Iowa Infantry at the Railroad Redoubt; A Failure of Command: The Confederate Loss of Vicksburg," by Jim Stanberry. Columns, reviews. $10.00. SOLD OUT. Let us know if you would like to see some or all of this issue on-line! If you need a Vickburg fix, try Terrence J. Winschel's *Triumph & Defeat: The Vicksburg Campaign* (Savas, 1999).

No. 2: "The 1st GA Regulars at Sharpsburg," Richard McMurry, editor.; "The 9th New York Infantry in the Battel of the Crater," by William Marvel; "The 148th Pennsylvania at Fort Crater (Petersburg)," by Austin Brightman. Columns, book reviews. $8.00

No. 3: "Dahlgren's Marine Battalions," by Jeffrey T. Ryan; "Chasing Banks out of Louisiana: Parsons' Texas Cavalry in the Red River Campaign," by Anne Bailey; "Final March to Appomattox: The 12th Virginia Infantry," by Chris Caukins. Columns, book reviews. $8.00 LOW STOCK

No. 4: "The 11th Mississippi in the Army of Northern Virginia," by Steven Davis; "The 32nd Wisconsin Volunteer Infantry," by John M. Coski. Columns, book reviews, volume index. $8.00

VOLUME ONE [Collector's Items!]:

No. 1: **PREMIER ISSUE!** "From Eacho's Farm to Appomattox: The Fredericksburg Artillery," by Robert Krick; "The Fredericksburg Artillery at Appomattox," Chris Calkins, ed.; "The 37th Illinois at Pea Ridge and Prairie Grove," by Michael Mullins. Columns, book reviews. $8.00. LOW STOCK

No. 2: "Duryee's Zouves: The 5th New York Volunteer Infantry," by Brian C. Pohanka; "Duryee's Zouaves at Second Bull Run," Brian Pohanka, ed.; "Rackensacker Raiders: Crawford's 1st Arkansas Cavalry," by Anthony Rushing. Colunms, book reviews. VERY LOW STOCK. $8.00

CIVIL WAR REGIMENTS:
A JOURNAL OF THE AMERICAN CIVIL WAR

BACK ISSUES (CONTINUED)

No. 3: "A Confederate Surgeon at Fort Donelson," Jim Stanbery, ed.; "The Pennsylvania Bucktails," by William J. Miller; "The 22nd Battalion Virginia Infantry," by Tom Brooks; "The Shoupade Redoubts: Joe Johnston's Chattahoochee River Line," by Greg Biggs. Columns, book reviews. $8.00. LOW STOCK

No. 4: "The 126th New York Infantry at Harpers Ferry," by Wayne Mahood; "The First Confederate Regiment Georgia Volunteers," by C. Pat Cates. Columns, book reviews, volume index. $8.00. LOW STOCK

We extend an invitation to you to visit our

completely revised website: www.savaspublishing.com

Book Catalog	Book of The Month	Civil War Regiments	Journal of the Indian Wars	Book Excerpts	Articles
Forthcoming Titles	Map Drawer	Author Interviews	Speakers' Bureau	Submission Guidelines	ORDER

Our site is regularly updated with excerpts, photos of authors, conference information, interviews, and new book information. Access our home page and click on "What's New" to see the latest additions!

Savas Publishing Company
202 First Street SE, Suite 103A, Mason City, IA 50401; 515-421-7135 (phone); 515-421-8370 (fax); cwbooks@mach3ww.com (e-mail); www.savaspublishing.com (website)